Football Babylon

Football Babylon

Russ Williams

Virgin

First published in Great Britain in 1996 by
Virgin Books
an imprint of Virgin Publishing Ltd
332 Ladbroke Grove
LONDON W10 5AH

ISBN 0 7535 0046 9

Typeset by TW Typesetting, Plymouth, Devon

Printed and bound by Cox & Wyman, Reading, Berks

In memory of the man
who bought me my first
football kit – my dad,
Tom.

Contents

Illustrations

Acknowledgements

Many thanks and much appreciation to: Alex Leith and Jim Drewett, for their tireless research; Julia, for typing it and coping with all the inserts and additions; Mal Peachey, for plying me with alcohol and asking me to write it; the countless contributors, for their time and help – you know who you are!

Introduction

It would be easy to label this book just another publication about football sleaze but, in fact, it's much more than that. *Football Babylon* documents everything from the saddest football deaths to the most bizarre. It examines very real issues in today's game, from brawls to bungs and the problem of drugs; it pours scorn on idle rumours and confirms your worst fears.

The stories contained in these pages should come as no real surprise. British football stands up well to intense scrutiny but its foreign cousins, sadly, do not. Some of the contents you will find shocking, others, hopefully, hilariously funny. From match fixing and cheating to football's courtroom dramas, it's all here.

Countless football personnel, both past and present, have assisted with the research and compilation of this book. Some of the stories they had to tell would make your hair curl. Inevitably, some of the more contentious yarns did not manage to slip through our lawyer's law-suit-alert machine, but the vast majority did.

Some names have been withheld to protect the guilty although nearly all the people involved in those stories are instantly recognisable to the discerning football fan. Some are household names, but their identity must remain forever secret – they know who they are; the question is, will you?

This book goes some way to lifting the lid on world football but it's fair to say that the best-selling football book of all time will be the one written by the player, or manager, who decides to throw caution to the wind and spill *all* the beans. It will take a brave publisher to commission that one.

The football world is a closed shop, a tight knit community where money and self-interest are the names of the game. Up to a point, football people are quite happy to talk about everyone and everything; penetrating further is the most difficult thing of all. You deserve to know what is going on even if, in some cases, it's only the beginning of the truth. Don't be under any illusion – there is far more to the game than the 70s, 80s and 90s and the oldest tricks in the book are as old as the game itself.

The nine months that it has taken to write *Football Babylon* have been hugely enjoyable (apart from my Repetitive Wrist Strain) and I hope the short time you spend reading it will be just as rewarding.

Irrespective of what I've written and heard, I still love this beautiful game – it's a game that touches people's lives in so many special ways. Fans, or emotional shareholders, are still the major powerbrokers in football and they deserve to know exactly what's going on, why it's going on and what's being done about it. To dismiss some of the contents as sensationalist would be a mistake. To keep an open mind would be more appropriate; after all, it's 'a funny old game'. Read on.

1 Death

THERE IS A SMALL BOY living in Indonesia who, when he grows up, unless he's smart and keeps his mouth shut, will ensure an uncommon amount of ridicule because of his father. In particular, the manner of his father's death.

Indragiri Hulu is hardly a place that you would expect to take its rightful place in football folklore – it doesn't sound right for a start and, when you see it mentioned in the same sentence as Hampden, Wembley, the Nou Camp and the Maracana, it certainly doesn't look right.

All great theatres of football have their own stories to tell but none are stranger than Indragiri Hulu. Every year, thousands of villagers from this tiny outpost near Jakarta choose to escape for a couple of days from their strictly religious lifestyles to watch and, if selected, play in the much coveted Independence Cup. One day is set aside for training and the other for the match itself.

As with any team, only eleven players can be picked but the training day is when, as long as you impress, a place in the team can be secured. Mistar, 25 years old and a veteran of the big game, was out to secure another Independence Cup appearance. Training was going well, hundreds of villagers stood attentively running their eye over their favourite players when, suddenly, disaster struck.

A herd of swines emerged from some nearby bushes and made a beeline for the training pitch. Spectators and players teamed up and charged the rampaging beasts in the hope that a quick dispersal would lead to a resumption of training – and hopefully a tasty snack for afterwards. Mistar, the Indonesian equivalent of Mark Hateley, soon discovered that being good in the air has its disadvantages, particularly when he was only up here because one of the swines had stabbed him with its large sharp tusks and tossed him several feet across the playing surface.

As a result of his horrific injuries, Mistar bled to death on the pitch. Training and the subsequent game were called off as a mark of respect.

His widow and son have to live with the memory of this tragic and almost comic death that, by its very nature, must surely qualify as the world's most bizarre on-field football death. The perpetrator also enjoyed a degree of notoriety by being the first murderer to be sentenced to be a kebab.

Animals 1 Humans 0. Until those lovable level-headed Turks decided to change things.

Anything goes in the fire and brimstone world of Turkish football where one minute you can be the flavour of the month and the next you are a pilloried useless lump of lard. Graeme Souness is a case in point. On arrival in Turkey, as the manager of Galatasary, he was portrayed as some sort of messiah – on the pitch, maybe, but as a manager, hardly. After only a few short months, he was appearing in British newspapers saying how unhappy he was. 'Souness stuck in Turkey', said one tabloid headline (what a surprise this must have been for Mum when she went to carve it). He was experiencing the difficult adjustment that all British footballers seem to suffer on moving abroad. However, it must be very hard to feel at home when, before kickoff, an animal is sacrificed on the pitch and the fresh, warm blood is then smeared over your players' faces as a good luck charm (without even bothering to enquire if they're vegetarians).

England Striker Les Ferdinand recalls with affection his time in Turkey with Bekiktas but found the sacrifices and blood a little disconcerting: 'This sort of thing never happened at QPR.'

Sometimes sheep are sacrificed (murdered) in front of team coaches, as Dean Saunders explains: 'We saw this guy walking this sheep like it was his dog into the middle of the road. All of a sudden he stops and cuts its throat. I think people in Britain are going to be shocked during the European Championships.'

Perhaps the strangest double ritual involving death was practised by a football team in Nairobi. The club were suspended from the league after they sacrificed a goat on the pitch before a game. The previous year the team had been suspended from the same league when, as spectators cheered, they urinated on the ball before kickoff for good luck.

My earliest recollection of death at a football match was watching Tommy Steele dying in front of 100,000 fans at Wembley Stadium as, once again, he attempted to sing 'Abide With Me' before the FA Cup Final. I remember commenting to my father that Tommy was the world's first reincarnated singer – he died last year, I thought, and now he's back this year to do it all over again. The FA soon got wise and Gerry Marsden took over, but that's another story.

Death is not an easy state to contemplate. When you're at school and growing up, it's the furthest thing from your mind. I remember occasionally thinking that, if I had a choice of how to go, I'd like it to be quick and painless – a bomb maybe, or a bullet to the head, anything but a slow, debilitating death. As far as I know we don't get any say, it's just the luck of the draw, but, if you could have a choice, dying at a football match would be my utopia. No fuss, just slipping away to the roar of the crowd and the smell of patties or something masquerading as hamburgers and, as you float out of your body, you would get aerial views of the game that no TV company could ever reproduce. Knowing my luck, I'd die halfway through the penalty shoot-out and spend forever wondering who won.

The great Dixie Dean died at a football match. The equally great Bob Paisley didn't. However, I'm sure that if Bob had been given a choice he would have chosen Anfield to spend his last 90 minutes on earth before the inevitable final whistle.

As commercialisation has taken a firm grip of football in the 1990s, it is now quite common for clubs to allow wedding ceremonies to take place on the pitch. Some benevolent clubs even allow supporters' ashes to be spread on the pitch, the goalmouth area being a firm favourite amongst the deceased. It's worth checking with your local club to see if any such acts have taken place recently because, if it's windy on match-day, you could get a lot more than tomato ketchup on your jumbo sausage.

Wembley has, for many years, adopted an ashes-spreading policy, although not on the pitch. Groundstaff consider human ashes too delicate a mixture to put on football's most famous turf, so any such remains are scattered liberally all over the perimeter dog track. It's not clear whether any dog racing fanatics' ashes have been scattered over the Wembley turf in a reciprocal move.

The finality of having someone's ashes tastefully dumped on their beloved team's hallowed turf is too much for some relatives to take. It's rather like Granny keeping Granddad's dusty leftovers in an urn on the mantelpiece and never *really* knowing if the contents are genuine. One Spanish supporter of the First Division club Real Betis came up with an ingenious alternative. His father's dying wish was to have his season ticket renewed and his ashes transported, by his son, to every home game. The son dutifully obliged, turning up for every home game with his father's ashes in a milk carton (I bet he didn't open it by following the written instructions) and placing them on his late father's seat next to him in the Benito Villemarin stadium. He initially took them in a jam jar, presumably so his father could get a clearer view, but he was banned from doing this after club officials said the jar could be used as an offensive weapon.

Deaths on the field of play were few and far between, until the commencement of organised competitive games at the end of the nineteenth century. Not only players, but also match officials, coaches, managers and club directors have met unnatural, brutal and untimely ends on or around the football pitch. Britain had a monopoly on pitch deaths until the rest of the world discovered the beautiful game at various stages of recent history.

Early records of football, or a similar ball game, vary globally, with tales ranging from the sublime to the ridiculous and often carrying social and political overtones. As early as the first century AD, the Chinese writer Li Yu spoke of a game played with a full moon ball, square goals and two captains where determination and coolness were essential.

Between 1170 and 1183, William Fitz, the biographer of Thomas à Becket, wrote of a popular ball game played by young men and watched by their seniors. Balls were made of inflated animal bladders and the unnamed game was a violent and physically demanding one which was described as life threatening for the spectators as well as the players.

No specific examples of pitch deaths are quoted but this is not to say that they didn't happen, because they almost certainly did. Attitudes to life were different then; common folk, or serfs, were considered two-a-penny, so it is understandable that somebody playing the game and losing their life would hardly raise an eyebrow, let alone warrant historical documentation.

Between the thirteenth and nineteenth centuries, football appears in English legal records, being denounced by the authorities as a violent game and a root cause of social unrest in which personal and collective scores were often settled. There were no team restrictions, no rules and no time limits – it was just good wholesome life-threatening fun. Goals could be two or three miles apart and the sheer physical exertions involved doubtless claimed many lives. Injuries, rather than deaths, were very common and only the strong went unscathed, so it was better to be a Tommy Smith than a Matt Le Tissier.

Medieval observers were more concerned with the wider social unrest caused by football. Occasional beheadings were apparently turned into kicking jamborees, with the headless corpse remaining stationary whilst the head was tossed to the crowd for a knockabout. (Head kicking is still practised in the 1990s, but even the meanest of hard men defenders will tend to leave their victim's head attached to the body.) During this period the spectators were never at risk, although the players certainly were as a plethora of rampaging youths chased the 'ball' which, I'm sure, took on less significance as 'the game' progressed.

By the early seventeenth century, football had spread to all four corners of England, despite Royal proclamations of disdain and local authority disapproval. Active measures were taken to move football out of the towns and cities and into more rural areas. Shrove Tuesday became a significant football day, together with animal sport and cock fighting, as it was the last chance for people to let themselves go before Lent.

Despite official disapproval of the game and various attempts to ban it, ordinary people loved it. Fote Bale, or Folk Ball, was here to stay. Sixteenth and seventeenth century puritans loathed it – it was the devil's recreation. This no doubt explains why no Amish team has ever entered the World Cup. Fines were introduced to prevent games taking place on Sundays and footballing speakeasies popped up all over Britain.

In sixteenth century Italy, a ball game was played that stressed the social and physical aspects of the game although up until comparatively modern times the world has viewed football as being a distinctly British pastime. This began to change in the nineteenth century, as influential church officials began to endorse and appreciate the game for what it was, despite its chequered history. Travellers, explorers and missionaries took the game to all corners of the globe and in Britain the first bold steps towards league football were taken, a far cry from the sophisticated modern game we know today, but it was a start.

In South America, the game caught on comparatively quickly after being exported to Argentina by English landowners setting up pampas ranches. Football had stumbled through at least eight centuries and the time had come for the game to walk, jog, and then run into the twentieth century.

Early organised football had a set of rules of sorts. It was physically dangerous and, like any other semi-contact sport, fostered injuries and deaths on or around the field of play. Some deaths were contributory, others accidents, some were deliberate and some were downright odd ones. Quite a few were beyond any human control, thus fulfilling the criteria of the insurance world's favourite 'Act of God' clause. From the early 1880s, records concerning football's mishaps became far more detailed and what follows is a chronological account of football-related deaths, spanning players, officials, managers, spectators and even animals.

In 1881, Swindon were forced to move grounds after a small boy died as a result of falling into the quarry that was situated next to their pitch. It's unclear whether this was enforced, or done as a mark of respect – maybe they moved because they feared their ground might suffer the same fate. Scotland's first contributory death occurred in 1892 when St Mirren's James Dunlop died of tetanus after suffering a cut to his leg during a game.

The first on-pitch death of the new football era happened in England in 1897. Aston player Thomas Grice was killed during a game when he stumbled to the ground and his belt buckle penetrated his stomach. The size of the buckle was obviously huge and more in keeping with the fashion of the day than with any need to hold up his shorts. Thomas could be described as football's first fashion victim, a condition that was admirably continued by countless players in the 1970s, though not with such terminal results.

South America got in on the death act in 1905. In Uruguay, Penarol's goalkeeper was killed in a collision with a Montevideo forward. After the match, rumours of the tragedy circulated amongst Penarol fans who then proceeded to set alight the carriages of the train carrying the Montevideo players. Luckily, no further injuries were sustained although the story does have a final twist: Penarol were owned by the railway company who, understandably, didn't appreciate the burning of their train and subsequently terminated their involvement with the club.

In the early twentieth century, unlike today, Christmas Day was considered a fine day for football. In 1909, James Maine of Hibernian died from internal injuries, sustained during a game at Fir Hill against Partick Thistle. The game was played despite deplorable ground conditions and, midway through the first half, the Scottish International was accidentally kicked in the stomach. He only appeared winded and was helped off the pitch, taken to the dressing room and allowed to go home after the game. During the night his condition worsened and he was rushed to Edinburgh Royal Infirmary where doctors discovered he was suffering from a ruptured bowel. After undergoing an emergency operation he failed to recover and died a few days later. Undoubtedly, had the accident happened some years later his chances of survival would have been far greater due to improvements in medical care. A testimonial match was arranged between Hibs and Hearts at Easter Road with all the proceeds going to James Maine's family.

During the 1910/11 season, Scottish club Morton were given a lamb by a local butcher every time they scored a goal. Centre forward Tommy Gracies, recipient of several lambs, decided to keep one, which he named Toby. The lamb became the team's mascot, but a few weeks later it mysteriously drowned in the team bath. Club historians are sketchy as to whether Britain's first dressing room death was sinister or just high jinks. If the players were involved, why would they be in a bath with a live lamb? Surely this sort of thing only happens in Australia?

Britain's first dressing-room death occurred on 19 February 1916. Former England International Bobby Benson went to watch Arsenal play Reading. Short of players, Arsenal persuaded him to play and not having played for over a year, the exertion killed him. After the game, he collapsed and died in the dressing room beneath Highbury stadium.

In today's game, goalkeepers are so cosseted by referees that you would think the men in green (or black) were members of Greenpeace. There is no doubt that goalkeeping is a hazardous position to play in, and the potential for injury is considerable: Dunbarton's goalkeeper James Williamson died as a result of the injuries he received in a game against Rangers in 1921.

Sometimes, non-life-threatening injuries that occur during play can have alarming repercussions. In 1923, Port Vale's full back Tom Butler died eight days after breaking his arm in a match against Clapton Orient. He suffered a compound fracture to his left arm in the final few minutes of the 1-1 draw. Septic poisoning was diagnosed and he died of tetanus in Hackney Hospital, London. Collections and donations raised £700 for his family.

English club Bury lost a notorious fullback in 1928. Sam Wynne had the unusual distinction of scoring four times in one game, playing for Oldham against Manchester United on 6 October 1922; he scored twice for Oldham (a penalty and a free kick) and twice for Manchester United (with two own goals). Fortunately for him, Oldham went on to win the game 3-2. He joined Bury and played his last game for them on 30 April 1928 when he collapsed whilst taking a free kick against Sheffield United at Bramall Lane. He died in the dressing room of acute pneumonia, with the match being abandoned immediately as a mark of respect.

In 1931, Celtic's brilliant young Scottish International goalkeeper, John 'Jock' Thompson, was involved in a collision with Rangers' forward Sam English during an old firm derby. Both men went for a 50-50 ball, with Thompson diving at the feet of English. Jock Thompson fractured his skull in the collision and, after being stretchered off the pitch, he was taken to hospital where he died five hours later. No blame was attached to English by either the press or neutral observers, but he was barracked and intimidated by Celtic fans thereafter and eventually, devastated, he moved back to Liverpool and later to his native Ireland.

Such is the passion and feeling for football in Glasgow, that incidents such as this promote an enormous outpouring of respect and emotion. In the lead up to Jock Thompson's burial, thousands of Celtic fans walked from Glasgow to his home town of Cardenden, near Cowdenbeath. The walk took about three days and they slept in fields along the way; even today, Celtic fans on their way to away matches at Dundee or Aberdeen make a detour to his grave and pay their respects.

Suicide has also touched British football, notably in July 1932. The Crystal Palace team turned up for the first day of pre-season training and goalkeeper Billy Callender joined them, despite the recent death of his fiancée Eva Leslie. Profoundly affected by his loss and presumably feeling that life was not worth living on his own, he took his own life on that day, hanging himself in one of the dressing rooms at Selhurst Park.

Sometimes, an event at a game, however tragic, can strengthen the camaraderie between players. On 1 December 1934, Gillingham were playing a home league game against Brighton and Hove Albion and their star frontman, Sim Raleigh, looked set to continue his impressive form since signing for Gillingham in 1932. His most extraordinary performance for the Gills was whilst playing for the reserves against Sittingbourne in the Kent League shortly after his arrival at the club; he scored a treble hattrick in a 12-0, one sided affair. Tongues wagged and, by the afternoon of his death, he was attracting considerable interest from many leading First Division clubs. The game was only five minutes old when Raleigh and Brighton centre-half Paul Mooney jumped to contest a high ball and collided in midair. Raleigh was taken off and, following an appointment with the obligatory magic sponge and smelling salts, he felt well enough to continue the game.

Teammates and supporters recalled Raleigh claiming he was 'quite all right' at half time. The second half got underway and, almost immediately, Raleigh brought most of the 4,115 crowd to their feet with a great run down the wing. Suddenly, he collapsed in mid stride. Once again he was carried off, but this time, following an examination by the club doctor, he was taken to St Bartholomew's Hospital where he arrived at 5.05 p.m. The club's attack leader had a swelling over his right temple and was unconscious. He underwent surgery within the half-hour but never regained consciousness and was formally declared dead at 9.55 p.m. His wife, Hilda, was by his bedside throughout.

Four days later, a verdict of accidental death was returned by the city of Rochester Coroner. Hospital doctors felt that he had almost certainly suffered a near-fatal brain haemorrhage during the game and it was sheer luck that he had managed to continue for so long. The Brighton player involved in the collision, Paul Mooney, continued playing in the game none the worse for wear. When he learned of Raleigh's death he was quoted in the *Times* as being 'most distressed' – the mental anguish following the accident certainly took its toll, with Mooney announcing his retirement after playing just a handful of further matches for Brighton. But for this tragic accident which cruelly ended his life, Sim Raleigh would undoubtedly have gone on to achieve greater fame.

Present-day players, thanks to modern medicine, are often able to continue playing even after sustaining horrific injuries or suffering from life-threatening conditions. In Britain, Paul Gascoigne, Ian Durant and Nottingham Forest's Steve Stone are all testament to the skills of the specialists and surgeons in that they have all been able to resume their careers after experiencing horrendous leg injuries. They truly are football's bionic men; they've been rebuilt and patched up with the medical technology that just a few short years ago would have been an impossibility. Today, leg breaks, compound fractures and severe ligament damage do not necessarily mean the end of a player's career. Club physiotherapy – so often a quick rub with the magic sponge and a quick whiff of smelling salts – has moved on. Players like Tottenham Hotspur captain Gary Mabbutt, who suffers from diabetes, and Birmingham City's Kevin Francis, who has a hole in the heart, manage to continue a fully active professional career through vigilance and the correct type of medical care. Former West Bromwich Albion player Asa Hartford underwent surgery in the early 1970s for a hole in the heart and was fortunate to carry on playing despite his condition. Some diseases and their contributory effects on the human body can take their toll: in February 1936 Sunderland goalkeeper James Thorpe died just a few days after playing in a match against Chelsea. The coroner was of the opinion that he died of diabetes – apparently the illness had been accelerated due to his 'rough handling' as a goalkeeper.

The chances of a similar death happening in today's modern game are remote, not only because of the medical factors but

also because of the increased protection offered to goalkeepers
by referees; the game's rules are such that 'rough handling' and
similar physical situations would no longer be allowed to occur.
Any discussion as to whether rule changes and player protection
are good or bad for the game is, perhaps, better reserved for one
of those rose tinted glasses-type retrospective debates down the
pub.

During wartime, football tended to take a back seat; the game
that was Utopia to so many people hardly got a second thought
during those troubled times. In World War I, football was
stopped by the authorities but did, temporarily, bring the
warring sides together during Christmas Day kickabouts in
no-man's-land between the trenches. It's worth considering that,
if enemies could drop their arms and engage in an amicable
game or two for one day a year, why on earth couldn't they do it
every day of the year? Just imagine the number of lives that
would have been saved and the misery avoided if governments
had sanctioned the settling of disputes by playing a game of
football. History could have read very differently: Poland could
have beaten Germany, thus avoiding World War II; England
would probably have lost to Argentina in 1982, thus losing the
Falklands; even Graham Taylor's England would probably have
beaten Iraq and a war in the Persian Gulf could have been
avoided. A simple suggestion but, considering Britain's international teams' performances over the last 25 years, it's probably a
relief that international disputes are not settled in this way.

Records from World War II became marginally more detailed
as far as deaths are concerned. As in World War I, profes-
sionally organised football was suspended and over 100
professionals lost their lives in the fighting. The Germans had a
habit of dishing out brutal and harsh treatment to their enemies. In Italy in 1941, eight Italian partisans were shot by the
Nazis at Inter's Arena stadium but by far the worst atrocity
occurred in 1942. As the German blitzkrieg of Russia gobbled
up vast areas of land, one notable game of football with a
difference took place. The Germans had a desire to be liked by
the locals and, in a gesture of perverse friendship, challenged

the Russian side Kiev to a game. Kiev beat the Nazis with some ease over a series of 'friendly' matches. The German powers that be found this a little unpalatable and called in reinforcements in the shape of the top German army side Flakelf. The Germans lost once again. The local commander ordered a replay, threatening the Kiev players with execution if they won again. They duly thrashed the Nazis. As a consequence, eight players were shot, two were sent to a labour camp and one escaped. The Kiev players had performed in the most intimidating of circumstances – it later emerged that the crowd almost entirely comprised German soldiers with machine guns who fired at the Russian players' legs. They then executed them as the final whistle blew. To commemorate the Match of Death, a statue was erected in Kiev which features three men in football kits and can still be seen in the city today. However, it is possible that the match never happened but was merely thought up by the then formidable Russian propaganda machine – as many sources deny the playing of the game as do confirm it.

Alan Hansen, TV pundit and former Scottish International and Liverpool centre-back, often castigates footballing mistakes with the phrase, 'he should be shot for that'. Rarely does this much-used expression come tofruition but on one notable occasion, it did. French player Alex Villaplane, who captained the national side in the 1930 World Cup in Uruguay, met a rather unpleasant death in 1944 when, following the liberation of France, he was shot by firing squad for collaboration with the Germans. Perhaps a similar fate should have awaited the Austrian team after the 1982 World Cup where they committed exactly the same offence.

During the postwar years, the Grim Reaper continued to make his presence felt in football. April 1948 saw an act of God spectacularly intervene in a game between the Royal Armoured Corps (Bovington) and the Royal Artillery (121st Training Regiment Oswestry). It was the 1948 Army Cup Final replay being played at the Command Control ground in Aldershot in front of a crowd of 3,000 people. The first game, played four days earlier, ended in a dull 0-0 draw and gave absolutely no indication that the replay would be any more eventful. However, during the second half, with the score at 2-0 to the Artillery, a mild thunderstorm passed overhead. All of a sudden, there was a flash of lightning and the referee and eight of the players dropped to the ground. According to newspaper and eyewitness accounts, most of the other players on the pitch swayed from side to side for a moment or two before they also fell to the ground. Eight players were taken to hospital where two later died. Some of the spectators also seemed to be suffering from shock. After the event, most of the players said they felt as if they had received a terrific blow to the back of the head. The general consensus amongst spectators was that the lightning had struck the referee's whistle, as he had been the first to fall. The referee survived.

Sometimes, the love of playing football carries over into a player's post-professional days with tragic results: on 29 March 1959, West Bromwich Albion's former England International centre forward (he played once for his country) Billy G. Richardson collapsed and died during a charity match at Perrybar, Birmingham. It was a match for ex-players and celebrities, and Richardson, according to one witness, 'was playing normally, then just keeled over and died'. He was 49 and still on the club's books.

In April 1962, during a match in South America, a referee gave a decision that one spectator in particular did not agree with. The fan ran onto the pitch and coldbloodedly stabbed the referee to death. Not to be outdone, another spectator shot dead the man who had just killed the referee. By this time it was pandemonium in the stadium; the crowd stampeded and another fan was crushed to death. During the following season, a Brazilian Flamengo supporter was shot dead by a sniper as he left the Maracana stadium.

San Andres FC of Mexico staged a match in Tetepileo in 1964 during a thunderstorm. One player was struck by lightning and killed and three others, plus the referee, were injured. In a curious twist of fate the ambulance carrying the casualties to hospital collided with a bus.

Away from the pitch, on 5 December 1966, 25-year-old Benfica star Luciano died in the club's jacuzzi. It had been working fine for twenty minutes, then the players began to receive fierce electric shocks. Luciano, who was completely immersed in the water at the time, gave a loud cry of pain and collapsed, along with two teammates. Colleague Jaime Garcia, an electrician turned footballer, managed to struggle out of the jacuzzi and turn off the electric current. Many of the players received serious burns but nothing more could be done for Luciano.

The old saying that lightning doesn't strike twice was spectacularly disproved on 25 February 1967. Worcestershire combination side Highgate United were playing an FA Amateur Cup quarterfinal match against Enfield. It was supposed to be the greatest day in Highgate's history, playing the mighty Enfield whose team boasted no fewer than eight England amateur Internationals, but it ended in tragedy.

After about 25 minutes of the match, played in driving rain, a bolt of lightning suddenly struck the pitch. Highgate's centre-half, 23-year-old Tony Alden, slumped to the ground. Spectators and club officials sprinted to him and Highgate trainer, Albert Bates, performed mouth-to-mouth resuscitation on Alden and two injured brothers, Eric and Roy Taylor, who were also Highgate players. The brothers recovered but Tony Alden was taken to Solihull Hospital where a medical team battled to save his life. The distraught Highgate manager, John Hewitson, remained at his bedside until Alden finally died at 1 p.m. the following day. It emerged that the bolt of lightning had rebounded off the ground and, in striking Alden, had caused irreparable damage to his heart. Naturally, after the incident the game was abandoned.

The grieving players and officials of Highgate United met to decide whether to forfeit the game, as a mark of respect, or whether to arrange a replay. They elected to carry on in the competition. Aston Villa offered the use of Villa Park and the match was played in front of 32,000 fans but even this failed to change the fortunes of Highgate – despite them playing in a donated Aston Villa strip, Enfield won the replay 6-0. The proceeds of the match, and a subsequent charity game at Birmingham City, went to Tony Alden's family.

In early 1973 in the 42nd minute of a Spanish second division game in Seville's Pasaron Pontevedra stadium, Seville's brilliant Under 23 International Pedro Berruezo collapsed on the pitch. He was rushed to hospital but found to be dead from heart failure on arrival. Berruezo should have heeded an earlier warning after collapsing in a previous home game against Baracaldo, once again with heart problems. His condition was then serious enough for him to spend five days in an intensive care unit but, amazingly, doctors declared him fit enough to continue playing football – which, quite clearly, he wasn't. Over 10,000 fans and mourners packed Seville's stadium for his farewell service.

When Perugia midfielder Renator Curt collapsed and died during a match against Juventus, club doctors at Perugia and his previous club Como were unsuccessfully accused of negligence in declaring him fit to play football. A heart condition was also suspected in the death of Portuguese player Joao Pedro who collapsed and died after a league game for his club Cuf against Barrierense. As in the case of Berruezo, Pedro had been alerted to his heart condition by the club doctor earlier in the season.

A quite bizarre football death took place in South Vietnam on 12 November 1974, when 27-year-old Nguyen Van Thang was shot and fatally wounded whilst celebrating his country's victory in an international tournament. Van Thang was killed after a friend of his pointed an unloaded gun at his head and pulled the trigger, only to discover that the gun was, in fact, loaded. With friends like that, who needs enemies?

Firearms were involved in another stadium tragedy on 11 December 1976. Haiti and Cuba were playing a World Cup play-off match when, after going behind to an early goal, Cuba equalised and someone in the crowd let off a fire cracker. The crowd behind one goal panicked and knocked over a soldier who was holding a machine gun. The gun went off, killing a girl and a boy in the crowd. In the ensuing chaos two people were trampled to death and a third fell to his death off a high wall. Outside the ground and unable to cope with his feelings of guilt, the soldier who started it all shot himself.

In 1977 Lazio star Luciano Re Cecconi, 28, died when a practical joke at a jeweller's shop went horribly wrong. Cecconi went into Bruno Tabocchini's jeweller's shop in Rome with his teammate Pietro Ghedin. For a laugh, Cecconi wiggled his hands in his pockets and proclaimed, 'Right, raise your hands, this is a hold up'. Unbeknown to Cecconi, Signor Tabocchini had only just had a hold up the previous Sunday and now kept a loaded Walther pistol under the counter. Signor Tabocchini reached under the counter, grabbed the gun and shot Cecconi. As he fell to the floor, Ghedin said, 'Don't you recognise us? We play for Lazio.' 'No! I don't know anything about football,' said the jeweller. Tabocchini was arrested on a charge of manslaughter but a court later decided that he had no case to answer, although there was a lot of suspicion that he was actually a Roma fan.

Planet Football's next notable death was Dixie Dean, the man who once told Joe Mercer, 'your legs wouldn't last a postman his morning round'. Dixie was a goalscoring legend, his record of 60 goals in the 1927/28 season still stands in 1996. He'd been forced to give up his licensee's job in Chester in 1962 through ill health and later went on to work for a pools company, but he always found time to visit his beloved Everton. There is a certain poetic irony in the fact that, on 1 March 1980, he died, aged 74, whilst watching the Merseyside derby at Goodison Park. No doubt the only slight disappointment to him would have been the result of the game that day – Everton lost 2-1.

To earn public recognition or praise from the late Bill Shankly was almost unheard of. So, when Jock Stein received a despatch from the great man describing him as 'immortal', it was a true indication of his status as colossus within the footballing world. Jock Stein, for many years, *was* Scottish Football, certainly as far as half of Glasgow and the rest of the world were concerned. The other half of Glasgow knew it but were loath to admit it.

On 10 September 1985, Jock Stein, the then Scottish national team manager, took his squad to Ninian Park for a vital World Cup qualifying game with Wales. The match was a 1-1 draw but was enough to send Scotland through to the 1986 World Cup finals in Mexico. Stein was already in the tunnel and, as the final whistle blew, he collapsed and died of a heart attack. Roy Aitken recalls: 'in the dressing room we should have been in a celebratory mood at the end of the match. Scotland had made it to Mexico. But there was near silence as we changed and waited for more news. It must have been twenty minutes later that we were told. I looked at physio Jim Steel's face and knew, without words, that the worst had happened.'

After the match, the Tartan Army, who had bellowed their team to qualification, stood in total silence and bewilderment outside Ninian Park in tribute to 'the big man'. Apart from the obvious, perhaps the greatest tragedy was that one of the greatest Scottish managers of all time didn't get the chance to participate in the greatest football tournament of them all.

In 1989, four years after the death of Jock Stein, 25-year-old Nigerian winger Sam Okwarajf collapsed and died six minutes from the end of a World Cup qualifier against Angola in Lagos. He died of natural causes, although it's difficult to understand how it can be natural at such a young age. Apart from being a Nigerian International, Okwarajf played his domestic football in the Belgian Second Division with Bercham of Antwerp.

World Cup year, 1990, saw two more football deaths, one in England and the other in Ireland. The bizarre thing is that they happened on the same day, 8 September. Both involved young men in the prime of their lives: David Longhurst, playing for York City against Luton Town, had a heart attack, collapsed and died, despite the efforts of his colleagues and a medical team. It was particularly distressing for Longhurst's girlfriend, Vicky, who was in the crowd. Hundreds of York fans sent flowers and tied scarves to the gates at Bootham Crescent as a mark of respect. On the same day, in Dublin, 27-year-old

William Christie was brutally shot to death as he sat on the substitutes' bench during an amateur match. There is a possibility that this death was a tit for tat killing as Christie had been arrested for murder earlier in the year but had been released after all the witnesses refused to testify.

Hungary's first (post-Communist) recorded football death happened in the 1993/94 season. Gabor Zsiboras, a 35-year-old Hungarian International goalkeeper with four caps, died after collapsing with a brain clot just before a practice match with the national team. During his shortened career (for a goalkeeper) he had played 361 matches for Hungarian club sides Ferencvaros and MTK. Obtaining documentary evidence of death within the Eastern Bloc before the collapse of communism is very difficult to say the least – it's a bit like dropping a grain of sand on the pitch at Wembley and then trying to find it.

1995 can be seen, in footballing terms, as The Year of Death. It could have been a karma problem or just plain coincidence, but to have a glut of deaths in the game all in one year certainly sets a historical precedent. The incidents, spread over three continents, vary greatly, but all have the same end result.

Nigeria was definitely not the place to be, with two deaths in as many months. In September, Igenewari George, brother of Ajaz Star Finidi, was shot dead by a stray bullet after fans rioted following an FA Cup match between Team Rangers International and Stationery Stores FC. In the murky world of African football, incidents such as these occur frequently and although, proportionately, the number of deaths is small, the Nigerian FA went on to ban Stationery Stores from all football activities for a year and ordered the club to pay the equivalent of £12,000 in compensation – a pitifully small amount of money considering a player had been killed.

In December 1995, Nigerian club Julius Berger reached the final of the African Cup Winners Cup with a 1-0 win over Maxaquende of Mozambique. Their celebrations were cut short when midfielder Amir Angwe collapsed and died of a heart attack mid-festivities.

Meanwhile, in South America, 4 February 1995 was the last

day on earth for 23-year-old Brazilian forward Augusto Candido. His club, Boom, were playing a Second Division match against Geel when Candido suffered a heart attack ten minutes into the second half and, despite efforts to revive him, died on the field of play. He left a widow and two young children.

South America is one of a couple of areas on earth where being a football official should carry a government health warning. Fervour amongst their fans makes the Italians look disinterested. Peruvian referee Felipe Compinez met a violent end after awarding a last minute penalty in a regional football competition: Social Santa scored from the penalty spot and took the title; rival fans took great exception to the referee's decision and stoned him to death.

Even youth football can be dangerous. In 1995, around 100 people were injured and a sixteen-year-old player was killed after fighting spilled onto the pitch during a Brazilian youth tournament. The venue was the Pacaembu stadium and featured the youth teams of top clubs Sao Paulo and Palmeiras. When Palmeiras scored the winning goal, hundreds of fans invaded the pitch and fought a running battle, resulting in the injuries and the death; ironically, the match was decided in sudden-death injury time.

Over in Europe, Davie Cooper's career was boys'-own stuff. He had spent twelve seasons at Ibrox Park following his £100,000 move from Clydebank in 1977 and then went on to play for Motherwell as well as earning 23 Scottish International Caps. On the morning of 25 March 1995, he was filming a soccer skills television show for Scottish TV on a training pitch next to Clyde FC's Broadwood stadium. He had just been coaching some 14-year-old children on taking free kicks and was rehearsing his lines for the cameras when, suddenly, he collapsed. Charlie Nicholas, who was also taking part in the filming, said in the *Glasgow Herald*: 'Davie had just asked me if I fancied going for a pint when we were finished and I said that sounded like a good idea. I turned away and when I looked back he was on the ground. We were all so shocked. Davie looked after himself and was very fit for his age. He didn't smoke and was not a heavy drinker and he looks the same way at thirty-nine as he did when he was thirty.'

The programme's director, Ian Hamilton, gave mouth-to-mouth resuscitation until an ambulance arrived. He had suffered a subarachnoid haemorrhage, which is where an artery weak spot suddenly gives way. Within less than 24 hours from hospital admission, Davie Cooper was dead. Glasgow's Southern Central Hospital had to set up a special phone line to deal with the hundreds of enquiries and goodwill messages. Following his death, the Rangers' fans decked the entire Copeland Road end of Ibrox in flowers, scarves and flags.

Teammate Ally McCoist summed up the club's devastation: 'This is a very distressing time, it's like we've lost a brother, someone who was with us and part of our lives. Ironically, Davie Cooper always said the greatest match of his career was playing for Scotland against Wales at Ninian Park on the night Jock Stein died. The day after he died the *Glasgow Herald* wrote: "Not since that day in Cardiff has Scottish football been left as devastatingly numb as it is today." '

After the collapse of the Soviet Union, Russia had become more like the Wild West than a country beginning a new optimistic chapter in its history, and football cannot escape the dangerous forces that now operate in the country. If money is involved, then so is organised crime. In the summer of 1995, in Donetsk, Russia's most crime-ridden city, Victor Bragin, president of Andrei Kanchelskis' old club Shakytor, was killed along with a relative and four bodyguards when a bomb went off under his seat seven minutes into a home game against Tavria Simferopol. He certainly wasn't the victim of a Western-style boardroom take-over battle, but the fact that he was surrounded by four bodyguards at the match suggests that he certainly wasn't top of somebody's Christmas card list.

Not wishing to tempt fate but, at the time of writing, 1996, has, so far, been death-free for world football. The passions aroused by football can induce, in some, a completely irrational side to their nature. Bravado and determination are one thing, but to publicly proclaim an intention to die does seem a weird way to manufacture pre-match hype: in the build-up to the 1995 South American Super Cup, World Cup winner and Flamengo ace Romario promised his side would start, play and finish the game 'like kamikazes'. He went on, 'We'll win or die in the effort.' Luckily, Romario and his teammates backed away from such drastic action after they beat the Argentinian side Independente 1-0.

Whether you believe in an afterlife or not, everybody loves a good ghost story. Ghosts, in a manner of speaking, are alive and well and have been known to make their presence felt at football clubs, although this phenomenon does seem to be monopolised by the UK. After his death in 1931 (documented earlier in this chapter), John 'Jock' Thompson, the young Celtic goalkeeper, was said to haunt the goalmouths at Parkhead. Is it possible that Celtic played for all those years with two goal-keepers? Celtic now play at their magnificent new stadium, Celtic Park, but if the legend is true, there is still one player who turns up at Parkhead every other Saturday expecting a game.

In the early part of the twentieth century, Herbert Chapman *was* Arsenal. He was the Gunners' revolutionary manager who built the team that went on to win three consecutive Football League championships. He died after contracting pneumonia whilst watching Arsenal's third team play. The club doctor had advised him to go home to bed but Chapman would have none of it, insisting he was staying at the game saying, 'I don't often get to watch the lads play'. Despite his death, his association with the club continues today – the marble halls of Highbury display a bust of Chapman and, according to legend, his ghostly footsteps can be heard pacing up and down the club's corridors with alarming regularity.

If there was a game where contestants have to connect famous historical figures with football clubs through obvious association, then few would disagree that Admiral Horatio Nelson would follow Portsmouth. Indeed, it does seem that Nelson's allegiances are by the seaside – but not in Portsmouth. His ghost is believed to be haunting the boardroom at Blackpool's Broomfield Road ground. Club officials have repeatedly been woken by the alarm system mysteriously going off in the middle of the night and the stadium manager seems to be able to sense a ghostly presence. The club believe that Lord Nelson's ghost is responsible as part of the boardroom is made of panelled wood which was originally part of Nelson's flagship, the *Foudroyant*, which beached off Blackpool in 1897. Manager John Turner offers some explanation for the haunting: 'It's an old maritime superstition that sailing folk take exception to anything on their ships being touched – that could explain these events. The alarm system has been repeatedly checked and the engineers were completely baffled.'

If the management of Oldham Athletic have displayed a haunted look recently, it would be wrong to assume that the team's performance was the sole cause. Oldham's Boundary Park is said to be haunted by a ghost called Fred, a particularly loyal fan who always occupied the same place in the stand and died during a game in the 1960s. Fred only appears early in the morning or late at night in the George Hill stand. The club's cleaners, after witnessing several visitations, refuse to work alone. Oldham's public relations man, Gordon Lawton, says, 'he frightens the cleaners to death; things move around up there and the cleaners don't like being alone. He moves mops and brooms and seems to have a particular liking for pens as well.' One notable encounter with Fred happened when Eileen (one of the cleaners) saw him in the kitchen below the stand. She was scared out of her wits but when she shouted his name, he disappeared.

All the deaths discussed so far relate, in some way, to the field of play. Stadium tragedies such as Hillsborough, Bradford, Glasgow and Marseilles obviously closely associate death with football, but in a different way. The underlying reasons for these, and other, disasters have been the subject of widespread debate, resulting in the introduction of stadium safety laws specifically designed to prevent similar incidents ever happening again. To reopen the debate here would only open old wounds and rake up painful memories for those concerned. Suffice it to say that everything there is to say on this matter has already been said.

2 Brawls

FOOTBALL IS A GAME OF EMOTION and when passions run high, rational behaviour can be abandoned. This is true both off and on the pitch. The do-gooders insist that the law-abiding behaviour of the players is of paramount importance, but these same people will never have experienced the thrill, excitement and adrenaline rush of a competitive professional sport. Cricket is a genteel sport where physical contact with opponents is almost non-existent – in football, it's completely different. In a perfect world, unsavoury incidents would never happen on the field of play but events can, and do, influence the players in ways which would be unimaginable in most other sports.

Whether we like it or not, brawls are part and parcel of football. The clever player is the one who keeps his head when all around him are losing theirs. When tempers flare, referees usually manage to calm things down – a couple of yellow cards, and maybe a red one, will normally do the trick. The history of brawls in football is an interesting one, mirroring the behaviour of different cultures: Northern Europe, for instance, rarely experiences seriously violent brawls; Mediterranean countries like to make them look worse than they really are; in Africa, they can be life threatening; however, it's in South America where the most frightening and ugly scenes have consistently occurred. The South American psyche undoubtedly plays its part: the Argentinian writer José Luis Borges summed up Latino attitudes to football by proclaiming, 'football is a post-colonial replacement for knife fighting'. It is, of course, rare to change the habits of a lifetime; attitudes are in the blood. If boxer Mike Tyson ever decided to change sports, he would feel right at home in South American football where the two sports combine very well.

The large majority of football fracas are your bog-standard handbag at fifteen paces-types of disputes. They happen week in and week out – usually a ten second rush of blood to the head and then it's back to reality and on with the match. Brawls usually have a predictable ending and none more aptly than when eleven Peruvian players from the same team were sent off in a cup tie in early 1980 – the club's name was Los Terribles.

As early as 1860, the boisterous nature of football claimed its first victim. Blackheath FC withdrew from the game when hacking was officially outlawed. Intent on staying butch and macho, they decided to set up a rugby club instead.

In December 1891, Blackburn were playing Burnley in appalling weather conditions. Tempers were frayed and a couple of fights ensued. After the second fight, ten of Blackburn's team decided they'd had enough and walked off the field. Only their goalkeeper, Herby Arthur, was left on the pitch together with the full complement of Burnley players. The game carried on regardless, with the strange sight of eleven players bearing down on one solitary player defending his goal. Miraculously, Arthur managed to save an incoming shot and grabbed hold of the ball, refusing to kick it back into play on the basis that he actually had no one to kick it to. The referee had no choice but to abandon the game.

In South America, as in England, football had started as a gentleman's game, played by the middle classes. As it evolved, it obviously became more popular and spread through all social classes. Passions rose and, as money started playing a part in the game's development, more people wanted some of the action. The Corinthian spirit soon went out of the window.

During May 1912, Argentinian team Estudiantes de La Plata had their ground closed down following an ugly incident during a match against Estudiantes of Buenos Aires. A group of de La Plata players had incited the crowd to attack the referee, whilst another player was happy to just verbally attack the poor guy. Two players were suspended for encouraging the crowd to assault the ref and a third player was suspended for insulting him. Future events in South American football make this incident look like a vicar's tea party – a precedent had been set and there was no looking back.

In the same season, Independiente won the Argentinian league by beating Club Argentinos 5-0. A pretty conclusive result you might think, but you would be wrong. Second placed Porteño claimed they had evidence that Argentinos had, for some reason, fielded a weakened team. Enough suspicion was raised that league officials agreed a play-off match between Porteño (who were only behind on goal difference) and Independiente and the winner would then become automatic league champions. Porteño scored first and held the lead right up to three minutes from time when Independiente equalised. After the game had restarted, Independiente won a corner. A goal-mouth scramble ensued and Independiente's players protested when a shot appeared to go over the goal line, only to be overruled by the referee. The mother of all arguments followed and the situation deteriorated, with three Independiente players being sent off. In protest, the rest of the team walked off the pitch, refusing to continue. The referee was then attacked by players and spectators alike and was forced, for his own safety, to abandon the match. The inexcusable behaviour of the Independiente team led to the inevitable: the championship was awarded to Porteño.

By 1916, Argentina and Uruguay had built up a bitter and intense rivalry. The meetings were eagerly awaited but were always potential powderkegs. One fixture between the two sides prompted a stampede for tickets and it was later discovered that too many tickets had been sold. The match was postponed and the fans were pretty miffed to say the least – they proceeded to set fire to the stadium. The blaze lasted for four hours and only the central pavilion remained standing.

If old scores can't be settled on the pitch, you can rely on South American fans to settle them off the pitch. In 1918, a match between San Martin and Vila Bargano in Argentina ended in a dull 0-0 draw. Rival supporters, probably frustrated by the sterile game they had just watched, decided to have a *Gunfight at the OK Corral*-type shoot out in the streets. Two fans were killed and an old lady walking nearby was injured by a stray bullet. It's easy to understand the pressure players must have felt when they knew rival fans watching them play were armed and dangerous.

It wasn't uncommon for these fans to take the law into their own hands. In the early 1900s British football teams used to travel to South America to play in exhibition games. Britain was the natural home of the game and the thinking was (in Britain) that British teams were the best, and wasn't it a good idea to go abroad to teach Johnny Foreigner a few tricks of the trade. Contrasting cultures led to some interesting events. For example, in 1923, a combined Scottish XI were playing in Argentina when they won a corner that, as far as the local crowd was concerned, was dubious to say the least. Fans surrounded the Scotsman attempting to take the corner kick, forcing him to kick the ball out of play for a goal kick. The game then continued as normal, as if nothing untoward had happened. Had the Scots insisted that the corner be taken properly, it's easy to imagine what might have followed.

Plymouth Argyle toured Argentina, briefly, in 1924. They were awarded a penalty in a match against Rosario. Plymouth's players were amazed when their opponents threatened to leave the pitch at once because they disagreed with the referee's decision. A light brawl and argument followed and a section of the home crowd invaded the pitch. It took twenty minutes for play to resume by which time Plymouth had dutifully forgotten about the penalty.

Uruguay showed the world that South America had become a soccer force to be reckoned with by winning the gold medal for football at the 1924 Olympic Games. Their neighbours Argentina, who had often beaten Uruguay, were upset that a team they considered to be inferior to themselves had won an important tournament. The Argentinians challenged the

Uruguayans to a pair of friendlies, obviously designed, in Argentine eyes, to humiliate Uruguay. The first match passed off comparatively uneventfully in Montevideo, ending in a 1-1 draw. The second match in Buenos Aires ended in chaos. The crowd encroached onto the pitch and, after five minutes, the players walked off. Argentine soldiers managed to get the crowd back, but they were so close to the touchlines that the Uruguayans said they didn't want to play on. A rematch was scheduled for the same stadium four days later and wire fencing was erected around the pitch. Argentina had the better of the game, scoring direct from a corner and then, despite a fight-back, going 2-1 up just after half time. The Uruguayans then began goading their opponents, and the home crowd. Argentine crowds are not known for their tolerant attitudes and they decided to show their dissatisfaction with the Uruguayans by throwing pebbles at them. As the stones rained down on them the Uruguayans decided to throw them back at the crowd. One of their players, Scarone, was arrested for kicking a policeman who was trying to stop him throwing stones. The game was never concluded because, once again, the Uruguayans walked off, 2-1 down with five minutes still to play.

The Uruguayans got their own back on Argentina by beating them in the 1926 World Cup Final. As if to underline the volatility of South American fans there followed serious rioting in Buenos Aires. A woman was stoned for waving a Uruguayan flag and the Uruguayan consulate and the Oriental club were stoned. Two people were shot dead.

Infamous football hooligans in late 1920s South America were the Argentinian 'Barras de Hinchas', a motley crew who followed a collection of teams. In essence, they were the prototype hooligans travelling to various stadiums armed with bottles and oranges which they delighted in using as weapons. It's difficult to contemplate grievous bodily harm being inflicted on someone using an orange, but it was an essential part of their armoury. One of the 'Hinchas' party tricks was to burn stadium benches, throw them on the pitch and swiftly follow up with a pitch invasion to attack rival players and fans.

Chelsea saw this bad side of Argentine football when they toured the country in 1929. During the fourth game of their tour against a Capital XI (a team made up from the four big clubs in Buenos Aires), a group of Barras de Hinchas invaded the pitch. One of them punched Chelsea's captain on the nose, and he slumped to the ground. Order was briefly restored but, shortly afterwards, violence erupted again. Argentine International Luis Monti kicked Chelsea's centre half Rodger in the groin. He promptly fainted and was carried off, whilst a more substantial punch up got underway, much to the delight of the crowd who considered this all part of the game. When order was eventually restored, the game was played to a conclusion – Chelsea lost 3-2. Before they could make a hasty retreat to their transport home, a local fan rubbed salt in the wound by kicking out all the glass panels in their changing room.

The South American men in black ran the gauntlet in the vast majority of games they refereed and respect for them amongst players was almost non-existent and, if it did exist, it was given only grudgingly. In June 1932, Señor Bruzzone was beaten up by Huracan fans after their team had lost a match 1-0 to Racing. In the same year, referee de Angelis was seriously assaulted on the pitch by fans of the team Ferrocarril Oeste (Western Railway) and referee Gomez was assaulted after the final whistle by fans of Buenos Aires team Gimnasia y Esgrima. Señor de Angelis was in further trouble when he refereed a top-of-the-table clash between Estudiantes and River Plate. Trouble started when he disallowed an Estudiantes equalising goal and he was surrounded and man-handled by angry players. He ran straight into the dressing room to escape the furore only to emerge, fifteen minutes later, and award the goal after all. The goal was dubbed 'El Gol de la Casilla' – the dressing room goal – as rumours circulated that the referee had been 'persuaded' to change his mind at gunpoint, by the Estudiantes president. The match finished in a draw.

The England versus Italy match, played in 1934, became known as the Battle of Highbury. Italy were the World Cup holders coming to England, the home of football, to play in a game that was dubbed by the press at the time as 'the most important football match anywhere in the world since the great war'. Seven Arsenal players were in the England side, including the great Ted Drake. 'Could Drake's Armada beat off the Mussolini invasion?'

Winning was everything to both teams; it was a game of national pride. The Italians – a product of the fascist pre-war uncertainty – were on huge win bonuses which included money, cars and exemption from military service. The trouble started when Luisito Monti broke his toe in a crunching challenge by Ted Drake. Monti's teammates claimed the incident was foul play and, when the decision went against them, they started to get shirty. As the game wore on it became increasingly violent. England player Eddie Hapgood suffered a broken nose in another clash and, for a while, the game looked like developing into all-out warfare. Eddie Hapgood's comments after the game summed up the feelings of the England players: 'It's difficult to play like gentlemen when somebody closely resembling a member of the Mafia is wiping his studs down your leg.' Despite their severe physical beating, England were 3-0 up at half time. In the second half, the Italians calmed down a bit and concentrated on playing football. They managed to pull back two goals but despite their incentives to win, ended up losing 3-2. Almost the entire England team reported finishing the game carrying injuries of varying severity.

Meanwhile, back in Argentina, concern was growing about the treatment and reliability of home grown referees. It was decided by the powers that be that British referees could be the answer as they were well-known for their impartiality and fairness. Somebody had to control the unruly players and defuse the passionate and violent crowds that populated Argentine football grounds: Isaac Caswell was the first British referee to adjudicate in South American football.

In 1938, whilst officiating in a match between Boca Juniors and Racing, he was stoned by rival supporters. Despite this unsavoury baptism, he went on to become very popular, paving the way for the arrival of scores more British referees. One of them, John Mede, had to send off all 22 players in a match between Huracan and Velez Sarsfield in 1950 after a violent mass brawl. The events and subsequent injuries were so serious that all the players were arrested and given prison sentences ranging from six to fifteen weeks.

The bitter rivalry between Uruguay and Argentina manifested itself again in 1952. Uruguay's Peñarol were playing hosts to Botafogo for a friendly match when Botafogo scored a perfectly good goal and were instantly attacked by all the Peñarol players. The brawl quickly grew as the club's reserves waded in soon to be followed by the local police, who were less than sympathetic to Botafogo's plight. The free-for-all lasted several minutes, forcing the game to be abandoned. John Arlott wrote in 1960, 'the struggle between defence and attack – the basic contest in football – is really, and always, the chief interest in any football: this is why a "friendly" match never quite rings true.' That statement is all very well for the comparatively sedate game played in Britain but, in South America, 'friendlies' should quite clearly be renamed.

In 1954, two of the game's most skilful international sides, Brazil and Hungary, were brought together in Berne. The stakes were high, with both teams eager to secure a place in the semi-finals of the World Cup. The match was refereed by Englishman Arthur Ellis (who later went on to star in BBC TV's *It's a Knockout*). It was a feast of football and goals but when Hungary went 3-2 ahead, Santos of Brazil and Boszik of Hungary were sent off for trying to strangle each other. Tempers flared throughout most of the game and by the time Hungary scored their fourth goal in the ninetieth minute, horrendous tackles were raining in on players. A second Brazilian, Humbert Pozzi, was sent off. If the match itself had seemed violent, there was far worse to come. Hungarian star Ferenc Puskas, who had been unable to play in the game because of injury, remembers the Hungarians celebrating their victory loudly and boisterously in their dressing room. The Brazilian dressing room was directly opposite and the Hungarians' jubilation irritated them to the point that they completely lost their cool. The victors' dressing room door was kicked in by a rampaging mob of Brazilians who then kicked Puskas' colleague Toth unconscious. A soda syphon was thrown at the Hungarians, the dressing room lights were smashed and a shower of bottles followed very quickly afterwards. As the Hungarians dived for cover a mass of bodies jumped on top of them. The fight raged for over ten minutes before it was stopped and a damage assessment could be made: Hungary's Toth was still out for the count and a Brazilian player (centre half Pinheiro) had a deep five inch gash on his head (it was later alleged, by the Brazilians, that Puskas had inflicted the wound by attacking him with a bottle). Another player was bleeding profusely from a facial wound. Almost every player had some sort of injury. Hungary had won the match on the pitch but who had come out best in extra time in the dressing room was impossible to decide because there had been no referee.

The day host nation Chile met Italy in a World Cup match has been dubbed the Battle of Santiago. It took place on 2 June 1962 but before a ball had been kicked, bad feeling between the two sides had become more than apparent. The Chileans resented the poaching of their players by Italian clubs and the situation wasn't helped after a couple of Italian journalists wrote articles running down Chile and casting doubts on its very substance as a nation.

BBC Television commentator David Coleman described this fixture as 'the most appalling, disgusting and disgraceful game of football ever played' – and he wasn't wrong.

Straight from the kickoff, English referee Ken Aston struggled to control this vicious match. After eight minutes of play, Giorgio Ferrini was sent off for kicking Chile's Landa. Despite getting a red card he refused to leave the pitch for the next ten minutes. The referee, at his wit's end, summoned the police who had to forcibly march Ferrini off the pitch. 'This is one of the sorriest, stupidest spectacles I've ever seen', commented Coleman to a watching TV audience of millions. Five minutes before half time, Chile retaliated when Leonel Sanchez, the son of a boxer, punched and broke Limberto Maschio's nose.

Amazingly, the referee and linesmen didn't see the incident, but David Coleman did, saying, 'that was one of the neatest left hooks I've ever seen'. A few minutes later, with Sanchez now a marked man, Italian Mario David attempted to kick him in the head. He missed but executed a perfect drop kick to Sanchez's neck. David got an immediate red card. The Chileans came out 2-0 winners, with Italy completing the game with only nine men.

In 1964, 318 people were killed and over 500 were injured following the outbreak of a riot during a match between Peru and Argentina. The trouble started after a Peruvian equalising goal was ruled out, precipitating one of the most bloody riots in South American football history.

Pele, according to popular consensus the greatest player the world has ever seen, was sent off for his part in a brawl in the second leg of the Brazilian championship final in 1965. His club, Santos, were playing Vasco de Gama when Vasco's Zeznho hit his opposite number Lima, who then proceeded to return the compliment. Both players were sent off, after which a fight erupted with five more players being dismissed. Pele was one of them.

World Cup year, 1966, saw a couple of notable incidents, one of them quite bizarre. Brazilian club Bangu were already league champions before they played Flamengo. The game should have been a mere formality and saw Bangu cruise into a 3-0 lead. Suddenly, the entire Flamengo team started fighting amongst themselves. Fists and boots were flying and eventually the referee sent nine Flamengo players off as the fighting spread to the terraces. Six players were each given a six month suspension from the game.

So close and yet so far would be the best way to describe an international match between Chile and Uruguay on 25 June 1967. The game was abandoned after eighty minutes following a mass brawl between the players. Nine Uruguayans and ten Chileans were sent off.

In the same year, Anglo-South American relations were severely tested once again. The 1967 World Club championship saw Celtic face Racing of Argentina. Celtic won the first leg 1-0 in front of 103,000 fans in Glasgow. The South Americans had shown no restraint in employing their time-wasting techniques. The second leg, played in Avellanda, got off to a bad start when Celtic's goalkeeper, Simpson, was hit by a stone thrown from the crowd before kickoff. Celtic had to replace him and, in hindsight, should have walked out there and then. During the match the referee refused two certain Celtic penalties but they achieved a breakthrough when he awarded them their third appeal. Gemmill scored whilst the referee was being jostled by Racing players. Curiously, he then awarded Racing an obviously offside goal (even Argentinian newspapers acknowledged as much). At half time, the Celtic players went to their dressing room to find that no water had been supplied. Racing took the lead through Cardenas in the second half and brutally held on to it, ably assisted by the home crowd who kept the ball for long periods whenever it was kicked into touch. With the aggregate score level at 2-2 a third play off match was arranged in 'neutral' Montevideo. Jock Stein had made a bad move and realised it when he discovered that 20,000 Racing fans had crossed the river Plate to see the game. Basile and Celtic's Lennox were sent off for fighting and Racing's Martin claimed he was smashed on the head by a policeman's truncheon (although Celtic observers described his acting as more convincing than Roger Moore's). Johnston was sent off for being kicked in the midriff by Martin – who then fooled the referee by going down as if poleaxed by the challenge. Finally, Hughes and Ruili were red carded for more fisticuffs and in all that mayhem Cardenas managed to score the only goal of the game, giving Racing the World Club Championship. One abiding memory of the match was the curly red hair of Celtic's Jimmy Johnston completely covered in Argentine phlegm.

After the match, Celtic fined each player £250 whilst Racing, oblivious to the diabolical behaviour over the three games, gave all their players a brand new sports car each. And they say crime never pays.

Tensions are bad enough when South American sides play

each other but if the ingredients are changed, and an Italian side is added to the equation, the results can be far reaching. In 1969, AC Milan travelled to Argentina for a game against Estudiantes de la Plata in the World Club Final. Milan had won the first leg 3-0 and, as a consequence, the reception they got in Buenos Aires was far from welcoming. The Argentine players took the defeat badly and decided to employ a policy of all out attack. Unfortunately, the type of attack involved was the physical kind. The Italians were consistently and brutally beaten throughout the entire game and despite no sending off, Argentina's President Ongania felt compelled to personally intervene in the aftermath of the match. He felt that his country's reputation (surely not on the football field) had to be upheld and ordered that goalkeeper Poletti and defender Suarez should be imprisoned for thirty days and banned from the international team. The second leg ended in a 2-1 victory for Estudiantes de la Plata but Milan won the championship 4-2 on aggregate.

In the same year, there was more bad blood between Brazil and Peru when they met at the Maracana stadium. Trouble started when Peru went 2-1 ahead. Future World Cup winner Gerson kicked a Peruvian on the knee and a forty minute brawl erupted. The match was stopped and the Peruvians ended up back in their dressing room. Only a message from Joao de Havalange, FIFA's president, could persuade them back onto the pitch. Brazil scored two more goals, ensuring a 3-2 victory. Brazilian manager Saldanha said at the obligatory press conference that he was pleased to see that there were no women in the Brazilian team.

International matches in Britain during the 1970s rarely passed off without incident. Passion and rivalry are potent forces, not just for the players but for the supporters as well. In the 1972/73 season the world's oldest international fixture, England versus Scotland, was played at Wembley. Alan Ball, easily spotted with his distinctive red hair, was surprised to be confronted by a Scottish fan who ran on the pitch and punched him in the face. The incident was ugly but Ball maintained his sense of humour by declaring, 'luckily, I saw him coming, I was able to ride his punch in a way Muhammad Ali would have been proud of'.

The traditional curtain raiser to the English football season is the Charity Shield match held every year at Wembley. On 10 August 1974, the match was between league champions Leeds United and FA Cup winners Liverpool. The players involved in the game were either established household names or well on the way to becoming them. Leeds player Johnny Giles decided, for reasons best known to himself, to punch Liverpool starlet Kevin Keegan flush on the chin, only to scurry back into a crowd of players unnoticed. By the time Keegan had regained his senses and picked himself up off the floor, Giles was over ten yards away. As Billy Bremner, the Leeds captain with a well-earned hardman reputation, was innocently strolling by, Keegan, who wrongly identified him as his assailant, attempted to exact his revenge. All hell broke loose as Bremner tried to protect himself and the situation was only calmed down when giant Leeds centre half Norman (Bite yer Legs) Hunter re-strained Keegan by placing his hands around the Liverpool striker's throat. Both players, because of Hunter's actions, were prevented from trading blows but not saved from being sent off. The situation was not helped by the further actions of Bremner and Keegan who decided to show their disgust at the decision by ditching their shirts as they left the pitch. Aside from a bruised fist, Johnny Giles afforded himself a wry chuckle and completed the match. In 1996, he wrote a weekly football column for a national newspaper, dubbing himself 'the man the players read'.

The unlikely setting of Mauritius witnessed an unexpected interruption to the normally smooth running of the National Championship in December 1974. The incident happened in a match between those two pillars of society, the Fire Brigade and the Police. The fire brigade were leading 3-0 when police player Callychurn was sent off for a second yellow card offence. The referee also awarded a penalty – and started a riot. The linesman's flag was snatched by Tootoo, the police captain and

Mauritian International, who then kicked the linesman. With 25 minutes to play the police suddenly walked off the pitch, refusing to carry on. The game was awarded to the fire brigade after an inquiry by the Mauritius Sports Association.

Chilean referee Sergio Vasquez sent nineteen players off in the second leg of a Pinto Duran Cup match between Chile and Uruguay in Santiago after the game degenerated into a free for all. Trouble flared after 78 minutes when Chilean defender Garcia had put through his own net. Chile's Diaz and Uruguay's Santelli started fighting on the field and the general mêlée began. Ten Chileans and nine Uruguayans got their marching orders for fighting, but it took fifteen minutes for them to get off the pitch as they had to wait in the centre circle until a hail of stones from infuriated spectators died down. Amazingly, a week after the match, Señor Vasquez, the referee, was suspended and fined 50 US dollars for 'letting things get out of hand'.

Leeds United were once again involved in a famous brawl in November 1975. Derby's Francis Lee (short and chubby) and Leeds United's Norman Hunter (tall, butch and menacing) were playing in a league match at Derby County's Baseball ground. The incident started after Lee made a rather tame shot on goal before being unceremoniously bundled to the floor by Hunter. As he got to his feet the unsuspecting Lee walked straight into a bone-crunching right-hand blow to the head. Lee, blood splattered nose 'n' all, was outraged to say the least and had to be held back by four Leeds players. Norman Hunter, realising he now couldn't be attacked himself, gave Lee a knowing smile – only to have it wiped off his face when the referee decided to send both players off. Lee was somewhat bemused by the verdict as, up to this point, he hadn't actually thrown a punch. As both players trooped off the pitch further words were exchanged and, suddenly, Lee snapped. He swung aimlessly with two right-hand punches at the big man – looking like a kid brother riled by his older sibling's taunts. Norman Hunter tried to fend him off but Leeds players Frank Gray and Billy Bremner, together with Derby's Charlie George, had to jump in to separate the warring factions. After the players had left the pitch the match was concluded with ten-a-side. Francis Lee recalled the incident in an interview with a football magazine saying, 'Norman threw a punch at me when I wasn't looking. The referee sent us both off yet I hadn't thrown a punch, so I just lost my temper as I was walking off. Fortunately, all I got was a split lip.'

1979 saw a first for English football when Charlton Athletic's Derek Hales and Mike Flanagan became the first teammates to be sent off for fighting each other. Trouble flared when Hales failed to reach a pass from Flanagan in an FA Cup third round tie against Maidstone United. After exchanging some colourful insults, the pair came to blows and were sent off. Flanagan walked out on Charlton and Hales was sacked. However, he was later reinstated after pressure from the players' union, the Professional Footballers Association, and went on to become club captain.

The 1983 South American Junior Championships saw what is possibly the longest brawl in football history. The tournament's deciding match between Brazil and Argentina was held in Bolivia and a draw was enough for Brazil to take the title. Argentina led 2-1 at half time. Brazil equalised in the second half and Argentina's Garcia was sent off for a bad foul which, frankly, was no worse than the fouls that had already littered the match. The final straw for Argentina came when the Costa Rican referee awarded Brazil a penalty. Brazil scored and all hell broke loose. Nobody could say for sure whether the fighting was started by the reserves or the players on the pitch. Argentine goalkeeper Islas was seen racing the whole length of the pitch punching and kicking like a madman. The Bolivian police made matters worse by joining in the fracas with truncheons drawn. The fifty Bolivian police officers then turned their attention to the sports photographers who were taking pictures of the brawl. Like a true coward, the referee was long gone by the time Argentine officials persuaded the players to sit in the centre circle as a protest. The match, and therefore the championship, was awarded to Brazil. Both sets of staff were fined heavily and the Argentinian goalkeeper was banned for 100 days.

After a brawl in the Bulgarian Cup Final in 1985, the Bulgarian government threatened to disband the two biggest clubs in the country – CSKA Sofia and Levski Spartak. They also threatened to ban five players for life, including Levski's goalkeeper Burislav Mikhailov who later went on to play for Reading. The final had been marred by violence and was won 2-1 by CSKA Sofia. Three players were sent off, five were booked and the cup was withheld by the Communist Party. Both chairmen were handed what the Bulgarian press ominously called 'Personal Punishments'. All was forgiven six months later; Mikhailov was allowed to carry on playing for Bulgaria and neither team was disbanded.

For most of the 1980s it was Britain – the cradle of football – that exceeded all brawling expectations. However, a certain Eric Cantona was also in action in an incident that didn't endear him to the French football authorities. In 1987, he was playing for Auxerre and was heavily fined for assaulting his own team's goalkeeper, Bruno Martini, during a game. Martini was left sporting a black eye and Cantona was left sporting his new nickname, 'Enfant Terrible'. More of Eric later.

Glasgow's old firm derby continued to shape Scottish football history in October 1987, ably abetted by a few Englishmen. The intensity of this fixture has to be seen to be believed. During this particular match the pressure on the players became unbearable and what followed was one of Scottish football's most famous punch ups. With almost a quarter of an hour of the game played at Ibrox, Rangers' goalkeeper Chris Woods collected a back pass and was preparing to throw the ball back into play. Before he managed to accomplish this, Celtic's Frank McAvennie ran straight into him, knocking him over. In normal games such an incident would hardly raise an eyebrow but in the Glasgow derby it's completely the opposite: Woods shoved McAvennie who then in turn retaliated; Rangers' central defender Terry Butcher joined the fray and also pushed McAvennie; then, Rangers' former England International

Graham Roberts threw a punch at McAvennie; the referee had seen enough and sent McAvennie, Woods and Butcher off; the crowd rioted. The incident didn't stop there because legal action was taken against all four players.

Arsenal were also involved in a couple of incidents in the eighties. In September 1988, ITN cameras picked up Arsenal's Paul Davis breaking Southampton's Glen Cockerill's jaw in an off-the-ball incident. Equally significant was a disturbance at Highbury on 4 November 1989 when Arsenal were at home to Norwich City. It was an entertaining game with six goals in the first 89 minutes. Then, Arsenal were awarded a penalty in the final minute but Lee Dixon's shot was saved. Following up the rebound, Arsenal's Alan Smith was bundled into the goal by Norwich's Mark Bowen. As most of the Gunners were trotting back to the halfway line, Smith and Niall Quinn got into a playground squabble with the entire Norwich team. Prompted by the crowd, the rest of the Arsenal team realised they were missing out on something and charged back downfield to spend a lot of time swearing, pushing and shoving. It was a pretty tame affair really with not one decent punch being thrown and David 'Rocky' Rocastle not living up to his nickname. Finally, the police came onto the pitch to break it up and Arsenal won the game 4-3.

More trouble came from the mercurial Eric Cantona in 1990 when he was playing for the French club Montpelier and received a ten-day ban for smashing his boots into team mate Jean Claude Lemoult. His time in France was rapidly coming to an end with a transfer to English football his next move. Cantona would go on to illuminate the English game after a fairly inauspicious start but wherever he went, controversy would not be far behind him.

The former Yugoslavia was a country packed full of outrageously gifted players. Following the break up of the nation its international sides were devastated by political instability and war. Before the break up, in Zagreb (Croatia) on 13 May 1990, Dinamo Zagreb were playing Red Star Belgrade in a crucial cup match. The political situation gave the game certain overtones that were impossible to ignore. Red Star were the top Serbian team and Dinamo Zagreb were among the top sides in Croatia. With Yugoslavia on the verge of unravelling, the match had been billed as Serbia versus Croatia. Although nationalist fervour was at its most dangerous and ethnic dissent was rampant, the doomsday forecasts for the game proved underestimated and inadequate.

The match started during a riot. Not an English-style riot, where a couple of mounted policemen can fairly easily restore order, but a full scale outpouring of Serb–Croat hatred and, far from trying to prevent it, the police joined in. Red Star fans fought a running battle with the Dinamo fans with the state police, who were mainly Serbs, joining in. This became too much for the Red Star players and staff to handle and they proceeded to wade into the police. Players and police clashed on the pitch and the first battle of the Yugoslavian war was underway. Days after the game, the Yugoslavian football league – one of the last threads holding the country together – was abolished. Only hours after that decision, the real war began.

Bitter English rivals Manchester United and Arsenal always enjoy competitive and explosive matches. On 20 October 1990, the two sides met at Old Trafford; Arsenal were top dogs, champions from the previous season, whilst Manchester United had not won the league for over twenty years. Trouble started when United's striker Mark Hughes found himself in the middle of a crunching sandwich tackle between Nigel Winterburn and Anders Limpar. What followed was a well executed pincer movement – United's Brian McClair went into the back of Winterburn whilst Hughes clattered into the front of him: the spark for a 21 man brawl. Anders Limpar was the first to react. He followed up his original nasty tackle on Hughes with a perfectly executed rabbit punch on McClair. Arsenal's Michael Thomas joined in, grabbing McClair by the throat and, with Dennis Irwin, Tony Adams and Neil Webb making good early runs from deep positions, the brawl was well and truly on. Arsenal Captain Tony Adams, leading by example, shoved McClair over the touchline as Michael Thomas and Paul Davis made a couple of pansy-like weak shoves on the Scotsman. United's Paul Ince made a customary late run into the danger area, surging through a crowd of players and attempting to grab hold of Limpar. Perhaps sensibly, Limpar turned his back on the snarling, berserk England international and walked away, but it was only when managers George Graham and Alex Ferguson intervened on the pitch that order was restored. Enough had been seen by the referee for him to file a detailed report, resulting in fines of £50,000 for both clubs along with extra fines for Arsenal boss George Graham and players Nigel Winterburn, Paul Davis, Michael Thomas, David Rocastle and Anders Limpar. No Manchester United players were fined.

The Spanish sunshine island of Tenerife is used to battles, usually between British tourists and the locals. The battle that took place in January 1993 was quite different in that it had an Argentinian connection. After Argentina won the 1978 World Cup, their players were in great demand and began to play abroad. Spurs were first to take advantage and Osvaldo Ardiles and Ricky Villa joined the club. More countrymen followed them to Europe, bringing with them their silky skills and fiery temperaments. The trend continued and came to include the footballing genius Diego Maradona, playing in Italy and then Spain. In January 1993, Maradona was in Seville's side playing Tenerife. Other Argentinians involved in the game were Simeone and Bilardo (the manager) with Seville, and Valdano, Redondo, Pizzi and Dertycia for Tenerife. Tenerife won the game 3-0; it included thirteen bookings and three red cards, amongst them Pizzi who scored two penalties. Following numerous violent exchanges, Maradona was also dismissed. There was a fight which involved Seville's manager and an encounter between Simeone and police officers all of which prompted an investigation by the civil governor of Tenerife. After the match the recriminations continued when Bilardo said that Valdano was 'a devil in white gloves'. Valdano retaliated, accusing Bilardo of being 'Argentina's public enemy number one' despite taking his country to two World Cup victories.

Merseyside fans experienced a mini player brawl in 1993

when Everton were hosts to Liverpool. Liverpool goalkeeper Bruce Grobbelaar started exchanging blows with Steve McManaman as Liverpool slid to a 2-0 defeat. Grobbelaar was furious with a poor McManaman clearance that led to Everton's first goal but both players kissed and made up after the game.

One South American side with an appalling disciplinary record are Gremio. Early in the 1992/93 season their players had been officially warned about their conduct after attacking a referee for awarding a penalty against them. In the same season, they met Peñarol in the South American Super Cup and eight Gremio players were sent off after brawling with police on the touchline following a major altercation which had already held the match up for ten minutes.

The mid-nineties have thrown up some memorable incidents spanning the whole gambit of severity and nationalities. Even UN peacekeepers managed to get in on the act in a match in the Autumn of 1995 when Ghanaian peacekeepers organised a confidence-boosting match against their local Rwandan hosts in Kigali. The game ended in a free-for-all after one of the peacekeepers punched the referee for awarding a penalty against them. Julian Beford, a local UN spokesman, said, 'when you put on a football jersey and tie up your laces you leave peace keeping behind'.

Sentiment is a wonderful thing, but it can become meaningless when a football match is involved. In 1995, a Brazilian derby, which was intended to promote peace between rival fans, ended in violence with two players being sent off and a further ten booked. The match between arch rivals Palmeiras and Corinthians had been called 'the game of peace' and was preceded by a series of symbolic acts of goodwill between fans. Both sets of supporters had walked to the stadium together and four tons of food was donated to a campaign against hunger. The irony was that the peace initiative had been taken following violence at a game between the teams' junior sides, when hundreds of fans had invaded the pitch and attacked each other with sticks, stones and bricks. Tragically, one sixteen-year-old died in those exchanges.

It's almost unheard of for a match official to be the antagonist but referee Luis Vila Nova was such a man. Whilst officiating in a Cesara state championship match in Brazil between Urbuetama and Ferroviaro in 1995, he was in the process of sending off Urbuetama midfielder Semilde when he took exception to verbal insults directed at him by another player and floored him with a fierce right hook. In hindsight, the referee should have sent himself off as well as Semilde but he didn't, and he carried on officiating to the end of the match.

1995 was the year of the kung fu kick. Eric Cantona of Manchester United was the first renowned exponent when, in a match at Crystal Palace, he was sent off and reacted to the baiting of Palace supporter Matthew Simmons. His actions resulted in a court appearance and what could have been a catastrophic premature end to his career. The second incident happened a couple of months later in South Africa during a match between Rabali Blackpool and Umatata Bucks. Blackpool player Ahmed Gora Ebrahim was substituted by his manager Walter Rautmann after only sixteen minutes of the match. He was not amused and showed his disapproval by marching to the touchline and ripping off his shirt before kung fu kicking Rautmann to the floor. The match was being shown live on national television. Ahmed Gora Ebrahim was immediately restrained and taken away in a police van whilst his manager was taken away in an ambulance suffering from a damaged kidney.

Another match that featured incredible scenes captured on live television was Blackburn Rovers' Champions League game against Spartak Moscow in Russia on 22 November 1995. Blackburn's fixtures had not been going well – their performances up to this point had been woeful and team spirit was close to non-existent. The match in Moscow was the return fixture; Blackburn had already been well and truly beaten by Spartak at Ewood Park. The match was only a few minutes old when David Batty and Graham Le Saux collided whilst going for the same ball. An innocent enough mix up for most sides, but not for Rovers. David Batty snarled an insult at Le Saux, prompting the fullback to attack Batty by clipping him round the ear with a left-hand punch. Their captain, Tim Sherwood, rushed to the two players to act as peacemaker but joined in the verbal exchanges. Sherwood appeared to bang Le Saux in the mouth with his elbow, prompting more pushing and shoving, as Batty made more menacing gestures towards him. The incident proved highly embarrassing to Blackburn Rovers who spectacularly crashed out of the Champions League. Rumours of unrest before the game seemed to be true but it was a shame that it manifested itself in such a public arena, as, usually, disputes like this are left to the training pitch and dressing room. David Batty soon left Blackburn Rovers for Newcastle United.

One of the fiercest Endsleigh Third Division games ever to take place happened at Gillingham's Priestfield on 25 November 1995, when they 'entertained' Fulham. Trouble started when Fulham's Mark Thomas tackled Gillingham's Mark O'Connor, leaving him with a double fracture of one of his legs. The incident sparked a mass confrontation. When referee Mick Bailey had managed to restore order, he sent off Fulham's on-loan Martin Gray by mistake. Nick Cusak quickly followed as the game degenerated once again. The referee described the last ten minutes at an FA hearing in March 1996 as, 'the most disgusting exhibition by professional footballers that I've ever had to witness'. All in all, the match featured two sendings off and ten bookings and, for the record, was won by Gillingham 1-0. The four hour FA disciplinary hearing saw representations from both clubs at the highest level. Fulham chairman Jimmy Hill, a vigorous defender of high moral standards in the game, stated that the match had been played in a cauldron-like atmosphere and although he was 'extremely disappointed', pointed out that no nastiness had emanated from Fulham's management team. The club fined Mark Thomas two weeks' wages and warned him that he would be sacked if he was ever involved in similar scenes again.

Gillingham were represented at the hearing by chairman Paul Scally and legal representative David Kenny. Scally said the game was 'an ill-tempered one during which there was severe provocation'. He also pointed out that, 'during the confrontation, not a single Gillingham player kicked or punched a Fulham player'. Both clubs were found guilty of misconduct under the Football Association's Rule 26 but they were cleared of a charge of 'failing to control their players' under Rule 24. Amazingly, both clubs escaped with an official warning – incredible, considering the events and the behaviour of the players.

Only ten months after Eric Cantona's antics at Crystal Palace, an almost identical incident occurred in a Kent Senior Cup match on 2 December 1995. Folkestone defender Dave Ward ran half the length of the pitch to vault over the advertising hoarding to headbutt a middle-aged fan. Ward, who had just been red-carded for violent conduct, had to be dragged away by angry fans during the match against Dartford.

Brazil's Gremio excelled themselves, even by their own shocking standards, in 1995. The side had kicked their way to the final of the Copa Brazil when they restarted their Copa de Libertadores campaign with another display of outright thuggery in a quarterfinal tie against Palmeiras. Gremio seemed intent on starting a riot and involving the police. This tactic was so common that their fans have a song called 'Bring on the Riot Police'. Trouble started as Gremio's Dinho (Brazil's version of Vinny Jones) head butted Valber. Valber retaliated by punching Dinho, leaving his face covered in blood. The referee acted quickly and sent both players off but, as they wandered behind the goal on the long trek back to the dressing rooms, Dinho aimed a kung fu kick at Valber's head. Another Gremio player then grabbed and held Valber round the waist whilst Gremio keeper Danriel punched him repeatedly. Then, the police, security men, club directors and substitutes all joined in, stopping the game for a further fourteen minutes. Intimidation obviously works – Gremio won the game 5-0 and eventually went on to win the whole tournament without further incident. Palmeiras manager Carlos Alberto Silva commented after his team's thrashing (on and off the pitch), 'the Gremio players encouraged the police to hit my players. All they want to do is fight'.

It's not only Gremio in Brazilian football that likes to bend the rules. In the 1995/96 season, Cruzeiro were saved from a rout by their neighbours Sao Paulo because too many of their players were sent off during the game. First, central defender Rogeiro was sent off for kicking an opponent in the face. His teammates protested in their usual animated fashion – so much so, that three more joined him on the walk to the dressing room. Brazilian football rules state that if less than seven players are left on the field of play the match has to be abandoned so it seemed fishy, to say the least, when Cruzeiro's Luis Fernando Gomes suddenly collapsed without anyone being near him. He was stretchered off. Sao Paulo were leading 1-0 and almost bound to score a hatful of others when the referee was forced to call the whole sorry affair off as Cruzeiro's team had been reduced to only six players.

It is rare in English football for a dressing room brawl to make the newspapers but in February 1996, an incident between Grimsby Town's manager Brian Laws and his star player, Italian Ivano Bonetti, caused massive interest in the press. Grimsby had been playing at Luton Town and been on the receiving end of a 3-2 defeat. In the dressing room after the game, manager Brian Laws was reported as 'going loopy'. A witness claimed that the flare up began as a managerial-type lecture to the players. Laws apparently spotted Bonetti not paying the slightest bit of attention but eating a chicken leg. He then blew a fuse when Bonetti commented the defeat had nothing to do with him. 'Yes, it fucking is', said Laws, 'it's every single one of you'. The two started shouting at each other, finally squaring up, before Laws allegedly decked Bonetti with a single punch. Bonetti, an ex-Juventus and Torino player, suffered a fractured cheekbone and stayed in hospital for several days – he looked as though he'd been twelve rounds with Mike Tyson, not the victim of one solitary punch. One newspaper report at the time suggested the bruising to Bonetti's face was caused by a flying chicken leg.

On 8 May 1996, following the removal of a surgical metal plate from his face, Ivano Bonetti announced that he was going to sue Laws. He said he was disappointed that the club had only fined the manager and added that it's time the fans learned the truth. Sadly for Grimsby fans, Bonetti confirmed that he would not play for the club again whilst Laws was still manager.

In November 1995, there was a massive brawl in the tunnel after an ill tempered Anglo-Italian Cup match between Ancona and Birmingham City. During the match, Ancona's president Francesco Contandini went to the side of the pitch to remonstrate with the Birmingham players. The Birmingham players claimed there was a bit of jostling in the tunnel after the match. Contandini called the game 'one of the most violent matches ever played in Italy'. He claimed he needed stitches for a cut above his eye which he sustained during the tunnel brawl. The Italian police interviewed several Birmingham players about the fracas and there was talk of extraditions and charges being brought against them. Birmingham's manager at the time, Barry Fry, interpreted the tunnel events quite differently saying, 'there was a lot of ranting, raving, screaming and shouting but not much else.'

Occasionally, trouble can happen after the final whistle, when the victors celebrate and the defeated wonder about what might have been. Exactly this happened in the 1995/96 South American Supercup between Flamengo of Brazil and Velez Sarsfield of Argentina. The first leg, in Argentina, had been a close affair with Flamengo running out 3-2 winners. In the second leg, Flamengo scored three more goals taking the final aggregate score to 6-2. Just before the final whistle, Flamengo and Brazilian International Edmundo started fighting with Velez Sarsfield defender Zandona. A pitched battle erupted involving all the players, including substitutes and coaches. It didn't affect the result as the referee had blown, during the exchanges, for full time.

As long as there's football there will be fights and brawls on and off the pitch: human instinct is tribal and fit, young men, according to some experts, are biologically programmed to be war-like. The rules of football encourage good behaviour, fair play and restraint and, if taken into context, the amount of brawls compared with the number of games played is a microscopic percentage. Provocation for players can be too much to handle, not only from the opposition but also from the fiercely partisan crowds. Some Italian pitches look more like a bottle bank than a football ground after matches. Officials have to cope with everything from coins to snooker balls being thrown at them; crude intimidation, but an everyday hazard in modern football. The critics suggest that crowd and player behaviour are interlinked – this may be true but suffice it to say that it only takes one nutter intent on trouble to cause problems with far reaching consequences.

3 Intimidation

LOVE AND MARRIAGE go together like . . . intimidation and football, and anyone who does not accept this is either naive beyond belief or they've been walking round with their eyes and ears closed for an awfully long time.

Vocal intimidation can be hurtful – just ask Eric Cantona. Managers and players verbally abuse each other on a regular basis and to a level most other professions would find intolerable. Crowds dish out vocal barrages against clubs, individuals and officials at every available opportunity. Some attempts have been made to curb obscene and racist chants, making it an offence, in Britain, to perpetrate such acts.

However, it's not these activities which constitute good old football intimidation but the more macabre activities – incidents where weapons, blackmail, personal threats and physical violence are the order of the day.

It's a sad indictment of modern day South American football that kidnapping is commonplace and wholly expected. Such is the way of things in Brazil that, when Brazilian International Romario failed to turn up for training at his club Flamengo, both the club and the police automatically assumed the worst. On this occasion, their paranoia was unfounded as it later emerged that the player had taken a tranquilliser and had merely overslept. Relief all round – for the club and for Romario's insurers.

The tentacles of intimidation stretch back as far as the game itself and it has made its presence felt at all levels. England's Jimmy Greaves commented at the time of the 1962 World Cup in Sweden, 'there are some good players here playing some rubbish. They are afraid to hold onto the ball in case they get killed.' Intimidation has even tainted youth soccer in America: in October 1995, a Miami youngster successfully sued the coach of a rival club for damages after the coach had urged his players to 'waste him' during a fixture between the two clubs. The boy was awarded damages of 180,000 dollars.

Scotland takes its place in football history with the first mild case of intimidation in 1881. It was in the Scottish Cup Final between Queen's Park and Dumbarton when, with the score at one apiece, a pitch invasion took place, allowing Queen's Park to score the winning goal. Dumbarton rightly protested, claiming it was entirely unfair to lose a match in the middle of a crowd disturbance. The authorities agreed and the game was declared void.

Pitch invasions were a popular way to try and influence the outcome of games in the 1880s and Aston Villa fans got this rather crude form of intimidation down to a fine art. In 1888, Villa were playing Preston North End in a fifth round FA Cup tie when Villa fans invaded the pitch in a futile attempt to get the match called off. They were at it again a few years later, in 1893, when, following another Villa pitch invasion, the Hussars of the British Army were called in to restore order.

It didn't take long for British referees to feel the wrath of the crowd. Championship rivals Sheffield Wednesday and Sunderland met in a crucial match at Roker Park in 1903; Wednesday won 1-0 and Sunderland fans showed their displeasure at the referee and his performance by stoning him as he left the ground.

Crowds can feel intimidated too, as was proved by the events surrounding the fourth old firm Scottish Cup Final in 1909. There had already been a 2-2 draw between the clubs and the replay finished in yet another, with the score at 1-1. Celtic and Rangers fans expected the replay to go into extra time but when it became clear this wasn't going to happen they rioted. Over one hundred people were injured as ingenious fans set alight to one of the stands, using whisky as fuel. They also hacked the goalposts to pieces for souvenirs and took great delight cutting policemen's hats into strips for similar purposes. The fans were incensed because, as far as they were concerned, both matches had been 'fixed' to end in draws in order to gain extra revenue. The fact that the replay didn't go to extra time merely served to fuel their belief. Following these events the final was deemed void, robbing Celtic of the chance of a third consecutive victory.

In the early 1900s, football was still very much in its infancy in South America but it didn't take long for Argentine club Racing to put their name on the intimidation map. In 1914, Exeter City were touring Argentina and, during a friendly fixture with Racing, the referee was threatened with a gun by one of Racing's officials. The move was as subtle as an air raid but seemed to work since Racing went on to win the match. None of the Exeter officials were brave enough to take up this unorthodox procedure with their hosts.

Even the weather can be employed to make things difficult for teams, as happened in 1928 when England played Spain in Madrid. Spain's manager, Billy Pentland, being fully aware of England's athletic style, ensured the match was played in the heat of May. England quickly went 2-0 up but, as they tired in the second half, the Spaniards drew level with the score at 3-3. Many of the exuberant crowd invaded the pitch, subjecting the England players to intimidation on a level rarely seen in Britain. The Guardia Civil despatched the fans back to the terraces, with the help of drawn swords, and the game restarted. Seconds later, Spain scored a fourth goal and, curiously, England slumped to their first defeat against overseas opposition (excluding Ireland).

Millwall Football Club, and their supporters in particular, have always had a bad reputation. Millwall's old ground, the Den, was always an intimidating place for opposing players and supporters to visit, the home fans being tough working class folk with a partisan attitude rarely rivalled in Britain.

The club first ran into trouble in the years immediately after World War II. In 1947/48, Millwall's ground was forcibly closed for a week because of crowd trouble. In the 1949/50 season, hooligans threatened the club's already tarnished reputation by invading the pitch and manhandling the referee. Not being quick to learn, in the same season, Millwall fans did exactly the same thing again, this time in an away game at Plymouth.

As we've already seen, firearms had already made an appearance in South American football, albeit in largely cameo roles. This changed during the 1950s in a famous case of intimidation and retribution. During a Mexican league match, Carlos Zomba scored four goals for Atalanta against Los Apaches. As he was leaving the stadium at the end of the match, a Los Apaches fan shot him four times in the legs, one for each goal. He never played again.

A curious illustration of the referee's intimidatory powers occurred in the Persian Gulf in April 1962 when referees were allowed to sport a rubber truncheon and had the authority to dish out some heavy on-the-spot discipline. Interestingly, during this experimental period, there were no registered fouls.

The basic length of a football match is 90 minutes and the only way the duration can be extended is by adding on stoppage time or playing extra time. Abiding by the rules this is absolutely true. However, in 1961, in Ecuador, spectator intimidation of the referee took one game into the footballing equivalent of the twilight zone. Brazilian club Santos (including Pele) were on a tour of their South American neighbours and, in the game concerned, Pele agreed only to play the first half. Noticing the Great One's absence, the crowd poured onto the pitch and menacingly demanded that he come back on for the second period. Naturally, the game could not be completed until the pitch had been cleared and the referee decided this would only be possible if Pele came back. He appealed to the Santos directors and Pele himself, who then agreed to come back on and complete the game. The interesting twist in the tale is that intimidation from the crowd had directly affected the referee's ability to play the match to its natural conclusion. Obviously, fearing more trouble, he refused to count the time when Pele hadn't been playing and, in the end, the match lasted for 115 minutes.

Santos were involved in another odd affair in 1962 when they were playing the second leg of the South American Champions Cup against Peñarol in Sao Paulo: the game finished almost two and a half hours after kick off. Peñarol were leading 2-1 when, after a succession of nasty incidents, trouble came to a head – the barriers surrounding the pitch were broken down and the crowd proceeded to storm the pitch. Sensing imminent danger, the referee declared Peñarol the winners and ordered the players off with only 52 minutes of play having taken place. Much talk and argument followed until the tournament's organising committee eventually declared the match null and void and further declared that a deciding game was to be played straightaway. Santos won 3-0, giving them the championship 5-1 on aggregate.

The great headache for any club is how best to protect officials, players and fans from violence and intimidation. Generally, as stadia standards have improved, so have the standards of protection and, during the 1980s and 90s, policing methods around the globe improved immeasurably. It's a shame such high standards were not practised in Paraguay in 1963 where, in a league match in Asuncion, the crowd invaded the pitch, overcame flimsy police opposition and attempted to lynch the referee. Fortunately, they didn't make a good job of it and, though badly beaten up, he made a full recovery after three weeks in hospital. This prompted the government of Paraguay to set up a special training course for riot police. Their objective was to provide commando squads to give protection for the match officials at important games.

Napoli supporters were involved in a scandal when, during a home fixture against Modena in May 1963, Napoli had a penalty awarded against them. This did not go down very well at all with the home fans – they rioted in the stands and then invaded the pitch, attacking the referee and Modena players as well as dismantling the goals. The game was abandoned and, in the crush, one fan was killed, prompting the Italian football authorities to close down the Fuorigrotta stadium for six months. Another six month sentence was dished out for intimidation and violence against a referee in Greece in the summer of 1963. Greek player Angelopoulos of Prae was suspended for all football for six months for attacking a referee during a game.

Football intimidation had a field day in 1964 with one of the most famous cases in the game's history, involving the then golden boy of Spanish football, Alfredo di Stefano (the Blond Arrow). Di Stefano had flirted with a film career in 1963, starring in a movie whose plot hinged on him being kidnapped on the eve of a big match; a prophetic tale, as it turned out.

At six o'clock one Saturday morning in February 1964 in Caracas, Di Stefano was rudely awakened in his hotel room to find that fiction had become a grim reality. A group of men forced their way into room 219 of the Hotel Potomac, showing him documents and identification which, they said, proved they were narcotics police. They insisted he accompany them to the police station for further questioning, claiming he had been a witness in an investigation. Di Stefano's team-mate Pepe Santamaria, who was asleep next door, awoke and heard the rumpus and went to help Di Stefano with his protestations of innocence. The men made it clear that Di Stefano had to go with them immediately and even refused to discuss the matter further with Real Madrid's directors, claiming that would be 'a waste of time'. The player was frog-marched out of the hotel.

Several hours later, a woman phoned the hotel switchboard, the police and leading Venezuelan newspapers with the bombshell that Di Stefano, the world's greatest centre forward, had been kidnapped. The kidnappers were members of the paramilitary Armed Front for National Liberation, whose previous publicity stunts had included the theft of art treasures and an attack on a government-owned ship. The group's plan was to embarrass President Romulo Betancourt and, in a country that eats, sleeps and breathes football, kidnapping a high profile star like Di Stefano was a perfect way to do it.

The government ordered every spare policeman onto the

biggest manhunt in Venezuela's history. However, for 57 hours the AFNL, led by a debonair man with a moustache called Maximo Canales, held Di Stefano under lock and key, before releasing him near the Spanish Embassy in Caracas.

Di Stefano said afterwards: 'When we left the hotel we climbed into a black car. I felt uneasy right away. There was no official markings on the car, you see. We had gone a little way when suddenly one of the men turned to me and said he was a revolutionary. They had guns, he said, but if I gave no resistance they would not harm me.'

Di Stefano said his kidnappers emphasised that he would come to no harm; they merely wanted to draw attention to what was happening in Venezuela and even apologised for inconveniencing him. He told the police he was blindfolded and eventually ended up in a small room with a bed, three chairs, a table and a toilet – a sort of kidnapper's executive box. He revealed he was worried for his own safety because, although amiable, his captors were young, armed and courageous. He feared a rescue attempt and being killed in the crossfire.

In order to while away the time, he played dominoes with his captors and they happily revealed that his kidnapping had been planned for some time. In fact, they had almost snatched him after a match between Real Madrid and Oporto but a car had got in between them and the team coach, so it had to be called off. Di Stefano was cared for by the AFNL beyond the call of kidnapping duty. When he had a pain in his leg, they called in a masseur to treat him. On the day of his release, Di Stefano said he couldn't quite believe it: 'I thought they were trying to make me feel better. But then off came the blindfold. "It's ended, Alfredo," said one of the boys. I suspected that they were only planning to change our hide-out though, even when they bundled me into the back of a car.' They dropped him a couple of blocks from the Spanish Embassy, wished him good luck and gave him three bolivars to pay for a taxi.

In a final comic twist to the saga, the first policeman on the scene refused to believe Di Stefano's claims as to his identity, so he took a taxi for the short ride to the Spanish Embassy, where he was greeted by the ambassador like a long lost brother. No word on whether the ambassador was a Real Madrid fan, but it's safe to assume the probability was high.

It's rare for a Football Association to change the points system but the Greek FA were forced to do just that in the early 1960s following years of player and crowd intimidation. The winners of a match would now get three points, the losers one point with two points each awarded for a draw. In other words teams were rewarded merely for completing a match.

The system was introduced because so many games had to be abandoned when referees gave penalties that could not be taken because players kept kicking the ball away from the spot or refused to leave the penalty area. Other games came to a premature end after players who had been sent off refused to go. Although a good points system, which undoubtedly would have worked in other countries, it still didn't solve all the Greek FA's problems. Even with the 1964/65 league championship at stake, on the last day of the season, the Greek temperament won.

That day, Panithinaikos were virtual champions, three points ahead of their neighbours, AEK Athens. If AEK won their final game at home to Olympiakos then they would equal the present points total of Panithinaikos who, therefore, only had to take the field in their last match against Niki because even if they lost, they would still get a point and win the championship.

At half time, the Panithinaikos players rushed off the pitch to listen to the radio and heard AEK Athens were winning 3-0. The situation was unchanged, Panithinaikos only had to complete the match to win the title. Then, in the second half, the referee ordered off the Panithinaikos player Panoussakis . . . but he refused to go. His teammates threatened him and begged him to go, but he refused. Club officials and the team manager ran onto the pitch to try and persuade him, but it was no good. Panoussakis still refused to go and the game was abandoned which meant no points for Panithinaikos and bye bye championship. Or so they thought. Amazingly, they still won the championship thanks to a miraculous second-half fightback by Olympiakos who ended up drawing 3-3 with AEK.

In the previous season AEK, Panithinaikos and Olympiakos were all involved in the abandonment of the 1963/64 Greek FA Cup competition. The cup was awarded to AEK Athens without a ball being kicked after the semifinal between Panithinaikos and Olympiakos ended in a riot. With the score at 1-1, the crowd, furious about a refereeing decision, began to riot. Safety fences were smashed, the goals were torn down and the pitch was littered with the debris of war. There was a history of trouble between the clubs; when they met in 1963 another riot resulted in three deaths. More than 100 people were also injured and 100 fans were arrested. Cars had been set on fire and the match officials had to lock themselves in the stand and wait for reinforcements.

During 1964, Africa suffered a wave of trouble and violence connected with football. In Gabon, Tunisia and Kenya referees were chased by mobs from grounds, and in Leopoldville, a referee was almost stoned to death for his perceived mistakes. In Northern Rhodesia (now Zimbabwe), three stadiums were closed down for long periods of time because of trouble. One of these was the Kenneth Mackay stadium in Bancroft where a referee had to run for his life five minutes before the end of a match after fans stormed the pitch in a game between the home team and Rokana United.

Around this time, a novel way of dealing with crowd intimidation and violence was developed in Rhodesia, whereby any unruly elements of the crowd were identified by police officers and sprayed with orange paint. The future for stamping out Rhodesian soccer violence was (now) bright – the future was orange.

Players are not beyond intimidating their own teammates – if it's felt their behaviour is 'unreasonable'. Following the final whistle of a Mitrupa Cup clash in 1964 between Bologna and Sparta Prague, one of the Bologna players offered the beleaguered Hungarian referee a sporting handshake, only to be cuffed round the ear by his own captain. In the same year, one referee was shown no mercy at all whilst officiating in a European Cup tie between DWS Amsterdam (making their

European Cup debut) and Fenerbahce of Turkey. Having seen their team beaten 3-1, the Turkish fans ran onto the pitch and attacked the Danish referee Tage Soerensen. He was rushed to hospital and was diagnosed as having a broken jaw, three fractured ribs and a whole host of minor cuts and bruises. His injuries could have been far more serious, perhaps even fatal, if he had not been rescued by Dutch officials.

In another European Cup tie in 1965, Manchester United played Benfica in the Stadium of Light, defending a slender 3-2 lead from the first leg of the quarterfinal. Sir Matt Busby had instructed his players to sit back and soak up the pressure for the first twenty minutes or so, only to be ignored by the mercurial George Best who fired United into an early 2-0 lead. United eventually won the second leg 5-1, an extraordinary and unexpected result which prompted the Benfica fans to invade the pitch. The fans weren't at all violent – they just wanted to congratulate the Manchester United players on a great performance. George Best remembers being chased by a knife-wielding Benfica supporter and then discovering the fan only wanted a lock of his hair as he reminded the fans of one of the Beatles.

No such camaraderie existed in the 1965 Intercontinental Cup which Inter Milan lost to Independiente 1-0. During the game, legendary Inter coach Helenio Herrera was struck by a rock, hitting him just above the eye. After the game, he said, 'the Argentinians were poor shots all round'. Stones also hit Inter players Piero, Suarez, Sarti and Brazilian Jair who said, 'after I was nearly hit by a dirty great rock I was scared to go near the touchline'.

Attitudes began to change in the 1960s, not only to football but to life as well. Youngsters were warned by adults of the dangers of the Beatles and the Rolling Stones and a youth culture swept through the whole of Britain and, later, to the rest of the world. With a new wave of optimism in the country, British life, and in particular English football, was about to enter its golden age. Ireland and Northern Ireland enjoyed a knock-on effect but, unlike the mainland, had to cope with a simmering historical and religious bigotry.

Linfield were one of the most famous Irish clubs, but were famed for 'the yob support which seemed to attract the lowest form of animal life in Belfast' (as one commentator put it). In 1966, Linfield met Glentoran in the Irish Cup Final and there was trouble even in the pre-match warm up. Glentoran's goalkeeper Albert Finney (not the famous actor) was hit by a brick thrown from the Linfield section of the crowd. He was not seriously hurt, but it was a clear message of hate and crude intimidation. 'I didn't see who threw the brick and I certainly wasn't expecting trouble that early on,' said Finney.

On the other side of the world, in Australia, Simmering played Favoriten in January 1966. Wiltschko, Simmering's centre forward, had an extraordinary run on goal. He dribbled past several defenders and, as he ran into the penalty box, sauntered past the prostrate goalkeeper. He then lay down and pushed the ball over the goal line with his head. The referee awarded the goal but cautioned Wiltschko for humiliating the opposition (some people will do anything to rid the game of fun and skill) whilst the crowd roared with laughter. By sheer coincidence, a former FIFA referee was watching the game, and protested after the final whistle that the goal should have been disallowed and the scorer sent off for intimidating his opponents. The goal stood.

Millwall were back in the news in 1967 and, once again, for the wrong reasons: Derek Dougan had scored a last-gasp equaliser for Wolverhampton Wanderers and, overcome with emotion, he turned round to celebrate with a fan who had run onto the pitch – only to discover that the man was a Millwall supporter who hit the startled Dougan on the nose. Maybe it was the same fan who travelled to Cardiff a couple of years later, and was so irked that the match was called off after half an hour that he marched up to the Cardiff City manager, Jimmy Scoular, to demand a refund. When Scoular told him it wasn't possible the fan punched him on the nose – so much for the customer always being right.

World Cup qualifying games are tense affairs, carrying the footballing hopes and dreams of every nation which competes in them. At the end of a successful qualifying campaign lies the greatest prize in world sport. The theory that international football is merely a substitute for war, although extreme, was taken to a frightening new dimension in 1969. This was the year that war really did break out over a World Cup qualifying game. A frenzied three-match play-off series between bitter South American rivals Honduras and El Salvador exploded in more ways than one. By the time a cease-fire had been agreed 3,000 people had lost their lives and over 100,000 had lost their homes.

The soccer war 'kicked off', officially, on 14 July 1969, although the trouble really started on Saturday 7 June when the El Salvador squad arrived in the Honduran capital, Tegucigalpa, for the first match of the play-offs. Both nations had a history of bitter rivalry, notably over land disputes, stretching back over many years. The atmosphere for the game reached new highs in hysteria levels, making Old Trafford look like Torquay when the reserves are playing at home. The match was to be played on Sunday, which meant the El Salvador players had just one night to experience Honduran hospitality. The Hondurans made sure it was a night to remember.

They laid siege to the El Salvador players' hotel, beeped car horns, threw stones at the windows and made makeshift drums from empty barrels; they set off firecrackers and whistled, screamed and chanted all night long. Funnily enough, El Salvador weren't exactly at the peak of their game the following day. Amazingly, they didn't concede a goal until the last minute of the game when Honduran striker Roberto Cardona popped in the winner. The Hondurans went crazy with delight. Back in El Salvador, the fans watching on live television did not take defeat very well at all.

One girl, eighteen-year-old Amelia Bolanios, shot herself in the heart, in front of her father, just after the final whistle. The El Salvadorean newspaper *El Nacional* reported the incident the following day saying, 'the young girl could not bear to see her fatherland brought to its knees'. El Salvador had a new national heroine, with Amelia's funeral televised live.

The first game is only a third of the story and, exactly one week after the first match, the Honduran squad arrived in San Salvador for the return game. They were transported to their hotel in a fleet of armoured cars to protect them from a baying mob hell-bent on revenge. A screaming crowd surrounded the Hondurans' hotel, shouting, breaking windows and pelting the building with rotten eggs and dead rats.

The following morning the armoured cars returned to ferry the players and officials to the Flor Blanca stadium for the match. The army completely surrounded the ground and, inside, the Guardia Nacional were brandishing trouble-deterring submachine guns. The pre-match build up included the ceremonial burning of the Honduran flag and the raising of a tattered dirty rag in its place. This met with massive approval from the home crowd.

El Salvador won the match easily, 3-0. The victory celebrations were wild, prompting Mario Griffin, the Honduras coach, to comment, 'we're awfully lucky we lost'. He and the team went back to the airport in their armoured cars, but the Honduran fans were brutally attacked. Hundreds were injured and two were killed. More than 150 Honduran cars were burnt out and hours later the shared border between the two countries was closed. The repercussions continued with the repatriation of immigrants, extradition orders and streams of refugees as the dispute escalated to government level.

On the eve of the third and deciding match, El Salvador broke off diplomatic relations with its neighbour. This only served to fire up even more the dangerously high level of friction between the fans. The match was switched to Mexico City, a neutral venue. The Honduran fans were on one side of the ground and the El Salvadoreans on the other. Between them stood 5,000 Mexican police armed with thick clubs.

The game was a classic, ending 3-2 to El Salvador who now qualified for the 1970 World Cup finals in Mexico. After the match, surprisingly, there was no real trouble, but two weeks later El Salvador and Honduras were at war. It started after El Salvador invaded Honduras and, just like in the football, their bigger and better-equipped army took an early lead, breaking through the Honduran defences almost at will.

Ryszard Kapuscinski was the only foreign correspondent in Honduras when the full-scale fighting started. In his book *The Soccer War*, he tells of the graffiti that sprang up overnight in the Honduran Capital, 'Nobody Beats Honduras' and 'We Shall Avenge the 3-0'. 'In Latin America', wrote Kapuscinski, 'the border between soccer and politics is vague'.

The fighting raged for over four days. Honduran bombers destroyed El Salvador's oil refineries and the conflict paralysed the Central American common market. Eventually, the Organisation of American States negotiated a cease-fire. Unlike the football, no one won the war, although El Salvador went on to get stuffed by all and sundry in the Mexico World Cup. Obviously, there were long-standing political undercurrents behind 'the soccer war', but football was the catalyst for hostilities. It's just a shame that they couldn't have settled the whole thing with a penalty shoot-out.

As the 1970 World Cup finals in Mexico drew closer, the world champions, England, were involved in a short tour of Colombia, specifically designed to acclimatise the squad to the high altitude rigours that lay ahead that summer. Bobby Moore, England's victorious World Cup winning captain, was again leading the team who were much fancied to retain the cup. The team stayed at the Tequendama Hotel in Bogota, where Moore and Bobby Charlton decided to go and have a browse around the Green Fire jewellery shop.

Afterwards, sitting innocently outside and minding their own business, the pair were approached and asked to explain the alleged disappearance of a £600 emerald and gold bracelet from the shop. Both men were astonished that the finger of suspicion was pointing at them, blissfully unaware of the well-established curious Colombian practice of accusing visiting celebrities of misdeeds, usually seeing them pay money to avoid publicity. If it could happen to singers and bullfighters, it could happen to the England football captain. Bobby Moore could not recollect even looking at the bracelet so he and Bobby Charlton made statements to the police and thought nothing of it.

England then travelled to Ecuador for a friendly game and, on their return to Mexico, stopped en route in Colombia. To his horror, Bobby Moore was placed under house arrest by the Colombian police and placed in the care of the president of Millonarios Football Club. Accusations were made against Moore by the proprietor of the jewellery shop, the shop girl and a mysterious third witness. The situation was now turning into an international incident as the England team were forced to leave Colombia for Mexico without Bobby Moore. Four days after his initial arrest and some timely diplomatic intervention (including Prime Minister Harold Wilson, who was electioneering back in Britain), Moore was released on bail to play in the World Cup where his performance outstripped even that of four years earlier.

This deliberate attempt at intimidation must have unsettled Moore and the squad; England went out of the competition losing 3-2 to West Germany. The case against Bobby Moore collapsed almost as quickly as it had begun but not before he had been persecuted a little more and threatened with further charges. The mysterious witness predictably disappeared and the owner of the shop, together with shop girl, Clara Padilla, were charged with conspiracy in 1972. The unanswered question is, who instigated the conspiracy?

A sinister footnote to England's Mexican World Cup in 1970 is the suspicion that goalkeeper Gordon Banks was poisoned. He was the only player out of the entire England squad who experienced stomach upsets, either an amazing coincidence or a blatant attempt at sabotaging a very important member of the England team. To this day nothing can be proved but other members of the squad are still convinced of dirty tricks.

Invading the pitch at a football match serves no purpose for the fans at all. Short-term satisfaction may be achieved but the long-term interests of the clubs involved are invariably jeopardised. Benfica found this out the hard way in 1970 when they were losing a match to Belenenses 1-0. Benfica's Torres was sent off which signalled the start of a pitch invasion. The crowd attacked the players and officials, resulting in Benfica's ground being closed down for eight weeks.

Referees and good news stories aren't usually mentioned in the same breath. However, sometimes a referee can get lucky. In 1972, Adolf Bueno (a very unfortunate Christian name for a ref) was blinded after an apple was thrown at him in a Spanish First Division game – intimidation at its crudest. He suffered damage to the retina of his right eye and initially gave up hope of ever seeing again. However, after a pioneering operation his sight was restored and, after a couple of months' recuperation, he managed to resume full-time refereeing.

Despite their unique points system, Greece considered 'smuggling in' foreign referees after a whole series of match abandonments in 1973. It's not clear whether they planned to supply fair skinned referees with a course of sunbeds and false moustaches but this move was seriously talked about after Panithinaikos goalkeeper Konstantinou punched the referee during a match, an incident which was viewed by the Greek FA as the final straw.

In April 1973, across the Mediterranean in Malta, referees went on strike to protest at the violence and intimidation against them. A game between Valletta and Birkirkara forced the issue when a referee had to run for his life, being chased by a mob of Valletta supporters who disagreed with a penalty he'd awarded against their team. In the same year, Argentinian referees also went on strike for exactly the same reasons.

In Kenya, they introduced a far more forceful way of dealing with unruly crowds. When Kenyan superclub Abaluhya met Ethiopian side Asmara in 1974, the game was stopped by a full-scale riot on the pitch. Kenyan police opened fire, killing two spectators. Argentina didn't introduce such drastic measures but in 1974, an attempt was made to clean up crowd behaviour. As a result of the events that occurred in a local derby between Newell's Old Boys (of Rosario) and Colon (of nearby Santa Fé), an automatic 30-day prison sentence was introduced for convicted football rioters. Colon fans had rained down bottles, bricks, sticks and stones on the referee for refusing to disallow a Newell's Old Boys goal which they felt was offside. The linesman was also hit on the head by a flying bottle; he was knocked unconscious and rushed to hospital. Newell's Old Boys finally won the game 3-2.

International teams in the 1970s were not beyond claiming feelings of intimidation as a reason for not playing fixtures. Because of the uneven number of qualifying games for the 1974 World Cup finals in Germany, Chile and the Soviet Union were forced to play-off over two legs. The first leg, in Moscow, ended goalless, but, even so, the Soviets didn't go through to the second leg as underdogs – because they didn't go to Chile at all. At the time, Chile had just undergone a bloody coup at the hands of the infamous General Pinochet which had involved thousands of dissenters being herded into the national stadium never to be seen again. The Soviets refused to go to Chile, saying they didn't want to play in a country where so much blood had been spilt. A bit rich coming from a country with statues of Stalin everywhere and with an appalling human rights record themselves. FIFA suspected it could have been a ploy to get the second leg switched to a neutral ground but this they refused to do. Nevertheless, on 21 November 1973, the entire Chilean team trotted out onto the pitch in the national stadium to face . . . nobody. With the Soviet team still on the other side of the world, they scored immediately. The match was abandoned and Chile went through to the World Cup finals.

Italian football also had problems in 1974. In April, AC Milan were banned from using their San Siro stadium for two matches after Juventus captain Pietro Anastasi was knocked out by a firework from a flare gun shortly after Juventus had been awarded a penalty. As a further punishment the Italian FA deducted a goal from Milan. The match finished 2-1 to Juventus but, after the goal deduction, went into official records as 2-0.

In the 1970s, British intimidation was a poor relation to the antics of the rest of the world. In March 1974, Newcastle played Nottingham Forest in an FA Cup quarterfinal at St James' Park. When Forest went 3-1 up, the crowd invaded the pitch, fought with police and attacked the Forest players. As a result, 23 people ended up in hospital with 103 being treated at the ground for injuries. With calm restored the game ended 4-3 to Newcastle. The ramifications of the events were far reaching, with the FA ordering a replay at Goodison Park which ended in a 0-0 draw. Newcastle eventually won a second replay 1-0 to go through to the semifinals. They eventually lost to Liverpool in the final.

A year later, at a Rangers–Celtic game, there were two attempted murders, two meat cleaver attacks, one axe attack, nine stabbings and thirty-five common assaults; statistics that would usually be synonymous with a small war.

In 1975, English fans brought shame on the nation at the European Cup Final in Paris. Don Revie's great Leeds United, a side illuminated by international players, reached the final after a series of gruelling battles on the pitch, but their potential night of glory turned into a night of shame. Leeds' uncompromising style of play had won them few friends on the Continent; during their campaign Duncan McKenzie was banned for three games and Gordon McQueen was sent off in Barcelona for punching a Spanish player. On 28 May, Leeds faced Bayern Munich in the final. It was a very physical match with two Bayern players, Andersson and Hoeness, injured and out of the game before half time. Bayern, as a consequence, were forced to reshuffle and Leeds dominated for most of the match. Leeds supporters couldn't believe it when two penalty appeals against Franz Beckenbauer were turned down and when Peter Lorimer's 66th minute goal was ruled offside they ran wild.

French riot police jumped in to quell the trouble whilst, on the pitch, Bayern scored two quick goals through Roth and Muller, to put the trophy beyond Leeds. Each goal served as a trigger for further outbreaks of fighting. Trouble continued throughout the night on the streets of Paris, prompting UEFA to ban Leeds United from European competition for four years.

Bayern Munich were involved in more amazing scenes in 1976 in a UEFA Cup tie in Madrid. Real Madrid were banned for a year from European competition after a drunk ran on the pitch and attacked Bayern's Gerd Muller and referee Erich

Linemayr. Following an appeal the ban was reduced to having to play their next three European home legs more than 200 km from Madrid.

The lengths some fans will go to in their attempt to sabotage or influence the outcome of games in South America should never be underestimated. Desperate men take desperate measures. In a vital Libertadores Cup match in Argentina, Independiente were losing 1-0 at home to River Plate. The goal had been scored in the fourth minute by Lopez and, in a typically bad tempered affair, River Plate were down to ten men. As time ticked by without any indication that Independiente would equalise one cunning supporter decided to sabotage the floodlights. The fans clearly thought that, without the light, the game would be abandoned and the referee would order a replay. Wrong. Initially, the referee was all for abandoning the game but was persuaded to change his mind by club officials who arranged for an electrician to repair the damage. The delay of 87 minutes was the longest in Argentine football history but the floodlights were switched back on and the final twenty minutes of play were completed. There were no more goals: justice was done.

Even in devout Muslim countries, football can change normal standards of behaviour. In 1977, Al Misro of Port Said were playing at home to Esco in a league match when Al Misro striker Nour scored – only to have his efforts ruled offside by Mr Ibrahim, the linesman. The goal, according to the rules of the game, was disallowed. In protest at the decision, an Al Misro substitute knocked out the linesman with an impressive combination of punches. After receiving treatment, Mr Ibrahim resumed his duties under intense pressure, only to be headbutted by the Al Misro goalkeeper, Radwan, on the final whistle. The two aggressors were suspended for life and Mr Ibrahim carried on officiating – after he had spent a week in hospital recovering from his injuries.

March 1977 saw a spate of football intimidation all over the world. A Guatemalan army team played a friendly match near Santa Barbara, America. After winning 6-3 they were attacked by a mob of locals as they boarded the team bus. The crowd used machetes, knives and wooden clubs on the soldiers, five of whom lost their lives.

The Nou Camp stadium is one of the temples of world football but has seen its fair share of trouble over the years. In a home match against Malaga in March 1977, Barcelona's Johan Cruyff was sent off for insulting the referee, Ricardo Melero. The crowd rioted and invaded the pitch before attempting to beat up the unfortunate Señor Melero. Despite their team winning the match 2-1, they also set alight a television vehicle and stoned the police. Fences and a moat were installed at the Nou Camp to prevent a repetition of any such incidents.

In the same month, in South America, the refs struck back. Despite intense intimidation during an international match between Ecuador and Uruguay, a referee sent off the entire Ecuador team for arguing over the sending off of one player.

Back in Italy, Napoli's ground was closed down for the eighth time since the war – a record – after linesman Agustino Binzagi was hit on the head with a Coca Cola bottle after he'd disallowed a goal which even the Napoli players agreed was a handball.

In April 1977, when Palermo were playing in an Italian Serie 'B' game against Ternana in Sicily, the crowd rioted at the end of the game. Following a disallowed but potentially match-winning Palermo goal the crowd became very agitated and poured onto the pitch. They were eventually repelled by police using tear gas after which the police ordered a helicopter to rescue the referee and linesmen from this very volatile and dangerous situation. In a scene reminiscent of *Apocalypse Now*, the chopper swept through the clouds of gas to rescue the officials.

This was not the first time a helicopter had been used to rescue a referee. A precedent was set in 1969 when Palermo (again) played Napoli. The game was abandoned because of crowd trouble and referee Antonio Shardella needed a police bodyguard to be ushered to the safety of the waiting helicopter.

Only three and a half months after having their ground

closed down for the eighth time Napoli were back in trouble. In a home match against Fiorentina a linesman was showered with bottles and bricks after Fiorentina scored. The Italian football authorities had no option but to close the ground down again; it would not be the last time the two parties crossed swords.

Boca Juniors, the Napoli of Argentina in the 1970s, were involved in two incidents in consecutive months during 1977. In October, Boca were victims rather than intimidators. Playing against Colombian side Deportivo Cali in a Libertadores Cup tie, Boca claimed their hosts did everything in their powers to disrupt them before the game. They claimed that their flight was deliberately delayed by the Colombians with police detaining some of the crew on drug smuggling charges. Nothing appeared to happen to the airline staff and Boca coach Lorenzo claimed it was a set up. The tyres on their team coach were punctured, making their arrival at the team hotel much later than it should have been. Then, an inordinate amount of beautiful women were sent to Boca's hotel where they stripped naked in front of them. It must have been hell.

Back in Argentina in November, Boca played a big home game against old rivals Estudiantes. Boca were only fielding a reserve team (maybe the first team had gone AWOL with the girls in Colombia) but the passion from the fans was still there. Linesman Carlos Aranguran was knocked unconscious by an object thrown by the Boca fans and the match was held up for nineteen minutes. As punishment, Boca Juniors were banned from using their ground for two matches.

One should never underestimate the passion and depth of feeling displayed for football by the Italians, even when playing amongst themselves in seemingly friendly kickabouts. In April 1979, a football match between the customers of two bars in Rome ended with unbelievable scenes. Bar Miki were beating Bar Acquario 4-0 when, suddenly, shots rang out from the crowd and all the players dived for cover. Only the referee remained upright, boldly standing his ground in the middle of the pitch. When the chaos had subsided the referee was adamant that all four shots had been aimed directly at Bar Miki's star striker. About a dozen spectators then suddenly ran on the pitch, some of them armed with pistols. One of this charming bunch approached the referee telling him to kneel down and lick his boots. Just as the referee was about to comply, the pitch invaders got nervous and ran away thus saving him from any further embarrassment.

Turkey is another European country where football and intimidation sit side-by-side with unnerving ease. In January 1978, Fenerbahce, the league leaders, only managed a 1-1 draw with lowly Altay. Upset by refereeing decisions, the crowd rioted; cars outside the stadium were overturned and inside the ground the referee was punched in the face and the press was stoned for about half an hour. Fernebahce's ground was closed down for the next two games, incensing the club's president Faruk Ilgaz who formally tried to defend the club by saying, 'the whole incident was an outside plot to unsettle the players. We are being punished unjustly because of shameful demonstrations. The mob created terror and endangered the lives of thousands. It was a plot.' Nice try, but essentially bollocks.

Just before the 1978 World Cup finals in Argentina, the terrorist group the Montoneros kindly announced that they would not disrupt the spectacle as it was 'a feast of the people'. In a football mad country even terrorists forget their ideals and principles for the World Cup. The news must have come as a welcome relief for the ruling military regime who had, to put it mildly, a disgraceful human rights record. Pressure group Amnesty International had been campaigning, right up to the start of the games, for a boycott. This was ignored and the finals went ahead. This World Cup was the one where Argentinian football would enjoy a renaissance rarely equalled in modern times. It was also the ticker-tape competition where it must have been a nightmare to be a stadium cleaner.

The tournament had its good and bad moments. One humorous episode involved two boisterous Scotland supporters who jostled and annoyed locals in the Cordoba press centre before being led away by a policeman. He either had a great sense of humour or completely miscalculated a suitable punishment for the two Scotsmen as he took them to a cinema where all three of them sat down to watch Walt Disney's *Fantasia*. Afterwards the policeman drove them to his home, served them coffee and then dropped them back at their hotel – he should have dropped them at the airport as Scotland weren't to last long in the tournament.

The disappointment of defeat can bring out the worst in people, as Mexican manager José Antonio Roca discovered after Mexico were beaten in the first round of the 1978 World Cup by Tunisia. The headquarters of the Mexican FA received hundreds of calls threatening not only Roca's life but also to blow up the building.

In the final itself, intimidation was crudely used in anticipation of victory. Host nation Argentina were swept along on a wave of nationalistic fervour. Their opponents were the beaten finalists in 1974, a team packed full of skilful artistic players most coaches could only dream of. Only Holland stood between Argentina and the greatest football prize of all. The hosts deliberately kept the Dutch waiting for five minutes before kickoff, leaving them entirely alone on the pitch in front of 100,000 fanatical, baying Argentinians – not the most sporting and hospitable thing to do. Argentina went on to win the final but the free kick count aroused some suspicion, with referee Sergio Gonell of Italy awarding 46 fouls against Holland and only 20 against Argentina.

In the same year Seville's Spanish International goalkeeper Francisco Ruiz Paco was sentenced to five days' detention for attacking a barracking spectator, a move that also earned him a £300 fine.

Even referees are human and can snap when under intense intimidation. In Peru, in October 1978, referee Hugo Bustamante knocked out Atletico Chalaco defender Escobar when he tried to prevent a free kick being taken quickly in a match against Colegio Nacional Iquitos. Players can also try the patience of opposition benches, sometimes with violent consequences. In a Brazilian match between XV De Jau and Santos in December 1978, XV De Jau defender Marco Antonio became so irritated by a barrage of personal jokes from the Santos bench that he kicked the ball straight at them and was sent off. As he walked past the Santos bench he kicked one of its occupants and was promptly punched unconscious by the Santos team doctor, who was himself sent off. More seriously, if that's possible, during the same month Real Madrid star Juanito was suspended from football for two years for repeatedly headbutting Adolf Prokop, an East German referee, as Madrid slumped to a 2-0 European Cup defeat in Zurich against Grasshoppers.

Our old friends Napoli were back in trouble again in February 1979. Lazio players Dario Pighin and Lionello Manfred-Onia were taken to hospital suffering from shock after they were bombed by fireworks at Napoli's Sao Paulo stadium as they warmed up for a league match. The match was delayed for over half an hour as Lazio brought on two reserves. The game finished 1-1 but, as a punishment, the Italian football authorities later declared the result a 2-0 win for Lazio. A month later, referee Luigi Agnollin was struck on the shoulder by a solid gold cigarette lighter thrown by Inter Milan fans in their 2-0 victory over Avellino. Inter's fans were obviously wealthy and upmarket but the referee was clearly a nonsmoker as he didn't keep the lighter – maybe Inter officials pawned it to pay the club's £500 fine.

Newly crowned Paraguayan champions Olimpia contested the 1979 Copa Libertadores against Bolivian team Jorge Wilsterman. During the game there was constant friction between the players and numerous missiles were thrown onto the pitch. One of the objects hit the referee, Jose Wright of Brazil. After momentarily stopping the game, Señor Wright sent off two Bolivians, quickly followed by a third and then a fourth. It was twenty minutes from the end of normal time and the floodgates opened: the 150 police officers on duty could not contain the baying crowd who poured onto the pitch, obviously intent on attacking the Olimpia players and the referee who managed to escape with a black eye, kick marks all over his body and, more importantly, his life – he had, miraculously, succeeded in hailing a taxi whilst being chased through the streets. Seven Olimpia players were injured, four of them seriously, but they did go on to win the cup.

It was the same story in the 1980s with incident after incident being recorded around the world. Africa was rocked by the scandal of intimidation in 1980 when, in November, Zambian clubs Green Buffaloes and Power Dynamoes played a typically boisterous match after which Green Buffaloes' midfielders Chris Kaoma and Peter Tembo decided to beat up one of the linesmen. At the same time, the Referees Association of Ghana threatened an all out strike because of constant attacks on their members by fans. In January 1981, things went horribly wrong after a passion-packed African Cup game between Canon of Cameroon and Bendel Insurance of Nigeria. Canon won the game which infuriated the home-based Bendel fans who threw stones and bottles onto the field before going on the rampage and burning several vehicles, including the Cameroon team bus. The Bendel fans caused thousands of pounds' worth of damage as trouble continued for several hours. Eight people died in the incidents.

Meanwhile, across the Atlantic, San Cristobal and Universidad Estatal were contesting a Dominican Republic Cup semifinal. San Cristobal were losing 3-0, probably because three of their players had been red carded for various violent offences. Their fans didn't take the prospect of defeat kindly; one of them ran onto the pitch with a large stick and beat up the referee who was so badly cut and shaken that he had to abandon the match.

Even pensioners are partial to a bit of intimidation every now and again, as was proved by a Ledbury Town supporter in 1981. Sam Phillips was banned from all the club's home games after taking part in a solo pitch invasion where he managed to attack the goalkeeper and tear his shirt. Mr Phillips was 82.

The intimidated can, and do, sometimes strike back. In March 1982, Panithinaikos star Mike Galakos threw back a full bottle of water that was thrown at him during a heated derby with Olympiakos. Sadly for him, the fan who was struck by the bottle managed to successfully sue Galakos for abnormal violent behaviour. Just before the 1982 World Cup, Peru blamed Cameroon witchdoctors for a wave of illness that interrupted their preparations. In retaliation, Peru's manager flew back to South America to enlist the dark forces of the Macumba priestesses who, considering both sides' World Cup performances, only served to compound any negative influence.

The 1982 World Cup finals in Spain witnessed an extraordinary intervention in a game . . . by royalty. France were playing Kuwait when, following a goal by Frenchman Giresse, the Kuwaitis stopped playing, saying they had heard a whistle at the time of the goal. The Kuwaiti players remonstrated with the referee claiming that the whistle was his and, therefore, the goal shouldn't stand. Suddenly, a Kuwaiti prince, accompanied by the President, came down from their seats in the stand to let the Russian referee know, in no uncertain terms, that the goal should be disallowed. After much discussion the referee agreed – to the obvious astonishment of the French team.

El Salvador's World Cup preparation went ahead, despite a bloody civil war raging in the country which claimed the life of one of their top players. Ismael Cisco Diaz was ambushed and killed by guerrillas on his way to a training session with his club Deportivo Aguilla. Diaz was rich by El Salvadorean standards, having interests in property and plantations, which led the national team players to speculate that the guerrillas may have demanded a contribution from him and killed him when he refused to pay.

As we already know, football can induce the most unreasonable behaviour in people. A German man made a very good case for the rapid introduction of video recorders in July 1982. The man wanted to watch an important World Cup game but his wife wanted to watch the film *For Whom The Bell Tolls*. Having only one TV in a football-loving household is a mistake as the man's wife found out – he threw her out of the front room window.

Greek police must have finally twigged that crowd intimidation and behaviour had got completely out of control when, after one match in 1982, the groundsmen found eight cigarette lighters, one electric shaver, a pair of glasses, a flower pot, a urine specimen, a spark plug and a transistor radio, all of which had been thrown onto the pitch by fans.

One of the most despicable and degrading intimidation techniques practised amongst supporters is the depositing of body fluids over each other. In January 1983 at the Pascual Guerrero stadium in Colombia, 22 people died as lower tier fans stampeded for cover when fans in upper tier sections urinated on those below. Hordes of drunken spectators were involved but amongst the dead were three women and seven children.

Mass kidnapping is very rare in football, but there's a first time for everything. Shortly after the start of a league match in San Sebastian, El Salvador, heavily armed rebels surrounded the field and forced the players, together with 200 spectators, to march to their mountain hideaway. The incident occurred at the end of 1982 but wasn't reported until March 1983 by which time most of the prisoners had escaped or been released. The act was a spectacular 'own goal' by the rebels who gained nothing but embarrassing publicity for one of the more bizarre raids of the three-year civil war. Officials believed the guerrillas' aim had been to snatch army personnel who played for San Sebastian's civil defence team. Ironically, on this occasion, the defence team's fixture had been changed and they were playing away from home.

Fine examples of intimidation continued to present themselves throughout 1983. In May, a game in Mexico had to be stopped three times; once because the referee was felled by a stone and twice because the noise from a band in the crowd was drowning out the messages from the referee's whistle. Inter Milan were awarded a 2-0 win over Juventus in May after their team bus had been attacked by Juventus fans injuring Giampiero Marini; before the outbreak of trouble the match had been a 3-3 draw. In September an African Cup match between Stationery Stores and Asecs was abandoned after a series of fights erupted on and off the pitch. The problem started at the beginning of the second half when the Asec goalkeeper was seen burying an object behind his goal. Enraged Stationery Stores players were convinced the burial was a black magic ritual.

No notable year of intimidation would be complete without a contribution from Argentina. Commenting on 1983, the magazine *World Soccer* reported: 'In Argentina the fans, in repeated scenes of violence on the terraces, attacked referees, club officials, players and other fans . . . the police attacked fans . . . club officials attacked referees and players . . . referees attacked the disciplinary committee for not being strict enough . . . players attacked referees and club officials and in the end also the fans . . . and the press, being attacked by fans, players and club officials, attacked everybody in sight.' Say no more.

In January 1985, a simple request to officiate at a Greek Third Division battle ended in deep embarrassment for the man in black, Stelios Rinious. The game was between Aianta and Anagenisi from the island of Salamis. The score remained 0-0 right up to the 85th minute when Aianta scored a disallowed goal. The home fans were not happy and, on the final whistle, all hell broke loose – 1,500 fans invaded the pitch, knocking down fences and overcoming the entire island police force (26 officers) before attacking the referee and linesmen. Not only were the officials beaten senseless but the fans also decided to remove their clothes. The referee was debagged and the linesmen's shirts were ripped off their backs. The three officials ran half naked around the stadium before being rescued by the police who hid them in an armoured vehicle for three hours until the situation had calmed down. The fans got a measure of support from the Aianta president Dimitrios Kutsuhis who said, 'I don't agree with the fans' methods, but I do understand why they were upset'.

Two leg aggregate matches in Africa are always dangerous affairs as was proved in the African Cup second leg game between Gallia Mascara (Algeria) and Ittihad (Libya) in June 1985. The Libyan crowd didn't take kindly to overall defeat – they won the second leg at home 3-0 but had lost the first leg in Algeria 4-0. Many of the 70,000 crowd stormed the pitch and brutally attacked the Mascara players, several of whom were cut and bruised with the Mascara president suffering a broken arm. The strange Libyan hospitality even extended to the local hospital where Mascara's general manager was attacked when he turned up for x-rays on suspected broken ribs.

In the same month, Nigerian players were accused of causing a riot when they played Ethiopia in the African Nations Cup. The match, held in Ethiopia, erupted in violence; Nigerian fans were beaten up and several players needed medical treatment. Eye witnesses confirmed the trouble started when several Nigerian players taunted the Ethiopians by holding out one hand and rubbing their stomachs with the other – a sick reference to the appalling famine Ethiopia was enduring at the time.

In 1985, Garcia de Loza refereed a Seville–Real Madrid clash, which finished 2-2, in front of 70,000 fans. Seville's fans were so outraged by Señor de Loza's performance that not only did he leave the pitch to a hail of bottles but, when the officials left the ground three hours later, there were still enough fans around for a further hail of missiles to rain down on them.

Middle Eastern passions for football tend to run high, especially if the game concerned is a World Cup qualifying game with a near neighbour. In late 1985, Iraq's leading sports newspaper printed the following command on the morning of a vital match between Iraq and Syria: 'In case of loss, God forbid, the people will not stand idle but will pelt those who disappoint their hopes with tomatoes and bottles.' Not only was Saddam Hussein the President of Iraq, he was also quite clearly doubling up as a newspaper editor.

Less than a year on from the Heysel tragedy, Liverpool were involved in another disturbing set of events. In April 1986, Ron Atkinson's Manchester United went to Anfield to be faced by deplorable intimidation even before a ball was kicked. As the Manchester team coach drew up outside Anfield a brick was hurled through one of its windows and, as the players stepped off the coach, some of them were sprayed with gas from an aerosol can. United's Clayton Blackmore was momentarily blinded and 21 fans were hurt. Ron Atkinson condemned this indiscriminate attack, referring strongly in post-match interviews to the 'hell of Anfield' and the prospect of a player being killed by a fan in the near future. Thankfully, his doomsday views have not yet come to pass in Britain.

On the night before the second leg of the 1987 Libertadores Cup Final between River Plate of Argentina and America of Colombia, the America players decided to go and have a look at the Argentine pitch. They were attacked and beaten by a mob of River Plate supporters. The next day River Plate won a very violent game and the Colombians wasted no time accusing River Plate officials of organising the attack the night before – which, of course, they denied.

In February 1987, a clash between Estudiantes and Boca Juniors was suspended after it spiralled into chaos. Estudiantes were playing at home and their fans tried to get onto the pitch to attack their own goalkeeper. Boca had taken the lead with Estudiantes keeper Bereto seeming to help the ball into his own net; the verdict was an own goal. When the home fans voiced their disapproval, Bereto turned round and pretended to conduct their chants with his hands – he got out alive despite wild scenes and the abandonment of the game five minutes before half time.

In February 1987 Scottish engineer Ricky McShane came up with a novel idea for controlling crowds – hosing them down. His suggestion was for a water ring main system to be installed beneath the perimeter running track area with hoses fixed around the ground at regular intervals. He admitted to one flaw in his scheme – the impossibility to pinpoint a single individual for a soaking – saying, 'In a pitch invasion, there are no innocent by-standers'. Only Belgium's police force showed any level of interest in his idea.

Using music as a form of intimidation seems an unlikely way of putting players off their game but, hardly surprisingly, the South Americans tried it. Argentina's River Plate played a friendly match against Mexico's Universidad Autonoma in the United States in the Spring of 1987. Without regard for subtlety, a large Mexican Tijuana brass band positioned itself directly behind the River Plate goal and began playing very loudly whenever the ball came close. River were not happy but managed to cope, scoring two goals to win the match 2-1.

Spanish football has been plagued by hooliganism for years. Occasionally, wild claims are made about the conquering of the problem but they never stand up to close scrutiny. In April 1987, Real Madrid president Ramon Mendoza proclaimed that he was winning the war against violence and intimidation saying, 'Since I took over, not a single object has been thrown on the pitch'. On hearing this, Real Sociedad's goalkeeper Luis Arconada felt compelled to remark 'At the Barnabéu Stadium [Real Madrid's ground] I either stand in front of the posts or outside my area in order not to be hit by cans or catapulted ballbearings.'

In December 1987, Greek Cypriot goalkeeper Andreas Charitou was hit by a rocket whilst playing for Cyprus against Holland in Rotterdam. By way of recompense, he accepted the offer of a free holiday from the Dutch tourism office. The device was a homemade smoke bomb rocket and the Dutch bomber claimed he only fired it to cause a sensation. Eventually, the game was replayed with the Dutch thrashing Cyprus 8-0. However, UEFA turned the result into a 3-0 win for Cyprus.

Fireworks have always been a vital ingredient in the Italian fans' arsenal. A Juventus fan threw a firework into the players' tunnel at half time in a game against Cesena in January 1988. The firework injured Cesena player Dario Sanguin who was on his way back to the dressing room. Juventus won the match and then lost it – the result was overturned because of the incident. A month later, Roma's Italian International goalkeeper needed heart massage to save his life after suffering a cardiac arrest as a result of being hit by two thunder flashes at the San Siro stadium in Milan. When the teams returned to the pitch for the second half, Franco Tancredi ran towards his goal. As he reached his six yard box in front of the Lion's Den (the San Siro version of the Kop), a toilet roll was thrown at him from the crowd. Smiling, he threw it back. He was still smiling when the thunder flashes exploded in his face. Only the swift action of the Roma doctor, Ernesto Alicicco, saved his life.

Two years before the Gulf War, Iraq and Kuwait engaged in a little football sabre rattling when they met in an international match. FIFA banned two Iraqi officials from all international competitions for two years for attacking the referee in an Olympic Games qualifying match. They had already attempted to bribe the referee for the same match and, when things didn't go Iraq's way, decided to physically assault the man.

Boca Juniors were the unfortunate victims of two violent intimidatory attacks in February and June 1989. Firstly, goalkeeper Navarro Montoya was knocked out when a smoke bomb exploded next to him and midfielder Simon was felled by a stone as he went to help him. Secondly, Boca's captain Claudio Marangoni had to leave the pitch with blood streaming from a face wound after being hit by a stone. Both incidents happened in games against Racing who were docked points on both occasions.

However unintentional, a bad injury can have flashpoint potential, as Malawi's national team discovered in June 1989. In a match in Addis Ababa, Ethiopia's star forward accidentally had his kneecap broken in a clash with Malawi's goalkeeper. The crowd were incensed and invaded the pitch, attacking three Malawi players. Police attempted to quell the disturbance by firing bullets into the air but failed to stop a further attack on Malawi coach Clement who needed stitches for a serious head wound.

In August 1989, Diego Maradona refused to return to his club Naples unless he received guarantees for his safety. Maradona claimed he was being threatened by a local branch of the Mafia called the Camorra. When the Italian season kicked off, Maradona was on a fishing trip 500 miles north of Buenos Aires. On 1 September, following persuasion by his club, he boarded a plane for Naples, only to storm off because there was no place in the first class cabin for his advisor Guillermo Coppola. He finally flew to Naples two days later under unprecedented security.

Ajax fans were at it again in late 1989, earning their club a one year ban from all European football. The Dutch fans halted a game against FC Austria in extra time after the Austrians scored. They bombarded the pitch with a hail of missiles including pipes, iron bars, lumps of wood and stones; the match was abandoned.

Greek referees went on strike in 1989 in protest against the rising tide of violence against match officials. The last straw for Greek referees was the beating up of Nikos Hrysanis by players and spectators after a cup tie in Crete. Referee Hrysanis said, 'More than a dozen fans started kicking and punching me about the head and face. Fans had blocked the entrance to the dressing room and tunnel and my linesmen and I didn't know which way to turn, the punches and kicks and blows were coming from all directions. I don't know how we managed to get to the dressing room.' They were finally rescued by the police.

For at least the last fifteen years, Colombian football has been controlled by drug cartels whose influence over the game is as legendary as it is unstoppable. Intimidation has played a huge part in the recent history of Colombian soccer. Intimidatory tactics are as common and guaranteed as night following day. Nobody is exempt – from officials and club presidents to the players themselves. In November 1990, in the Copa Liberta-dores (the most corrupt South American competition), Nacional of Colombia defeated Brazilians Vasco De Gama 2-0 in the second leg of the quarterfinals at home in Medellin. After the match, Vasco De Gama officials alerted the South American Football Confederation that the match referee, Jose Daniel Cardellono, had been threatened by six armed men who then offered him $20,000 to ensure a Nacional win. The approach had been made right under the Federation's noses, in the referees' dressing room, prompting concerns of Federation corruption. Suspicion of wrong doing was strong enough for the Federation to order the match to be replayed at a neutral venue in Santiago, Chile. Once again Nacional won but, in future, all Colombian teams competing in the Copa Liberta-dores would have to play all their home games on neutral ground.

Zambian President Kenneth Kaunda was forced to intervene and rescue a player from certain death during a game in February 1991. Zambian's Nkane Red Devils were playing Algerian side Jeunesse Sportive Kabylie in the African Champions Cup when Mennedy Malitoli missed a vital penalty for the Zambians in a penalty shoot-out. Malitoli was brutally attacked by his own fans and a shocked and tearful Kenneth Kaunda was forced to order his rescue by the local police.

The Vasco De Gama–Flamengo derby in Rio De Janeiro entered a new era of terror in November 1991 with unprecedented (even by Brazilian standards) crowd violence. Four fans were shot and wounded and fifty others were injured in the fighting. A homemade bomb, containing a mixture of broken glass, a screwdriver and gunpowder, caused a fourteen-year-old boy to lose one of his feet. Further crude explosives, knives, wooden clubs and bottles were also confiscated by police who made a large number of arrests.

Former Scottish International and Liverpool and Glasgow Rangers manager Graeme Souness unwittingly inflamed an already extremely volatile situation after the conclusion of the 1995/6 Turkish Cup Final between the country's biggest rivals Galatasary and Fenerbahce. (Manchester United found out in 1993 just how intimidating Turkish fans can be when Eric Cantona and Co. were spat at and bombarded with missiles after playing Galatasaray.) The first leg of the final saw Galatasaray scoring the only goal of the game and the return match, on the opposite side of the Bosphorus, was a typically tight derby match. With the game in extra time, Dean Saunders scored the winning goal for Galatasaray in the 116th minute. The stadium went deathly quiet as few Galatasaray fans had been brave enough to make the journey. Before the winning goal the stadium had been a sea of fireworks, waving banners, chanting and gunshots. (In Turkey it's traditional for fans to fire handguns in the air, especially after games, and the morning papers invariably follow up with reports of mothers and babies being killed whilst watching from balconies.) The state of shock lasted until the final whistle when Graeme Souness,

Galatasaray's manager, ran to his supporters' end and grabbed a huge eight foot high flag from one of the fans. He paraded it to the centre of the pitch, spearing it erect in the centre circle – effectively a dagger through the heart of the Fenerbahce fans. Souness soon realised that this had not been a wise move and ran for the tunnel, sensibly choosing not to reappear. The cup presentation by President Demirel could not be seen for all the police riot shields being held up to protect players and officials from a hail of missiles and fireworks. 'You can go fuck your mother with the cup,' chanted the fans. Police used alsatian dogs and truncheons to regain order. Outside, armoured cars helped disperse other troublemakers. Three people were wounded in knife attacks and the windows of both team coaches were smashed. There's no doubt that Graeme Souness' actions infuriated the crowd, however innocent his intentions. He was charged by the Turkish FA with ungentlemanly conduct and this was, no doubt, a contributing factor in his departure from the club a few weeks later.

In 1996, Falkirk FC claimed fan rage caused manager John Lambie to resign. Caretaker manager Gerry Collins said, 'When fans tried to run John and his wife off the road after a match, it made him think twice about football. He doesn't think football's worth that kind of strife and that's why he quit.'

The sad thing is that John Lambie isn't the first and will not be the last manager to be hounded out of a club in such a way. Intimidation is a powerful weapon and that's why it will continue to play an active part in the game – whatever the authorities try to do to stop it.

4 Match Fixing

ATCH FIXING IS the sinister side of football that no one in the game likes to talk about or admit to. Match fixing, without doubt, cons the ordinary supporter, robbing them of the general rule that 'anything can happen in a game of football' as long as it's legal. Their faith in the team they support – moral and financial – is completely abused and treated with disdain by the 'fixers', who are self-centred, greedy, dishonest people who have no place in the game. Human nature dictates that when a vocation involves money, or the making of money, a significant number of people find it impossible not to be tempted into corruption. Mammon is alive and well within the world of football.

The problem stretches back as far as the game itself, involving conspiracies, politics, money, mysterious third parties, incentives and even the Church. Betting syndicates are not uncommon; they attempt to blackmail, bribe and set up players and officials to cooperate with their highly illegal activities. It's not just clubs involved in championship challenges or relegation and promotion issues who participate in, or fall foul of, match fixing; cup competitions and even youth football haven't escaped. A perfect example is a York District League youth match between Heslington and Moore Lane. Both clubs were suffering massive fixture backlogs and so agreed to fabricate the result of a game the two sides were due to play against each other. This they did, announcing to the local press that the game ended 0-0; they even had the gall to give the local press a match report, including comments about the referee's performance. Both teams were rumbled and they were each fined and relegated. The disturbing thing for the football authorities was that, if dishonesty existed at this level of football, what would be the implications for the professional game where the stakes are much higher?

Assuming desperate teams take desperate measures the spectre of game tampering and match fixing, in one form or another, will be here to stay. Britain, once again, has the dubious honour of recording (discovering) the game's first match fixing incident but if a world trophy were awarded for the crime, Italy would have been winners with monotonous regularity. The eminent British sports journalist Brian Glanville has, throughout his career, focused his attention on match fixing and corruption in football. Events in Italy during the 1960s and 70s led Glanville to write openly about what was going on, and make accusations that shocked Italian football to its very core.

The 1960s were a golden period for match fixing. In Greece, 'honest' referees were considered almost impossible to find – so much so that, in 1962, an impartial German had to be flown in to referee a match between AEK Athens and Panathinaikos. International football has not been untouched either; suggestions were made that the Austrian national team 'sold' a vital match to cover their gambling debts. The Austrian players, apparently, had a penchant for playing cards and gambling away large sums of money. This pastime was officially banned in 1964.

Comical scorelines only serve to confirm the manipulation of whole clubs: it was claimed that, in 1979, a Yugoslavian team struck a deal with their opponents in an end of season clash; they won 134-1. In 1993, in South Africa, East Blackpool beat their opponents 68-0, prompting the minister of sport to understate, 'I think something fishy is going on'.

Cheating, although far less widespread than match fixing, obviously exists in football as well. Technically, taking a throw-in ten yards further up the pitch from where the ball went out of play is cheating. Other methods employed by some players and clubs are slightly more subtle and worthy of discussion. The old adage that cheats never prosper isn't necessarily true when the beautiful game is involved. What follows is the (as near as you can get) definitive guide to match fixing, from the innocent and guilty parties, through the methods employed, to the consequences and repercussions.

In 1898, Stoke City played Burnley in an end of season test match in which a draw would ensure that both teams kept their place in the First Division. The two sides secretly agreed to draw the game and, as a consequence, the match was a farce. The 40,000 crowd were clearly not as stupid as Stoke and Burnley thought and soon cottoned on to what was really happening – they kept the ball whenever it went out of play along with all the replacements. The uproar was sufficient for the FA to cancel test matches and replace them with automatic relegation and promotion.

In the season before the outbreak of World War I, West Bromwich Albion were involved in a scandal over attempted match fixing. Jessie Pennington was offered five pounds, for himself and every other West Brom player, if they lost to Everton on 29 November 1913. At that time, £55 between eleven players was a lot of money but it didn't influence them and the game was drawn. Afterwards, Pennington reported the fixer to the police and handed over the evidence. The man was arrested and sent to prison for six months.

Two of the modern giants in English football had their reputations sullied in 1915 after being involved in a match fixing scandal. The game in question was Manchester United versus Liverpool at Old Trafford on Good Friday, 2 April 1915. The score was predetermined in a Manchester pub a couple of days before the game. Suspicion was aroused when bets were placed all over the country at odds of 7-1 for a Manchester United 2-0 victory. In the match itself, Liverpool were completely inept and dutifully lost 2-0. The police started to investigate the incident when a bookmaker refused to pay out on successful bets. Eventually, a Liverpool player admitted the scam and nine players were suspended and later banned.

Manchester United's Enoch 'Knocker' West was given a life suspension after being found guilty of match fixing but the ban was lifted in 1945, when he was 62. Three other guilty players had the ban lifted and went on to fight for their country in the Great War. One, Sandy Turnball, was killed.

The Italian leagues' first documented problems were in the 1930s, a decade of massive change for Italy. One famous incident involved Juventus fullback Allemandi who was offered £550 to play badly against Torino. He accepted the money even though he did not honour his obligations. Actually, he played very well and even managed to stop a certain Torino goal by clearing the ball off the line. At the time, there were whispers, rumours and counter rumours that other players must have been involved since Juventus were surprisingly beaten. Allemandi was suspended for accepting the money but, shortly afterwards, the Italian FA relented and reinstated him to the game. It obviously did not do his future prospects any harm since he went on to captain the Italian team in the 1934 World Cup finals.

Stupidity and impatience had disastrous consequences for French club Red Star in 1950. They were playing well and on course for promotion to the First Division when they were found guilty of trying to affect the result of a league match by offering bribes to opposition players. They were disqualified from Division Two and missed out on promotion even though they had finished top of the league although how many games they had fixed to be in that position was never established. In addition, their president was suspended and their trainer banned for life.

During the 1954/55 season in Italy Serie 'A', Udinese achieved their best ever position, finishing second. Their success was short lived, and partly explained, when they were found guilty of buying one match as well as being implicated in many other instances (none of which were proved). They were relegated to Serie 'B'. Match fixing was rife in Italy during the 1950s and relegation was little deterrent, as Udinese proved the following season. They were playing Pro Patria in a game that was so obviously fixed that it prompted Signor de Barnardi, the referee, to say, 'funny business was going on. So much of it, that I felt like putting away my whistle and leaving them to it.'

At this same time, Catania were also found guilty of match fixing – just one more game in an estimated 150 fixed matches that season. However, the unusual thing about this incident was that a Catania fan and security official chose to do the bending himself, not for money but for power-trip, egotistical reasons.

The 1957/58 season saw one of the worst outbreaks of bribery in the history of the Italian league when it was thought that between seven and twelve Serie 'A' games were fixed. Accusations were flying left, right and centre as approaches were made to clubs at the highest levels. Sampdoria president Alberto Ravano claimed to have been approached three times and Achille Lauro, the millionaire president of Napoli, certainly suspected foul play when he fined his whole first team for what he described as 'a deliberately poor performance' in a 1-0 home defeat to Sampdoria.

Sometimes, seemingly natural results have crooked undercurrents which only come to light years after the event. In 1958, Brighton won two key matches against Watford and were promoted to the Second Division. Some years later, Jimmy Meadows, the former captain of Watford, publicly alleged that his team had been paid a remarkably small sum of money to lose both games. Glen Wilson, the captain of Brighton, seemed to confirm this when he told the press that the allegations were true and that he didn't know what would happen to him. Nothing did; no action was ever taken due to lack of hard evidence and the passage of time.

In March 1958, Gianni Azzini, Padova's International centre back, was suspended for life and Atalanta relegated to Serie 'B' following a conviction for bribery. Sampdoria, an interested party in Atalanta's struggle against relegation, had accused them of match fixing following a shock 3-0 win at Padova. Luckily for Azzini, his suspension was lifted a couple of seasons later when 'the thinness of evidence became plain'. It turned out that the main witness against him was an ex-girlfriend whom he had promised to marry in the close season – she had eventually got tired of waiting and left him.

In the late 1950s, countries behind the Iron Curtain got in on the act when an unnamed Polish club (how cruel for their fans) were suspended for attempting to fix a series of promotion battles by offering money, liquor and prostitutes to the opposition.

Dynamo Bucharest had several players included in a hit-list of twenty Romanian sports stars suspected of 'tampering their results'. Match fixing would later become something of a national sport in Romania with major accusations and revelations shocking world football in 1996.

Red Star were back in the spotlight in the 1959/60 season. The Nantes goalkeeper pretended to accept a bribe from a Red Star official but, in fact, reported the approach to an FA official. Although the incident was substantiated, the French FA made no official announcement, and Red Star continued to play in the league. It was only when a newspaper published photographs of Red Star's *already* banned trainer coaching the players in secret that the scandal broke. As punishment, the French authorities once again suspended Red Star's president along with the club treasurer. Furthermore, the team were thrown out of the French league in disgrace (although they were reelected some years later).

Bari, the team which replaced the disgraced Atalanta in Italy's Serie 'A', were clearly unready for the top flight and each season was a struggle against relegation. It wasn't long before they were trying to bribe their way out of trouble and, towards the end of 1961, they were caught in the act, automatically relegated and given a deficit of ten points, making sure an immediate return to the top was impossible.

Bulgarian football had its first scandal in January 1963. Newly promoted Rakowski FC from Dimitrovgrad were trying to escape relegation from the First Division when they were accused of trying to buy a referee. The club were found guilty after the full story of the previous season's promotion bid also came to light. It emerged that the entire town had got behind

Rakowski, pooling money to finance the match fixing efforts. The mayor, the chief of police and several factory bosses were found guilty of syphoning off public funds to finance the team. The plan was to buy referees; it worked and they won promotion. Cash was also used to bribe opposition players and subsidise team support on away trips. The club were relegated and several shady characters were jailed. The mayor, the chief of police and the town surveyor each received heavy fines.

Belgian Club Waterschei were promoted to Division One at the end of the 1962/63 season. Unfortunately for them, their negotiations to fix a match with Tilleur were overheard by the manager of their overnight hotel. Tilleur fullback Niessen, who used to play for the opposition, was suspended for his part in the proceedings and Waterschei were relegated to Division Three.

The Bulgarian Cup ran into trouble in September 1964 when the competition was temporarily suspended after most of the top teams had deliberately lost their first round matches so that they could concentrate on the race for the league championship. All of the clubs found guilty were severely reprimanded – and then reinstated in the Cup.

When Ipswich beat Sheffield Wednesday 2-1 at Portman Road in December 1962, no one batted an eyelid or suspected anything underhand. Although rumours about match fixing had abounded in the English game for quite some time, nothing had been proved. However, the revelations of Jimmy Gauld, the former Everton and Charlton forward, published in the *Sunday People* on 12 April 1964, rocked the game to its foundations. The paper revealed that three Sheffield Wednesday players, Peter Swan, Tony Kay and David Layne, had fixed the match to stage a betting coup. They had made sure Sheffield Wednesday were beaten 2-0 by Ipswich and each of them had won £100 by betting on their team to lose.

It turned out that Jimmy Gauld's disclosures were just the tip of the iceberg. He went on to reveal that two other matches, Lincoln and Brentford in the Third Division and York and Oldham in the Fourth Division, had been fixed on the same day.

Within weeks, the number of players implicated in the affair had grown alarmingly and, in total, over 60 players were interviewed during the police investigations. Dick Beattie, who had played for several Scottish clubs, was amongst the accused as were Walter Bingley (Halifax), Jackie Fountain (York), Harry Harris (Portsmouth), Ron Howells (Walsall), Bert Linnecor (Lincoln) and Peter Wraggs (Bradford). The players were charged with 'conspiracy to defraud' and suspended for life by the FA. The court case ended at Nottingham Assizes on 26 January 1965, with ten players, out of the thirty-three who appeared in court, being jailed. Jimmy Gauld, at the heart of the scandal, received the heaviest sentence and was jailed for four years and ordered to pay £5,000 costs. The other nine were jailed for between four and fifteen months, effectively ending several promising careers. One of the convicted was Tony Kay who could have possibly taken Nobby Stiles' place in Alf Ramsey's England team. His defence counsel realised the blunder and commented, 'he has given up, for £100, what has, in fact, been one of the greatest careers of any footballer. He was tempted once, and fell.'

In 1965, the Yugoslavian FA took the drastic step of not publishing referee appointments, stating that, in future, clubs would not know which officials had been appointed until the referee arrived at the ground. There must have been a fail-safe system, otherwise any Tom, Dick or Harry could have turned up to officiate, bribed or not. The move followed several complaints by referees claiming they had been plagued by mystery phone calls threatening beatings if they didn't 'bend' a game.

Hertha BSC were relegated to Germany's Division Two in 1965 after the authorities found they had made illegal payments to players. Hertha submitted a dossier to the German FA alleging that half the clubs in the Bundesliga were guilty of the same crime. The average incentive payment was said to be the equivalent of £1,200 and Werder Bremen and Borussia Dortmund were two of the main culprits, according to Hertha. The unofficial record was reported to be £8,500, paid by Nurnberg

FC to Swiss forward Rolf Wuthrich. Nothing was proved against the other clubs and Hertha were still relegated.

More Yugoslavian match fixers were rooted out in November 1965, when two players, two referees, three clubs and sixteen officials were suspended indefinitely for their part in a bribery and corruption scandal. The clubs involved were Hadjuk, Zeljeznicar and Tresnjevka and those banned included the managers and coaches of all three clubs and two Zeljeznicar players. Hadjuk were found guilty of giving Zeljeznicar 1,500,000 dinars to lose a match in May 1964 and Tresnjevka were found guilty of a similar offence, committed the previous month, when they gave Zeljeznicar 5,000,000 dinars (about £1,500). Not surprisingly, Zeljeznicar were sitting comfortably in a mid-table position throughout this period. The plot was simple, as Zeljeznicar 'lost' both games it allowed Hadjuk and Tresnjevka to amass 23 points each, two more than relegated Novisad, and thus ensured their survival in the league.

November 1965 saw another scandal rock Yugoslavian and Italian football at the same time. During the 1964 European Cup semifinal between Borussia Dortmund and Inter Milan, Inter's Luis Suarez ruthlessly kicked Borussia's Kurrai in the groin, right under the nose of the Yugoslavian referee Tesanic. He waved play on, when Suarez should have been booked at the very least. The Germans vigorously protested, Kurrai played on and Inter won 2-0. Later, the following letter appeared in Zagreb's *Sportske Novosti* newspaper: 'While I was on holiday in Italy, I found, to my consternation and embarrassment, that one of our referees had allowed himself to be bought for a handful of notes and has lowered himself to the position of a beggar. I learned, in fact, that two referees were staying here in Milan at Inter's expense, and that the Italian club were also giving them daily pocket money. What I want to know is, who permitted our referees to accept an invitation like this? And, how can these referees control a match in an impartial manner?' Good question.

The letter stirred up a hornet's nest – the referee mentioned turned out to be none other than Mr Tesanic along with one of his linesmen from the game, Mr Skoric. The other linesman, Constantin Zecevic, had refused Inter's advances. A committee of Yugoslavian referees, adjudicating over the allegations, found that Tesanic and Skoric had taken presents from Inter Milan for 'services rendered' and the pair were suspended indefinitely.

Infamous Italian agent Desiderio Solti had several brushes with the authorities over his activities. Solti's connections with several Italian clubs were well known and suspicions were aroused about his possible involvement in the 1965 Liverpool versus Inter Milan European Cup semifinal. Liverpool won the first leg at Anfield 3-1 and Inter won the second leg 3-0, with Bill Shankly claiming that match referee Ortiz de Mendibl was attempting to fix the tie. Two of Inter's goals had been dubious; one scored by Corso from an indirect free kick, the other when Piero knocked the ball out of the hands of Tommy Lawrence, Liverpool's goalkeeper. Liverpool player Ian St John spoke for the whole club when he said, 'we knew something was up when we couldn't even get a throw in'.

In another vital European Cup game on 2 October 1968, between Inter Milan and Malmo, it appeared that the French referee was totally biased in favour of the Italians. He disallowed a goal by Roy Andersen for Malmo which would have made the aggregate score 4-1 to the Swedes. He claimed the goal was not given because of an infringement on the goalkeeper although still photos of the goal clearly showed that Andersen was at least four yards from any Milan player when he headed the ball in. In the end, Milan won 5-3 on aggregate and Malmo's captain, Kristensson, was sent off for asking, in English, how many minutes of the game were left. Nothing concrete was proved against the referee but the two decisions did seem highly irrational.

German club Arminia Bielefeld were twice involved in match fixing scandals in the early 1970s, although punishments and fines weren't dished out to the guilty parties until the Spring of 1973. Eleven players were banned for between three and four months and eight of the eleven were Eintracht Braunschweig players. The ringleader, Ditmar Erler, was fined 2,200 DM and banned for four months for accepting money (about £260 a man) to lose a vital league match against Arminia Bielefeld in the closing stages of the 1970/71 season.

Arminia were clearly throwing their money around because they managed to fix their game with Shalke in the same season. Four Shalke players, Klaus Fischer, Herbert Lutkenbohmert, Rolf Russman and Hans Jurgen Wittkamp, were all fined 2,300 DM and banned for two years after being found guilty of throwing the game, which Shalke lost 1-0. Arminia had offered Fischer and his teammates the equivalent of £10,000 to lose the match. The German FA made it clear that no convicted players would ever play for West Germany. Fischer recalled, 'for me and my teammates it was the end of the world. We were a long time without playing. We went nearly two years living in hell, training alone, with no idea of what would eventually happen to us. Yes, I was wrong. I made a ridiculous error. I was young I suppose, I didn't think and committed what I know now to have been an inexcusable mistake. There's no one to blame but myself, it was my own fault.' His ban was later lifted.

British journalist Brian Glanville, wholly aware of match fixing methods (and the top suspects), was in very little doubt that Leeds United were victims in 1973. Leeds played AC Milan in the European Cup Winners Cup Final and lost 1-0. The Greek referee, Mr Michas, 'made a fiasco' of the final; he refused three or four Leeds penalty claims, sent off Norman Hunter and thoroughly looked as though he'd been 'got at' by the Italians. After a UEFA investigation, Michas was suspended and later struck off their refereeing list – but Milan still won the cup.

Glanville's revelations in the *Sunday Times* also led to the banning of Italian agent Desiderio Solti. It was alleged that Solti had attempted to bribe the Portuguese referee Lobo ahead of the 1973 European Cup semifinal between Derby County and Juventus. UEFA accepted that Solti did indeed attempt the bribe but, curiously, also accepted Juventus' assertions that Solti was acting completely independently when he travelled to Lisbon to see Mr Lobo. Juventus claimed Solti was simply one of their fans, and the Club had no way of controlling their supporters' actions. Derby County manager Brian Clough summed up his disgust by saying, 'no cheating bastards will I talk to. I will not talk to any cheating bastards.' It was evident to him who the guilty parties were.

Brian Glanville managed to sum up the whole Italian situation in one sentence: 'Do UEFA not know that it was an open secret that, for a decade, the big Italian clubs and probably (no, more than probably) the international team were wheeling and dealing in referees, bribing them rotten wherever they could, frequently manipulating matters so that they had the referee of their choice appointed for the important games.'

Juventus had always denied any connection with Solti, re-iterating that he acted alone. The *Sunday Times*, as part of continuing investigations, published a letter by Solti, signed on behalf of Juventus, which had been part of the negotiations concerning the dates for the two legs of a Fairs Cup tie against Dutch side FC Twente. The letter proved beyond doubt that Juventus had lied about not knowing Solti. UEFA still did not act on this new evidence; there was a suggestion from them that Juventus should sue Solti but nothing ever happened.

The 1974 World Cup finals in Germany attracted more claims of bribery, this time by Poland's coach Gorski. Poland played Italy in Stuttgart and, after the match, Gorski claimed that well-heeled Italian supporters had tried, without success, to bribe his players. Some time later, further allegations emerged when Polish players claimed they'd been offered thousands of dollars a man to lose, or draw, the game. These offers were made during the game and by the Italian players themselves. Gorski was officially gagged by the Polish authorities.

Six years later, in 1980, Brian Glanville spoke to the Polish captain, Denya. He confirmed that the Poles *were* offered money 'during the game' with Italy on 23 June 1974. The Poles refused and went on to win 2-1. Other players interviewed by Glanville said money was offered not on the pitch but in the grandstand, by six Italians who weren't on the bench that day.

No actual sum of money was mentioned, simply because the Poles rejected the idea outright. The Poles claimed a further attempt at bribery was made in the dressing room area during half time, when it was suggested to them that a 2-2 draw would be a very good result. Italy lost 2-1 and FIFA refused to investigate the claims, saying it was strange that the Poles were willing to talk about the events six years after the match but not before.

Questions were raised over the refereeing of the 1975 European Cup Final between Leeds United and Bayern Munich. Bayern were in very shaky form that day but won the cup with two strangely controversial goals; one from what seemed a non-existent penalty and the other when one offside man passed forward to another. Rumblings were made to those fearless and devoted investigators UEFA, but they rejected the protest, suggesting that the match referee received only a gift of a banner and a beer mug.

In 1975, match fixing in Hungary had become so much of an embarrassment to the country's communist government that they banned the book *Why is Hungarian Football Sick?* The author wrote of wholesale corruption: results were pre-arranged; money openly changed hands between the bribers and the bribed; players acted through unscrupulous intermediaries and it appeared that there was a fixed money rate for vital league points. In one case, cash was paid in the dressing room corridor as the teams waited to go onto the pitch. When questioned, the cheats said they were collecting an old loan.

It is almost unheard of for a supporter to bring a charge against a referee but that is exactly what happened in 1975 when Argentine referee Jorge Alvarez was arrested on a charge of 'sports fraud' after a match between Newell's Old Boys and FC Oeste. Visitors FC Oeste gained a 2-2 draw, scoring both goals in the last eight minutes. The first was a hotly disputed penalty, the second in the final minute, after Señor Alvarez had stopped what seemed like a perfectly valid home attack at the other end. Newell's fans rioted after the match, with Señor Alvarez sustaining a very serious eye injury. He was arrested by a Newell's fan, accompanied by five witnesses, and charged under a little known Sante Fe Province law. The immediate result of the action was a referees strike in Argentina. When Alvarez was cleared of all charges, the men in black went back to work.

One of the greatest names in post-war Belgian football, Josef Jurion, was banned from the game for life in June 1976. Just a few weeks before the ban, Jurion had been the manager of First Division side La Louviere whose set-up had been found guilty of attempting to bribe Berchem players before an important match which was likely to affect the relegation struggle. La Louviere won the game 2-0 but were relegated to Division Two, with a threat of further relegation should further revelations come to light. La Louviere were also fined the equivalent of twenty per cent of all their ticket sales from the 1975/76 season, a good deterrent if ever there was one.

Possible bribery and match fixing occurred in the unlikely setting of a Caribbean World Cup qualifying game between Haiti and Trinidad and Tobago in 1977. The game was played in Port of Spain and was refereed by an El Salvadorean, with two fellow countrymen as linesmen. No fewer than four West Indian goals were disallowed for no tangible reasons. The West Indians lost the game but decided to pursue a complaint about the officials, who were later suspended on suspicion of match fixing.

To the match fixer, it's palatable to use personal funds to make the necessary inducement, but it's far more sensible to have a scheme that raises funds for illegal activities and leaves a little bit left over as well. One such ingenious system was dreamed up by Paris Saint Germain president Daniel Hechter, who launched his own cottage industry in football dishonesty. The ruse was simple: Hechter had been printing two sets of tickets for matches; one set was sold through normal channels and the second set was sold privately by officials and players. The club's attendance figures were based on the official set of tickets, whilst the funds from the under-the-counter ticket sales were used for illegal inducements and boosting the signing-on fees. These large fees were thought to be directly responsible for PSG's signing Carlos Bianchi from Reims and defender Ramon Heredia from Atletico Madrid. Hechter admitted his part in the scandal, saying, 'this system has been used in five league matches. But let's face facts – in most of our First Division clubs the players are given under-the-table payments in addition to their regular wages.' Daniel Hechter's claims, if true, served little purpose for it was he who had been caught. He was banned from football for life.

Britain's reputation for impartial refereeing was tarnished in 1978 when Scottish referee John Gordon and linesman David McCartney were suspended for their part in AC Milan's UEFA Cup second round match with Levsky Spartak of Moscow. Before the match, Gordon and McCartney were escorted on a shopping trip to Milan where, in a menswear shop, an AC Milan official settled their bill. AC were fined £8,000 and offered a feeble explanation of the events, saying that the shop would only accept lire and the two British officials didn't have any Italian currency on them at the time. Milan's sports director, Sandro Vitali, later said, 'we didn't ask for the money back later because we wouldn't dream of behaving that way to any guest of ours'. The clothing purchased was estimated to have been around £400 per man. Milan's president, Felice Columbo, stated: 'It was a naive gesture of courtesy. UEFA fined us, I think, recognising our good faith but meaning to tell us that we must not have this kind of relationship with officials. We are taking note for the future.'

John Gordon had been a FIFA registered referee since 1967 and was widely believed to have been naive rather than a party to cheating, but, there is no doubt, he should have known better. No suggestion was made by UEFA that Gordon or McCartney had not acted impartially. UEFA's Directive for Referees sets out, very clearly, standards of behaviour declaring, 'referees and linesmen must refuse firmly but politely any exaggerated and too-generous form of hospitality. Souvenirs and gifts shall not be accepted before the game, only afterwards. Acceptance of valuables is strictly forbidden.'

World Cup history was tainted again in the 1978 finals in Argentina. In the second series of group games, Brazil faced Poland and Argentina played Peru. Brazil beat Poland 4-1, alerting Argentina to the exact score they needed to progress in the competition – they had to beat Peru 4-0. As Scotland had already found out, Peru weren't a bad side, but Argentina simply had to win the World Cup.

Although never conclusively proved, there is a theory about this which was first told in the *Sunday Times* and elaborated on by Simon Kruper in his book *Football Against the Enemy*. The story went that the ruling Argentine military junta had practically promised the nation World Cup victory. This meant that Peru had to be bribed to fix the game, and the Generals of Peru, short of money, were only happy to help out a fellow junta.

The arrangements were allegedly made by Admiral Carlos Lacoste, a World Cup organiser and, at the time, vice-president of FIFA. Argentina shipped 35,000 tons of free grain to Peru and (it was rumoured) arms shipments were part of the deal as well. As an added incentive, the Argentinian Central Bank suddenly freed $50 million in credits for Peru. Argentina's manager, Cesar Luis Menotti, barred his goalkeeper and substitutes from his pre-match team talk. In the match itself, Peru managed to squander several easy chances; they played four reserves, a defender up front and their goalkeeper Quiroga (a naturalised Argentinian known as El Loco, the madman) played more eccentrically than usual. Argentina won 6-0 and reached the final.

The story was originally published in 1986, as a letter in the *Sunday Times*. Its author, Maria Laura Avignola, was put on trial in Argentina for 'moral turpitude' but was acquitted. Although no concrete evidence has ever been unearthed, she claimed the sources for her letter were civil servants and football officials who wanted their anonymity preserved for fear of retribution. A wise move in a pre-Carlos Menem Argentina.

One very comical match fixing chapter in South American football history happened in December 1978. During the Rio Grande Championships in the south of Brazil, Gremio had to lose to Juventude to avoid a tough match against Caxias in the next round. Gremio came onto the pitch with the intention of being defeated but, after ten minutes, their young forward Victor put them 1-0 up. Gremio's supporters started to boo Victor for his 'mistake' but then the referee awarded a non-existent penalty against Gremio, bringing whoops of joy from their fans. The score was now 1-1. However, Ruverval then scored another for Gremio to make it 2-1. In the second half, after receiving further special instructions, Gremio's goalkeeper Remin allowed Juventude to score three times. In the closing minutes, Gremio scored one more, just to please their supporters. Their mission was accomplished; they'd lost 4-3 and secured an easy passage through to the next stage. The comedy of the situation provoked strong reactions in Brazil and it was branded 'the biggest scandal in Brazilian football for years'. The chairman of Gremio admitted in a television interview that his team had instructions to lose, blaming the organisers of the championships who were then severely reprimanded.

The great Italian betting scandal made the news in 1980 after a Rome magistrate launched an official enquiry into claims that players in Serie 'A' had placed upwards of £20,000 on the results of games which were then fixed in accordance with their gambling predictions. It was a simple system that relied entirely on the fixers' unique and privileged positions as players. The clubs allegedly involved were AC Milan, Lazio and Juventus. By March 1980, more than a dozen players had been interviewed in connection with the charges.

At the time, journalist Brian Glanville was continuing his investigation into match fixing and bribery and, with the betting scandal now raging, the Italian press decided to launch a blistering attack on him and his newspaper, the *Sunday Times*. The Italians claimed that they (Glanville and Co.) were only printing stories about Italy in order to destabilise them as Italy were in England's 1980 European Championship group – a farcical claim considering what was happening in Italian football at the time.

The betting scandal came to a head with the arrest of eleven players and the president of AC Milan, Felice Columbo, in April 1980. Armed police swooped in a nationwide operation to arrest the players, many of them as they were leaving the field of play. The police acted on the confessions of two members of a Rome gambling syndicate who claimed that they had bribed players to fix matches. The accused players were: Giuseppe Wilson, Bruno Giordano, Massimo Caccetiore and Leonello Manfredonia of Lazio; Giorgio Morini and Enrico Albertussi of AC Milan; Stefano Pellegrini of Avelino; Sergio Girardi of Genoa; Guido Magarini of Palermo; Mauro Martia and Luciano Zeccinini of Perugia.

The scandal grew bigger and the centre of the investigation focused on the Lazio versus Milan match which, it was claimed, was fixed. Lazio midfielder Montenesi feigned injury because he knew the match was going to be fixed – he said that a fruit and vegetable seller had given the Lazio players £60,000 which was to be divided amongst them after losing the match. AC Milan won the game 2-1.

It emerged that a syndicate were successfully making huge sums of money on the illegal betting market after paying top players to fix the results of games. Some players bravely took the money but didn't fix the matches which, considering the type of paymaster involved, was a risky thing to do. Others, who did take money, were also profiting from illegal betting on the results.

Investigators were faced with a wall of silence that was sensationally broken by two members of the illegal betting syndicate. Massimo Cruciani and Alvaro Trinca informed the police that they had lost over £1 million because the players had not 'played ball'. In a formal complaint to the Rome prosecutor they named 27 players as having been directly involved in match fixing on behalf of the syndicate. The black list included 21 players from Serie 'A' (including Rossi, Savoldi, Albertossi and six Lazio men).

Paolo Rossi was confronted with the accusations and insisted his name being on the list must have been a mistake. Lazio's Montenesi admitted to a newspaper that he feigned injury in the match against Milan because he got cold feet about fixing the match despite his £3,000 share of the bribe. Unbelievably, Montenesi later denied ever making the statement. On 19 March 1980, two players from Serie 'B' both admitted accepting cheques from syndicate member Massimo Cruciani after successfully fixing a Perugia–Avelino match at a 2-2 draw. On 18 May, ten players were banned for varying lengths of time and, as punishment, AC Milan were relegated for the first time in their history.

Following the enquiry, a whole host of punishments were dished out, the main ones being: the relegation of AC Milan for fixing a 2-1 win over Lazio; life suspensions for Milan president Felice Columbo, goalkeeper Ricky Albertosi and Lazio goalkeeper Massimo Cacciatori; Lazio were fined £6,000; five point deductions to be made at the start of the next season for Perugia and Avelino as punishment for their fixed 2-2 draw; a further eight players were banned for a period of three to five years including a three year ban for Paolo Rossi. It was ruled that the cases of 38 people, including 33 players, would be the centre of judicial proceedings after the 1980 European championships. All 38 charged individuals were freed by the court in late 1980 because match fixing was not a criminal offence in Italy, but the bans from football still stood.

Juventus still stood accused of fixing a 1-1 draw against Bologna; AC Milan player Stefano Ciodi told a newspaper how a Bologna player friend of his had asked him to place a bet of £1,000 on a draw with an illegal betting ring. At the time of the game, a rumour circulated that, after Juventus went 1-0 up when Franco Cuasio's long shot had been fumbled into the net by the Bologna keeper, the scorer ran panicking to the bench demanding, 'what do we do now?' only to be told, 'let them equalise'. The equaliser came in the form of a bizarre own goal scored by the Juventus stopper, Brio. By the middle of 1980, Juventus had still not been punished. Bologna's general manager and players were banned for their part in the fix and the team were also docked five points for the following season.

Considering this was Italian football, it was amazing that

enough evidence ever came to light for such a successful investigation to take place. The shock waves were felt throughout the Italian game for quite some time and it's worth noting that match fixing on a similar scale has not been detected in Italy since – which is not to say it hasn't happened. Paolo Rossi was fortunate to have his three year ban reduced to two, enabling him to play a full role in the 1982 World Cup finals in Spain. After a poor start, Rossi scored the goals that led to them being crowned World Champions.

Meanwhile, across the Mediterranean in Spain, following a game between Betis Seville and Real Sociedad, Seville's captain, Antonio Benitez, confessed to a blatant approach: 'the day before the game I got a phone call at our hotel offering myself and the team £5,000 for a draw or £10,000 for a win'. Betis drew the match 1-1.

In his confession, Benitez described the post match events: 'when we were on the way home we travelled by train into Chamartin station and then had a coach out to Madrid airport. While we were waiting to check in, a man and a woman of about fifty came up to me and gave me a plastic bag. I didn't open it until we were on the plane and found it contained the promised 750,000 pesetas wrapped in newspaper. We shared it among the eleven first team players, reserves, masseur and the kit man. Our coach, Luis Carriega, wasn't involved.'

The only team that could have benefited over the result were Real Madrid but, despite the confession, nothing could be linked to them or proved against them. The Spanish league declined to act against either Betis Seville or Real Sociedad as the payment was 'a third party bonus situation' rather than match fixing. An interesting viewpoint – at best it was an incentive payment, at worst it was match fixing.

Question: what do you do when you're a priest in Italy and need a new bell for your church but don't have the money to buy one? Answer: have a friendly sympathetic local football club called Avellino who throw a game and give the money directly to you. This happened in the Spring of 1980 after Avellino met Foggia.

Swiss club FC Wettingten were found guilty of match fixing in 1980; a Wettingten official succeeded in bribing local rivals FC Aarau to allow his relegation-threatened team to beat them 7-2. FC Wettingten were fined for the crime but avoided relegation.

In the summer of 1980 half a dozen Malaga players were suspended for varying amounts of time for accepting money to give away a game against Salamanca. Bribery investigations were also launched in Yugoslavia after a series of strange results, including two matches which finished 22-0 and 19-0 in the 1979/80 season. Yugoslavian football had to sort itself out (again) in mid 1981 when it was discovered Second Division club Maribor had paid around £15,000, out of a private account, to more than 30 referees over a period of five years. The revelations came from two former club officials and, following police investigations, all the guilty referees were banned.

Belgian club Beerschot were accused of widespread bribery and corruption by newly relegated Berngen. The claims were taken seriously when ex-Beerschot defender Dahling received death threats to the lives of his three children if he carried on testifying.

At the end of 1981, a scandal blew up involving the Steahul Rossu club of Romania. It turned out that officials from the local car factory, who were the team's backers, handed over large sums of money which were in turn used to line the pockets of referees and opposing players (they certainly wouldn't have been interested in Romanian cars). Steahul Rossu were promoted in 1980 by obvious means, but in the 1980/81 season they finished mid table – they were third when the scandal first broke.

In January 1982, Perugia stopper Mauro Dello Martira was banned by the Italian FA until 1985 for his part in a football betting syndicate. His 'family' took good care of him as he was put in charge of youth football with America's New York Cosmos. In February of the same year, Greek Second Division referee Constantine Pellidis was sentenced to four months in jail for accepting a bribe. He helped Panetolikos to win a match, accepting £1,130 for his efforts.

Italy's national team were accused by an anonymous source of trying to bribe Cameroon to fix a match in the 1982 World Cup. Italy made a very bad start to the tournament but a 1-1 draw with the Cameroons was enough to send them through to the second stage; if Cameroon had won, they would have gone through at Italy's expense. Among the players said to have accepted money was Roger Milla. Italy and Milla vociferously denied the claims and FIFA decided there was no case to answer – just as well really as Italy went on to win the tournament.

By far the most obvious piece of dishonest skulduggery in the 1982 World Cup was the match between Germany and Austria in Gijon. It was the final group two qualifying match and their fate rested on this late game. Germany needed to win but a 1-0 win would see them, and the Austrians, both go through. The teutonic chums set about the task of qualifying with typical efficiency. West Germany scored early on and Austria did nothing for the rest of the match; come to that, neither did the Germans who just posed and postured their way through the match. It was an unbelievably slow and boring game which is known in Germany as 'anschluss' – the great Gijon scandal – and although no outright cheating, bungs or dishonesty were ever proved, the facts speak for themselves.

TV money and financial spin-offs caused the fixing of a Libertadores Cup semifinal in Rio De Janeiro in October 1982. River Plate of Argentina ended up in a stronger group, where club officials wanted them to be because of massive TV and gate money. The other side in the match, Chile's Cobreola, ended up $60,000 richer for their help. The money was paid by River Plate and other clubs, Flamengo and Penarol in particular, who wanted River Plate in their group for the same cash reasons. Each club paid Cobreola $20,000 for the match to be fixed as a draw. River Plate were so confident they would go through that they had already negotiated and signed a $50,000 TV deal for a game against Flamengo.

Allegations of match fixing surfaced in Turkey in early 1983 after a match between Istanbul's two biggest clubs, Galatasaray and Fenerbahce – which Fenerbahce won 1-0. Trouble started when referee Cumhur Demir ignored a Galatasaray penalty appeal four minutes from time after Yugoslav striker Hogic was tripped by a defender. The game was halted for over a quarter of an hour and Hogic was so miffed that, at the end of the match, he attempted to punch the referee but was held back by team mates. In a post-match television interview Galatasaray manager Ozkan Sumer accused Fenerbahce's president Ali Sen of bribing the referee. He claimed that whenever Fenerbahce played at home they owed their success to penalties 'created' by referees. The allegations were never confirmed because of poor quality video evidence but, for their troubles, Hogic and Sumer were banned from football for five weeks.

Sensational further bribery claims were made in a 1983 television interview given by the then Argentina and River Plate fullback Enrique Wolff concerning Argentine attempts to bribe Poland's 1974 World Cup team. The Poles had already been approached by the Italians but Wolff claimed that he had offered the Polish players £1,000 per man to make sure that Argentina, not Italy, went through to the second round. His claims were backed up by central defender Ruben Claria but denied by other players including Mario Kempes who said, 'none of my money went into anyone else's pocket' – hardly convincing. The records show that the Poles beat Italy 2-1, thus sending Italy out of the tournament. A draw would have seen both teams through, and Argentina back on the plane. Something definitely went on and, unless the result really was legitimate, it seems Argentine money won the day.

A total of 26 people were arrested on charges of match fixing in Hungary in the spring of 1983. The matches were fixed to make a killing on the pools and Robert Kock claimed that Fradi's 2-0 away win over Ujpest Dozsa was one of the fixed games. He also intimated that Hungarian International Gabor Poloskei was assaulted because a game fixed against Csepel did not turn out as the fixers wanted it to. Among the accused were two top Hungarian referees and 215 players, several of whom faced criminal charges. The brains behind the operation was Tibor Molnar, nicknamed the Toto King, who was said to have made over £130,000 from the scam.

When Graziano Bini scored the winning goal in Inter Milan's 3-2 away win over Genoa in May 1983, TV and newspaper journalists noticed that there was little or no celebration for his last-minute strike. Relegation-threatened Genoa needed the points while Inter stood no chance at all of catching Roma at the top of the league. An investigation into a fix was launched; players, coaches and officials were interviewed but nothing was proved. A little while later, Milan newspaper *Il Giorno* ran a story alleging that Milan players Bini and Bagni were physically attacked by their own team mates after the match for breaking the fix. The investigation continued and Inter were cleared on the dubious grounds of 'insufficient evidence'. However, the case was re-opened in October 1983 following the seizure of television film and more interviews with players, officials and journalists. A new twist to the story emerged when Inter were accused of trying to buy a UEFA Cup second round tie with Dutch club Groningen on 26 October 1983. Groningen coach Hans Berger said he was offered £55,000 to 'fix' his players for the second leg which was to be played in Bari as Inter's home ground, the San Siro, was closed under a UEFA ban. Groningen had won the first leg 2-0 and days before the second leg, Groningen president Renzo De Vries complained about the approach to the Dutch Federation who passed the claims on to UEFA. De Vries later reported that he himself had been approached on the day of the match. Inter Milan won the match 5-1 and the Dutch coach and president stated the allegations in public after the game. Inter's president Ivano Fraizzoli was dismissive saying, 'It's all a pack of lies. Anyway, how could you buy a whole team with such an amount?'

Groningen presented a dossier of evidence to UEFA which named Dutch agent Appollonius Konijnburg as the go-between. They claimed he had admitted acting for Inter Milan and threw in the offer of a new stand in addition to the already offered cash. On 17 November 1983, a UEFA disciplinary commission was set up in Zurich and Berger, De Vries and Fraizzoli gave evidence, only to see the whole proceedings adjourned until 15 December as Konijnburg was ill. Incredibly, at the reconvened meeting Inter Milan were let off due to 'insufficient evidence'. It's difficult to imagine how much evidence is needed in order to find the corrupt parties guilty.

On 29 February 1984, Brussels' public prosecutor announced that investigations had revealed that the last and decisive match of the 1981/82 season between Standard Liege and Waterschei had been fixed. Liege and Belgian star Eric Gerets, Liege president Roger Petit, trainer Raymond Goethals and Waterschei player Roland Jannsen were all arrested. Goethals had persuaded his squad to hand over their win bonus (£385 each) to Waterschei to ensure victory. The method of transfer was pretty straightforward with Petit giving the money to Gerets who would then make contact with a player from Waterschei and hand it over. The authorities were bemused as to why they did it – Standard Liege only needed a draw and Waterschei were set to finish mid-table and had an appalling record against Liege anyway. When the punishments were revealed, Eric Gerets (who had just been transferred to and sacked by Inter Milan) was suspended from football for three years; Petit and Goethals were banned for life; thirteen other players received bans of between six months and three years; Standard Liege were fined £15,000. In December 1985, Eric Gerets had his ban reduced and was back playing for Belgium. This once bitten twice shy policy of reducing bans is all very well and good but, surely, a life ban would be more appropriate as players who are found guilty could easily succumb to temptation again, despite their protestations to the contrary.

In the summer of 1986, Iallo Allodi, formerly associated with Inter Milan and Juventus, resigned as general secretary of Napoli as a result of a new betting scandal. The allegations came to light when Turin police, who were conducting a drugs investigation, tapped a phone line and heard a conversation between Allodi and Udinese's general manager, Cordi. The conversation gave details of the forthcoming match between the two clubs. They agreed the score would be 0-0 and that one Udinese player would be assigned the task of provoking Maradona so as to get him sent off. The game was indeed drawn (it was 1-1) and Maradona was sent off five minutes into the second half. Allodi denied the charges, insisting, 'I have always been a clean man' – but he resigned anyway. Allodi was also the general manager of the Italian national side during the 1974 World Cup when they were accused of trying to bribe the Poles.

In 1987, a new scandal erupted in Yugoslavia when a newspaper claimed that prominent communist party members were heavily involved in match fixing. The newspaper story appeared in the state controlled *Slobodona Dalmacija* and followed an inquiry by Split's public prosecutor. The article proclaimed, 'Yugoslavian soccer is run by the Mafia' and alleged Split law officers had taped conversations which 'could be fatal for several socio-political figures, high ranking officials and members of the police'. Inquiries followed the arrest of a director of a top club who just happened to have a large quantity of foreign currency in his possession. Yugoslavian FA president Slavko Sajber gave some indication of the magnitude of the problem when he said, 'these people are dangerous and well-organised, and important and criminal proceedings must be instigated. They have been handling millions of German marks and US dollars for these transactions.'

When Turkish clubs Kocaelispor and Bursaspor were relegated at the end of the 1986/87 season, little did they know that their predicament had been determined by match fixing. Two of their relegation rivals had conspired to fix a match so as to relegate Kocaelispor and Bursaspor and ensure their own survival. The match fixing claims interested the Turkish government who demanded that the two clubs be re-instated in the Turkish First Division. The ministry of sport banned all league competitions for two weeks – until the Turkish FA finally agreed to their ruling.

Far East betting syndicates got involved in the Merlion Cup in Singapore during 1987. Four Canadian Internationals were accused of accepting bribes totalling £60,000 following Canada's two matches against Singapore. Chris Cheuden, Igor Vrablic, Hector Marinaro and David Norman were all charged by Canadian police, immunity being granted to a fifth player, Paul James, who agreed to testify for the prosecution. Bob Bearpack, who coached the team in the tournament, said that he was aware that his players had been approached by a local gambling syndicate and that he'd repeatedly told them to resist the temptation of taking bribes.

Rarely does a referee talk openly about bribes and match fixing; silence is often safer, and far less controversial. Top Swedish referee Ulf Ericksson broke with protocol in May 1988 when he said that bribery attempts before International and European ties were very common. He refused to name clubs but said that he'd never been offered a bribe in Britain.

There was more trouble in Yugoslavia in August 1988, when Pristina and Celike were both penalised six points for fixing their last league game in which Celike scored three goals in the last five minutes to win 3-2 and escape relegation. Pristina were heavily fined and Celike were relegated after all – as an additional punishment.

Newly promoted Portuguese club Famalicao were relegated from the First to the Third Division at the end of the 1987/88 season after it was discovered they had paid £3,500 to the president of Macedo De Cavaleiros to lose a vital match. Angry Famalicao fans, distraught at their club's demise, showed their disapproval by pulling up railway tracks and blocking main roads with tree trunks and rubble.

In January 1989, Colombian soccer was in uproar after the kidnapping of a referee by a group who had sworn to 'rub out' referees who do not control games properly or who have taken bribes to favour a certain team. Armondo Perez, the kidnapped referee, claimed that he negotiated his release by providing the kidnappers with the names of people (including referees) who were involved in match fixing which, at the time, was rife in Colombia. A timely example of bent refereeing also happened in the same month when, in a vital match between Armenia

Quindio and Independiente Santa Fe, the referee added twelve minutes of injury time during which Santa Fe managed to score an equaliser. In protest, 2,000 fans stormed the pitch, attacking the referee and the Santa Fe players, seven of whom were badly injured.

In 1989, the Colombian government tried to clamp down on match fixing following a string of dubious matches. Action included the restructuring of the league and refusing to rent state-owned stadia to those teams that chose not to comply. The designation of match referees was also taken out of the control of club officials. The start to the next Colombian season was held up for three weeks because of government investigations into the affairs of clubs suspected of being financed by drug cartel cash. The money was obviously being used to fund numerous illegal activities including the bribing of referees. The government chose to investigate the finances of every club in the Colombian league and had the power to refuse licences. Their task was not easy – some clubs were so disorganised in their administration that they hadn't even registered their club colours for 33 years.

In January 1990, the Colombian league was suspended and the 1989 title declared null and void after referee Alvaro Ortega was shot dead by gunmen as he was entering his hotel after refereeing a match between Independiente Medellin and America. Señor Ortega was 27 and hit by six bullets. Medellin failed to qualify for the championship finals as a result of the match. A man later rang a newspaper and said that the Mafia had lost a lot of money betting on the result of the game and that other referees who were not willing to co-operate would be placed on a hit list and face a similar fate. As a result of this chilling new threat several leading Colombian referees instantly resigned.

Two days after Ortega's murder, another referee, Jose Torres, was kidnapped and released a few hours later in a drugged state – a warning from the drug cartels. The Colombian government restated its policy: the use of stadiums would not be permitted unless clubs voluntarily stated that they were under no outside pressure from drug cartels and betting syndicates; tournaments

Hardman Billy Bremner suddenly discovers that he's not that tough after all. Would you have argued with Dave Mackay?

Top left A Kuwaiti prince holds a press conference during his intervention in a game at the 1982 World Cup

Bottom left Arsenal and Manchester United players square up to each other in 1990

Below The Wimbledon players get ready for more after-match touchline interviews

Above Diego Maradona and fellow Argentines attempt to send off the referee after awarding a penalty to Germany in the 1990 World Cup Final

Top right Swedish riot police prepare for the kick-off at the European Championships 1992

Bottom right Galatasaray's subs bench patiently waiting for their chance to get at the opposition in 1994

Left A perfectly coiffured Mo Johnston – such a sweet, innocent-looking boy!

Below Paolo Rossi rejects the advances of a Polish player in the 1982 World Cup

Right Diego Maradona – undrugged?

Below Brazil's Jorginho pleads innocence after amputating a Uruguayan player's legs in the 1995 Copa America

Above 'Excuse me. I'll have another suitcase of money please'

Left Controversial football agent Eric Hall, in cunning disguise, getting ready to complete his first mid-match deal

would also be suspended if there were any complaints of clubs being pressured, bribed or blackmailed. In retaliation to the drug cartels, a group called the 'Cleansers of Colombian Soccer' threatened to kill all shareholders of clubs who had a proven connection with drugs. The group said they would not allow the new season to start in May unless Colombian football was totally free of drugs money and match fixing. They admitted responsibility for six murders including Independiente Medellin president Pablo Correa and Deportive Pereira president Jhavier Piedrhati – in Colombia, even the good guys are bad. All six people who were murdered were allegedly part of a group who bet on football results in a massive operation manipulated by the drugs barons. The Cleansers of Colombian Soccer also threatened the national team coach, Francisco Matura, with death if he picked players for the World Cup in Italy who played for corrupt clubs. This would have decimated the squad. After being sent home from a pre-tournament training camp, for safety reasons, the Colombians chose to ignore the threats and take part in Italia 90 unscathed.

Scandal marked the opening of the 1989/90 Libertadores Cup when Paraguay's Sol De America and Olimpia conspired to fix a match so both would qualify ahead of Chile's Colo Colo. America needed to win to go through but Olimpia could afford to lose, as long as it was by no more than one goal and they managed to score four themselves. In a completely open game, with absolutely no marking, America won 5-4 – just what the doctor ordered for both to qualify. Colo Colo protested to the South American Confederation, but their appeal was turned down as there was no concrete proof of match fixing; some officials actually defended the notion that the Paraguayan clubs actually had a right to fix the result. Such are the unbalanced ethics of South American football.

Rumours that a match was going to be fixed circulated well before the March 1990 meeting of leading Calcutta clubs Mohammedan Sporting and Mohun Bagan in the All India Airlines Trophy. Both sides needed to avoid defeat to be sure of qualifying; a defeat for either would have let in the Punjab State

Electricity Board. Nobody was surprised when the rumours became reality and the game was a 2-2 draw. An inquiry was immediately launched where it was decided that a fix had taken place: both coaches, the referee and one of his linesmen were suspended.

French club Marseille were highly successful under the egotistical stewardship of Bernard Tapie; they won the French title in the early 1990s and the European Cup in 1993 – only to have it taken away after a string of dishonest behaviour brought shame on the club. Police enquiries gave the authorities no option but to take legal action. At the centre of the initial investigation was the 1993 match between Marseille and Valenciennes which Marseille won 1-0. Two Valenciennes players, Christophe Robert and Jacques Glassman, claimed that they were phoned in their hotel room (in the presence of Argentinian midfielder Jorge Burruchaga) by Marseille midfielder Jean-Jacques Eyedelie, who had then passed the phone to his general manager Jean-Pierre Bernes. It was agreed that Robert would be paid 250,000 francs (£30,000) for Valenciennes to take it easy during the match. Christophe Robert said that his wife, Mary-Christine, collected the money from Eyedelie in the car park of Marseille's team hotel. Following the disclosure, police arrested Robert and found 250,000 francs in used notes buried in his mother-in-law's back garden. Robert's wife was also arrested and both were cautioned on corruption charges; Jean-Jacques Eyedelie was also charged after surrendering himself to police.

Marseille's subsequent win virtually guaranteed them the title but condemned Valenciennes to the relegation play-offs, where they were defeated 2-0 by Cannes. Marseille were also in trouble in Europe after claims by Gennadi Kostylev, the coach of CSKA Moscow, who said that his players were offered cash to ease up against Marseille in the Champions League the season before. The teams drew 1-1 in Moscow, with Marseille winning 6-0 at home. Criminal investigations were delayed for long enough to test the patience of FIFA, who penalised the French authorities by expelling Marseille from defending the

Champions Cup in September 1993. FIFA also issued a further threat to expel France from the 1994 World Cup if a speedy conclusion wasn't reached.

Bernard Tapie quit Marseille, the club he had nursed to greatness, in December 1993, after the club were stripped of the French title. The European Cup was handed to AC Milan and Marseille were given a European ban which coincided with the launch of a thorough financial enquiry. There had been whispers and innuendo at the club for some time before the match fixing revelations surfaced. Questions had been asked about Tapie's methods of keeping Marseille at the pinnacle of the French game. The Valenciennes scandal was the first concrete proof of wrong-doing and the decision was taken to come down hard on Tapie.

During the ensuing trial, Bernard Tapie looked under considerable pressure when his alibi for having no part in the Valenciennes match fixing episode was disproved. Tapie claimed that he had been having a meeting with the mayor of Bethune, Jacques Mellick MP, at the time of the approaches. This was proved to be absolute fiction – the meeting didn't take place. The really damning evidence against Tapie and Marseille was provided by Jean-Pierre Bernes, a former coach of the club. Bernes stated under oath that Marseille had spent £1.2 million a year providing incentives for opponents to throw matches; some of the money was also spent on buying referees. In 1994, Bernes himself had been suspended on match fixing charges and was heavily fined; he knew precisely what Tapie had been up to and how he did it. Tapie was cited by Bernes as being the godfather of match fixing. 'It was Bernard Tapie who decided which match to buy,' said Bernes in court. Every year, four or five games were fixed and had included those against Nantes and Aek Athens in 1989 and even the 1993 European Cup Final against AC Milan. Jean-Pierre Papin, on the bench for Milan during that match, blurted out that he knew of at least two Milan players who had been bribed to take it easy.

During his testimony, Jean-Pierre Bernes told the judge, Monsieur Pierre Phillippon, that he feared for his own safety after giving evidence – a hint of the unsavoury characters involved in the scandal and the lengths they may go to silence people. In May 1995, Bernard Tapie was sentenced to a year in prison for his part in match fixing. In a statement issued on 2 July, he admitted that millions of pounds had been given as loans to players or used to buy players from other teams. It's likely that Chris Waddle was purchased this way. Tapie appealed against the corruption charges, anxious to overturn the verdict so it wouldn't interfere with his blossoming political career – in France, anyone found guilty of corruption or bankruptcy can face a five-year ban from elected office. Nevertheless, Bernes, Tapie and others were convicted of buying-off the Valenciennes players, and Marseille was stripped of its French title in 1993 and relegated to the Second Division in 1994. In April 1995, the club was placed in receivership – the money had run out for the players' wages and they were $48 million in debt. Tapie was jailed and Marseille banned from purchasing any new players; all new signings had to be free transfers – which explains Tony Cascarino's move to the former French champions.

One interesting sideline of the investigation was provided by the evidence of the Croatian fixer Ljubomire Barin, who alleged that Marseille were not the only big European club who had been involved in match fixing. The names of Bordeaux and Bayern Munich were mentioned, with an inference that the irrational refereeing of the 1975 European Cup Final between Bayern and Leeds had involved a degree of fixing.

In September 1993, UEFA kicked Dynamo Tiblisi out of the Champions Cup for trying to bribe the referee of their preliminary round tie against Linfield. UEFA found the Georgian club guilty of offering $40,000 to the referee and his linesmen before the game. The match took place on 18 August 1993 and Dynamo won 2-1.

Another part of the world where match fixing has become part of the football furniture is the Far East. Anyone looking for a real soccer scandal need look no further than Malaysia. In 1995, over 80 players were barred from playing in the

Malaysian Premier League for match fixing and 22 of them faced the interesting punishment of being banished to remote regions of the country under Malaysia's Restricted Residence Act. During the investigations, it quickly became apparent that the cancer of match fixing had spread to nearly every team in the sixteen-side league. Teams admitted taking cash payments from bookmakers to fix games but, despite 125 players being interviewed by police, lack of witnesses often proved a problem. Four players who did get their collars felt all played for the state team Sabah, and were arrested on evidence provided by the team's coach Kelly Tham, who got suspended himself after his much-fancied side were on the end of a series of uncharacteristic drubbings.

The Malaysian scandal spawned the biggest bribery investigation in football history but actually first surfaced in Singapore, who had a team in the Malaysian league. Singapore's Czech striker Michael Vana and a local referee were pulled in for questioning in August and charged with match fixing and corruption. Vana subsequently jumped bail and decided to fly back to Prague. By the time he was ordering his inflight duty frees, the Malaysian authorities were starting to make more sense of the curious end of season results. Vana's Australian team mate, Abbas Saad, was quickly arrested and banned for life by the Singapore FA for his part in the match rigging. The Malaysian sports minister, Muhyiddin Yassin, declared that all the country's players and officials would have to declare their assets to the government for scrutiny. A 'bribery watch' committee was set up, including former players, whose job it would be to watch match videos to try and identify suspect performances. Players were also offered free counselling and special courses aimed at suppressing any urges to chase money and luxury. Because so many players were banned, the Malaysian FA were forced to rely on their youth policy to replace the disgraced stars. Whilst all this was going on, match fixing allegations surfaced in Britain concerning Bruce Grobbelaar, Hans Segers and John Fashanu. Also involved was a Malaysian British-based businessman and a Malaysian betting syndicate. The tentacles of Far Eastern match rigging may now have spread to Britain.

Probably the most damaging thing that can happen to somebody in football is to be convicted of match fixing only to have the ruling overturned in the future; more people doubt the individual's innocence, even though the evidence may prove it without a shadow of a doubt. Dutch international referee Dick Jol was banned by the Dutch FA (KNVB) in October 1995 following claims on a TV show that he had placed bets on games that he refereed. Jol consistently denied the allegations and, in April 1996, an Amsterdam court ordered the Dutch FA to lift its ban.

At the beginning of April 1996, the Romanian Football Association admitted that corruption and match fixing were rife in the national league. The admission came after the national coach, Anghel Iordanescu, threatened to resign over the issue, stating that he couldn't possibly preside over the team in Euro '96 because the Romanian FA had consistently ignored his claim that sleaze had firmly embedded itself in the game. Three frantic days later, the Romanian FA promised that the problem would be tackled and Iordanescu dropped his threat. FA chairman Mircea Sandu told a highly charged press conference that Iordanescu was right and said: 'Of course there are rigged matches in the championship, but to have evidence is not so simple. You have to discover them . . . It is our shame that the problem has not been analysed.'

Match fixing in Romania is a national joke – so many teams do it that one television channel screened a programme showing the highlights of fixed games, complete with theatrical dives by goalkeepers and fluffed chances by forwards. At some matches, fans sing songs of ridicule when confronted with otherwise inexplicable results. There is, however, an historical reason for the emergence of match fixing. Many Romanian clubs were artificially created to glorify communist ideals and highlight key enterprises and they survived on state hand outs. Following the collapse of communism in Eastern Europe, they are struggling to make ends meet and, aside from selling players abroad, sources of income are few and far between.

The new free market system means that clubs which get relegated often close – not least because they can't pay the players' wages. These clubs offer bribes and incentives, usually to mid-table clubs with little to play for. Anghel Iordanescu said, when confirming his change of heart: 'Nowhere is soccer a clean game, but in Romania it has passed its limits.' For the final part of the 1995/96 season, when bribery and match fixing is traditionally at its height, the Romanian FA undertook to monitor games. Iordanescu had the last word: 'I am not naive,' he said, 'things won't change easily but, at last, I have pushed the alarm bell.'

Match fixing won't go away; it's a story that will run and run.

5 Cheating

ACCORDING TO THE Oxford Dictionary, 'to cheat' involves a person, or persons, behaving in a dishonest or deceitful way in order to win or gain advantage and there could not be a more perfect verb to sum up football's desperate sins. Whether blatant, subtle, ingenious or downright cheeky, football has experienced all kinds of cheating.

Subtlety was not the name of the game in an 1891 meeting between Stoke and Aston Villa. Stoke were awarded a penalty with a minute of the match to go, so the Villa goalkeeper deliberately kicked the match ball out of the ground. By the time the ball was retrieved, the 90 minutes were up, so there was no time for the penalty to be taken. Following protestations from Stoke, the laws of the game were changed to allow the playing of extra, or injury, time; stoppages were not to be deducted from normal time.

A slightly more well-thought-out method of cheating was employed by Argentine club Estudiantes, who often trod the fine line between cheating and intimidation. Juan Ramon Veron, Estudiantes' player of the 1960s, admitted: 'We tried to find out everything possible about our rivals individually – their habits, their characters, their weaknesses and even about their private lives so that we could goad them off the field, get them to react and to risk being sent off.' This win-at-all-costs mentality rubbed off on the Argentine national team and was perfectly demonstrated by Carlos Bilardo's team which reached the 1990 World Cup Final despite being poor. A stark contrast to the team of four years previous which won the World Cup in Mexico with some style – and a little help from Diego Maradona's hand.

There was uproar at the Under 19s South American championships in 1979 when it was noticed that one Paraguay player looked remarkably mature; defender Lisandro Cabera had a four-year-old son. Two Chilean players were also sent home because their passports had been falsified. A further investigation back home in Chile led to the players being jailed, along with coach Pedro Garcia, team co-ordinator Enrique Jorquera, two tourist agency employees and two registry office officials.

Greece, the country that had illegally imported referees, was back in trouble in 1980 after revelations that top clubs were illegally fielding top South American players who had entered the country on forged documents supplied by the clubs and so evading the two foreigners per team rule.

Two Spanish referees, Donato Pes Perez and Manuel Fandos, were loaned to Colombia for six weeks in 1981 in a vain attempt to bring some sanity to Colombian football. They claimed they had to go into hiding to avoid people trying to bribe them and they also received numerous death threats. The fairness of the Colombian game was rendered non-existent – the National League was populated by managers who were controlled by drug barons, armed referees struggled to control matches and crowds terrorised games. One popular Colombian trick was to throw two or three balls onto the pitch whenever they felt their team's goal was under threat.

In 1981, Inter Milan won the unofficial World Junior Championships in Mar Del Plata. They beat Tahuli of Bolivia on penalties and Inter's star player was a boy playing under the name of Massimo Ottolenghi. However, it emerged that Ottolenghi was, in fact, Massimo Pellegrini and, at fifteen years old, was a year over the age limit for the championship. Inter Milan's junior squad manager Giuseppe Fiore openly admitted the fiddle and said: 'Both players were in our squad. But we were told only boys born in 1967 could take part so we decided to use Pellegrini with Ottolenghi's name. After all, other teams were using over-age players on the quiet and Pellegrini wasn't that much over the age limit!' The cheek of the man.

Such blatant cheating is disturbing because it's so obviously pre-meditated. Another type of cheating is the win-at-all-costs mentality which is applied irrespective of the consequences. German goalkeeper Harald Schumaker decided that the only way to stop Patrick Battiston of France, who was clean through and bearing down on his goal, was to lunge into him at head height. Schumaker made the conscious decision to stop Battiston (the French were leading Germany 3-1 at the time) in the semifinal of the 1982 World Cup. A prostrate Battiston was rushed to hospital and, unbelievably, Schumaker stayed on the pitch to successfully nurse the Germans through a penalty shoot-out and into the final. To come back from 3-1 down was an achievement in itself but if Battiston had not been fouled by Schumaker, and had scored, France would have certainly progressed to the final to play Italy.

A year later in Argentina, Estudiantes were leading Sarsfield Velez by one point in the league. When they played each other, the first half was fairly incident free and goalless but the action was just about to start. During half time, four explosions were heard in the Velez dressing room. Coach Juan Carlos Lorenzo dashed out to say that four fireworks had been thrown through the dressing room window and some of his players had been injured. Lorenzo insisted that his team could not come out for the second half of the match.

Interestingly, Sarsfield officials would not let anybody from Estudiantes see the injured and by the time the police had arrived their coach was about to leave. However, they could not prevent a police doctor from boarding the coach. He found one player with slightly red eyes (probably from rubbing) and one player who said the explosion had made him deaf, although he managed to answer all the doctor's questions. Upon investigation of the dressing room, the police discovered that the window had been opened from the inside. Clearly, this was a ploy by Velez to try and get the match awarded to them, therefore securing the title. The Argentinian FA had other ideas

– they ruled that the final 45 minutes of the game should be replayed. Estudiantes won 1-0 and took the title.

Italy's young footballers were in trouble again in the 1987 World Under 16 Championships in Canada. Fiorentina's Ricardo Secci was so desperate to play in the competition that he lied about his seventeenth birthday, telling the organisers that it was 28 July instead of 28 August. The deadline was 1 August. He was not alone in bending the rules – Ghana were also thrown out of the competition for fielding three over-age players.

Ronald Koeman, the Dutch International, so often the executioner of the English national team, was fined and suspended by his club PSV Eindhoven in May 1988, after publicly praising a professional foul by teammate Hans Gillhaus. Koeman said that the foul, committed in a vital league match, was 'worth gold to us'.

In April 1991, AC Milan couldn't face going out of the European Cup. They were losing the second leg 1-0 to Marseille when a floodlight failed. With three minutes of normal time remaining the Milan players walked off, claiming they couldn't see properly. This clearly was not true and referee Bo Karlsson had to order them from the tunnel to complete the tie. Milan knew that they were virtually out of the competition. They paid dearly for their attempt at cheating when UEFA banned them from European competition for a year.

Chilean International goalkeeper Rojas claimed he had been struck by a flare whilst playing in a crucial World Cup qualifying game in Brazil. Chile were losing 1-0 and, if the score remained that way, they would be eliminated. After 65 minutes, Rojas played injured and got himself stretchered off, with Chile refusing to play on. It later transpired that Rojas had inflicted the injuries on himself in a bid to get FIFA to reverse the result. FIFA took a very dim view of the incident and were furious when they discovered that Rojas had been aided and abetted by Chile's manager, physio and doctor. Chile were banned from the next World Cup and all the perpetrators were given bans by FIFA.

Italian club Torino, whilst being investigated by the fraud

squad in 1994, were found to have cooked their books in order to siphon off under-the-counter cash from transfers. Investigators found that Torino had made £465,000 from the phantom transfer of Alkessandro Palestro, the son of one of the club's secretaries who was not registered with the club and was, at the time, studying at university.

6 Bungs

BUNGS OR ILLEGAL payments are, in effect, sweeteners offered to people to ensure a deal is concluded. Payments can be made in various ways from carrier bags full of money being handed over at motorway service stations to the slightly more upmarket briefcase full of money changing hands at a top London hotel.

Payments in kind are not uncommon; there is one manager who used to insist on a crate of champagne as a gift for his cooperation in a deal. The world of bungs is a seedy one and many observers of the game have no doubt that they are part and parcel of present day football. Often intermediaries do the dirty deed and it's rare for the bung makers and takers to be caught red handed.

Illegal payments are just as bad as a blatant bung. Cash incentives are a historical fact of British football stretching as far back as the turn of the century and they were still going strong in the 1990s when Tottenham Hotspur Football Club were investigated by the Inland Revenue for a series of 'illegal payments' in the form of cash loans to players.

The story of bungs begins in 1884. The old invincibles, Preston North End, probably the best club in the history of the game, were banned from the FA Cup for being unashamedly professional under their manager Major William Sudell who admitted paying players for their services. He had to or he wouldn't be able to compete with other clubs who were doing the same thing, only not being so honest about it. Accrington Stanley found themselves in a similar position and, after much debate, the FA agreed to allow payments to be made to players. As a consequence, football's balance of power shifted to northern England from its former stronghold in the south.

Scottish football was slightly less tolerant when it came to paying players. In 1890, Renton were banned from the newly formed Scottish League after only six games; they had played a team called The Edinburgh Sainti who were deemed to be professional.

In 1900, a maximum wage of £4 per week was introduced for players in England but not in Scotland. This opened up the game to the possibility of a plethora of scandals as the players, who were, after all, the stars, earned the same wages as the men who went to watch them. Today, a good comparison would be Paul Gascoigne earning only £200 per week – no wonder the players were deeply unhappy.

Burnley goalkeeper Jack Hillman was banned for a year for trying to bribe Nottingham Forest players in 1900. Hillman was anxious for Forest to throw the match and offered them £2 a man via their captain, MacPherson. The latter refused the offer on the grounds of dishonesty, much to the disappointment of Burnley who were staring relegation in the face. They were 2-0 down at half time, at which point Hill upped his offer to £5 per man. Forest went on to win the match 4-0 and Burnley were relegated. At the FA hearing, Hillman claimed he had only been joking because Nottingham Forest had recently been beaten 8-0 by West Bromwich Albion.

In 1904, Second Division Glossop were fined £250 for wholesale mismanagement and deception. Four of their directors were suspended for three years, their secretary was censured and six of their players were suspended for six months. The players were also forced to change their status from amateur to professional although, at the time, it was possible to earn more money as an amateur as all players received expenses. The FA expressed very keen interest in Glossop's accounts, especially when they investigated the transfers of two players, Irvine Thornley and Frank Norgrove, to Manchester City. Illegal payments between the clubs surfaced during the enquiry in October. City were fined £250 and five of their directors were suspended (three of them for three seasons and one for life). Irvine Thornley was suspended for the rest of the season. The public was outraged and football's maximum wage of £4 was blamed for the problems. Manchester City were a huge club at the time, but one of the outcomes of the proceedings was the emergence of Newton Heath, another Manchester club, as a force to be reckoned with. They still are, only today they are known as Manchester United.

1904 was a busy year for the FA, who were even stuffier than they are today. Sunderland were fined £250 for making illegal payments and their directors and secretary were suspended for three years. In between all the bung enquiries, the FA still found time to introduce a law ordering that players' shorts had to be long enough to cover the knee when they were in the standing position.

Middlesbrough Football Club were censured by the FA and fined £250 for making irregular under-the-table payments to players. The maximum wage a player could earn in a year was £208 and they had found a way to increase this amount on the side. The background to the story is very interesting. In 1905, Middlesbrough became the first club to spend £1,000 on a player, paying Sunderland the cash for the services of Alf Common in a desperate attempt to avoid relegation. Common's transfer infuriated FA chairman Charles Clegg who was all for scrapping transfer fees. Clegg was chairman of Sheffield United and had had Common in his employ, until he begged to go back to his native North-East. Clegg let Common go for the princely sum of £375 and, understandably, was furious when, three months later, he joined Sunderland for £1,000. To make matters worse, Common returned to Bramall Lane after his transfer to Middlesbrough and scored the winning goal. Clegg was not a happy man and, acting on a tip-off from a shareholder, instigated the investigation into Middlesbrough's accounts. As a result, eleven of Middlesbrough's twelve directors were suspended for three years.

1905 was most famous for the scandal involving one of the

most popular players in the land: Manchester City captain and Wales outside-right Billy Meredith, nicknamed the Prince of Dribbling, was the Gary Lineker of his day and enjoyed a spotless reputation as something of a goody two shoes. His world fell apart when he was accused of offering Aston Villa captain Alec Leake £10 to throw the match between the two clubs to help City win the title. 'I am entirely innocent and am suffering for others', said Meredith on learning of his suspension. But the matter didn't end there. Meredith was sent a letter by City manager Tom Maley, pledging illegal financial help during his suspension in return for him staying away from the club and refraining from talking to the press. Meredith showed the letter to an FA Commission but, in doing so, confirmed his guilt in taking illegal bungs. As a result of his admissions to the commission, a total of seventeen Manchester City players were deemed to have accepted illegal payments. They were fined a combined total of £900, suspended for six months and banned from playing for the club again. Tom Maley was banned from football altogether and fined £250. City were forced to auction off their players, raising £2,600 which, considering the first £1,000 transfer had just been made, was a pitifully small amount of money. Meredith went on to make amends for his stool pigeonry by becoming a member of the players' union. Tom Maley, nicknamed All-Of-A-Sudden Tom, for his quick-fire manner of speaking, became a schoolteacher in Scotland, only returning to England when the FA finally lifted his ban.

Fulham's George Parsonage wasn't happy with the £10 signing on fee, the maximum stipulated by the FA, when he was approached by Chesterfield. He was reported to the FA for asking for more money, admitting to the subsequent enquiry that he had asked for £50. In his defence he claimed it was a joke but the FA didn't see the funny side and banned him for life – the maximum penalty they could hand out. The ten pound maximum signing on fee remained in force until 1958.

In 1919, Leeds City were expelled from Division Two for illegal payments, allegedly made during the war. 'We will have no nonsense, the football stable must be cleansed', said League president John McKenna. Port Vale played the remainder of City's fixtures and Leeds United were formed to replace them. City's manager Herbert Chapman was implicated in the scandal, though he denied any knowledge. They were expelled after refusing to hand over financial details and were subsequently deemed to be the worst of a bad bunch. City's players were put up for auction and fetched £10,000.

Six years later, in 1925, Arsenal director Henry Norris was found guilty of financial irregularities and was forced to drop out of football – apparently, he had made unlawful payments to a chauffeur.

Sunderland were implicated in more trouble in 1957 when they were fined £5,000 for making illegal payments to players. The following year they suffered again when they dropped out of the First Division for the first time in their history. Brian Mears, a member of the Football League Management Committee and the FA Council, said proof against clubs was the hardest thing to get. Lots of clubs decided that the only way to get the players they wanted was to make an illegal payment – black market forces were ruling the roost.

When Len Shackleton was transferred to Newcastle, the fee was £13,000. Shackleton is reported to have also been given £500 as a signing on fee and told the club he would put the money in his building society account for safe keeping. Newcastle's Stan Seymour was mortified – he couldn't do that; people would put two and two together and know exactly where it came from. Instead, the club is said to have suggested that Shackleton could take £20 out of the safe every time he needed some cash.

When Jimmy O'Neil moved from Everton to Stoke, his wife Angela said they could do with a new cooker. Stoke were only too happy to oblige. Illegal approaches to players were common: whilst on the platform of King's Cross Station after playing for England against Scotland, George Harwick and Wilf Mannion were each offered £5,000 signing on fees by a director of a Second Division club.

Former England captain Alan Mullery recalls how he had

asked for £1,000 to sign for Fulham as a sixteen-year-old. He had been told by Roy Bentley to ask for the cash and, more to the point, was also told that he would get it, because the club wanted to sign him. Fulham offered him the standard £10 fee plus £12 a week. Mullery slid the contract back up the table and asked for £1,000 point blank. He was told to get out but returned the following day for further talks. He still refused to sign the contract and Fulham threatened to report him to the FA. After a weekend of frantic worry, Mullery was called back to the office and, as a compromise, the club said they would pay him the £1,000 if he was not in the first team within three months of his seventeenth birthday. Mullery signed and just two weeks before his birthday he was in Fulham's first team – he didn't get the £1,000 but a place in the team, and more money, suited him fine.

Money was also used by managers as a tax-free win bonus. Len Shackleton said one of his managers used to give the players £25 each for winning important league games. Most clubs didn't really care about the welfare of their players but were happy to make fortunes out of them. Things were slightly different for Trevor Ford when he played for Aston Villa: he used to go out with the manager after the match to play snooker and, if he had scored a goal, they would bet £5 a game; the manager never won a game – it was his way of giving Ford £5 for every goal he scored.

In April 1957, the FA Commission published its findings into Sunderland's illegal payments. Jimmy Hill acknowledged the fact that they had enticed players to join the club by offering them illegal payments. Even though it was wrong, Hill must have had some charitable feelings as, just a few years later, he was the man behind the introduction of a minimum wage for players.

There was a flurry of activity in the illegal payments department in Britain during the late 1960s. In the 1967/68 season, Peterborough United were relegated from the Third to the Fourth Division and fined £500 for making illegal payments to players. In mid-1968, Port Vale were fined £4,000 and expelled from the league for a similar offence. The next season they were re-elected and have since maintained a clean bill of health. Sadly, Peterborough didn't learn their lesson and, twenty years later, they were fined a further £2,500 for the same offence. European Cup holders Manchester United were fined £7,000 in 1969 for 'administrative irregularities' and Derby County were fined £10,000 and banned from the Fairs Cup for the same offence in 1970.

Manchester United were in trouble again in 1980 when a Granada Television programme made allegations of 'bungs' paid to the parents of schoolboy soccer stars in return for their sons' signatures on the club's books. Granada said washing machines, fridges and cookers were the main incentives although some hard cash was paid. Such under-the-counter-benefit-in-kind payments have been made in British football for years but Manchester United will go down in football history as the club who signed Hugh McLenehan from Stockport County for a fee of three freezers full of ice cream.

The integrity of French football was again called into question in 1982 when an illicit payments scandal blew up. The allegations centred around St Etienne who ran an 'under-the-counter slush fund' to pay players extra money during their glory years in French football. Club president Roger Rochet admitted to tax investigators that St Etienne did run such a fund and coach Robert Herbin and international midfielder Jean Francois Larios confessed that they had received money from it. A television programme alleged that money from the fund was also used to support local politicians sympathetic to the club's aims and ambitions. St Etienne were told to pay £1 million in unpaid tax or face going bust. They paid the tax.

Fulham Football Club were fined £15,000 for illegal payments in 1978 and, five years later, Spurs were fined £8,000 for the same offence. The dodgy dosh had ended up in the pockets of Argentine Internationals Ricky Villa and Osvaldo Ardiles. (Spurs and Ardiles would both have to face the music over more financial irregularities in the 1990s.) In 1989, Wimbledon were fined £10,000 for making unauthorised tax-free loans to players. The Dons had recently beaten Liverpool in the FA Cup Final and, no doubt, their fans and managers thought the players deserved a bob or two on the side.

It's a tough life being a Swindon fan. It's either promotion or relegation every year but things got a bit out of hand in 1990 when Osvaldo Ardiles was manager. He steered the club through promotion to the top flight for the first time in Swindon's history but the celebrations didn't last long – an investigation into the club's affairs revealed that they had been making unusual payments to their players and, instead of being promoted to the First Division, Swindon were relegated to the Third.

It was hardly surprising that Swindon were investigated since former manager Lou Macari and chairman Brian Hillier had been suspended and fined for betting against Swindon in a 1988 FA Cup match against Newcastle. Swindon lost 5-0, not surprising really when you consider that the top two men in the club had absolutely no faith in the team at all. Investigators found that transfer fees had been manipulated and that a number of players had received illegal payments; petty cash was being paid to club officials as perks and gate receipts were understated. For the betting offences, Swindon Town were fined £7,500 by the FA and Lou Macari was fined £1,000 and censured. Chairman Brian Hillier was suspended from football for three years for breaching FA rules.

The second set of charges resulted in the arrest of Lou Macari, Brian Hillier, former chief accountant Vince Farrar and club captain Colin Calderwood on 1 May 1990. Hiller, Macari and Farrar were all charged and released on bail. At the end of the court case, Macari was acquitted; Farrar got a six month suspended sentence and Hillier was sent to prison for a year but, on appeal, that was reduced to six months. All these irregularities went on before Ossie Ardiles joined the club and, following an appeal, Swindon were reinstated to the Second Division.

In 1991, Chelsea were fined a record £105,000 for illegal payments. A company linked to the club was found to have paid £100,000 over the market price for the Scottish home of former England defender Graham Roberts who signed for Chelsea from Glasgow Rangers.

June 1992 saw a routine check of Tottenham Hotspur's PAYE files by the Inland Revenue which revealed serious financial irregularities – a can of worms had been opened. As the taxmen probed deeper into the club's affairs, more and more irregularities were uncovered and a full-scale Inland Revenue investigation began. Spurs commissioned city accountants Touche Ross to do a thorough review of the club's affairs. The irregularities under Irving Scholar's regime were numerous and scandalous. Amongst the revelations uncovered were ex-gratia payments to players that would result in considerable back tax liabilities for Spurs. Belgian Nico Claesen had been given a secret payment of £42,000 when he joined Spurs in 1986 which had not included the statutory PAYE deductions. Icelandic international Gudni Bergsson also benefited from a payment which was, like Claesen's, made via his former club. Irving Scholar authorised both payments.

Paul Gascoigne's and Chris Waddle's pension papers were backdated by two years and loans to both players, used to buy houses around London, were illegal. Scholar also gave a secret undertaking to both players, guaranteeing them ex-gratia payments of up to £120,000 after they had left Spurs. A letter from Scholar to Gascoigne's agent Mel Stein promised to pay the player '£70,000 net of all UK taxes, up to a maximum of £120,000 gross'. The implications of such payments were, in the words of Touche Ross, 'like having a gun held to the club's head'. The special inquiry at Tottenham began on 17 July 1992. A few months later, in November, the Inland Revenue demanded a payment of £500,000, with the promise of more to come.

The transfers of Chris Waddle to Marseille and Paul Gascoigne to Lazio both involved payments to the football agent Dennis Roach who, as the *Sunday People* reported, was being paid by both sides in the deals which was in total breach of FIFA, UEFA and FA regulations. Scholar brought Roach into the equation and, even after Italian fixer Gino Santin was detailed to finalise Gascoigne's Lazio transfer, he received a pay-off payment of £27,500. However, this was not the end of the line for Roach who continued to receive money. A Spurs document stated: 'It would appear that Mr Roach has been on the pay-roll of the club, unknown to Mr Solomon and Mr Berry, having been paid £64,400 in the year ending 31 May 1991. It would also appear that Lazio may also be paying Mr Roach in connection with the Gascoigne sale. This is forbidden both under Football League and FIFA regulations.'

Most damaging of all were the irregular payments made over three transfers: the £250,000 transfer of Mitchell Thomas from Luton to Spurs in 1986; the £425,000 signing of Paul Allen from West Ham in 1985 and the £387,500 transfer of Chris Fairclough from Nottingham Forest in 1987. Thomas had been given a £25,000 loan when he joined Spurs but papers forwarded to the Football League Tribunal at the time of transfer omitted to mention it. Thomas also received a letter stating that, in effect, the money was never going to have to be repaid. The loan was made three weeks before he actually became a Spurs player. Allen and Fairclough also received loans before joining Spurs – £55,000 and £25,000 respectively – and neither payment was disclosed to the Transfer Tribunal.

When Irving Scholar left Spurs the club was in big trouble. Terry Venables desperately searched for a business partner to save the club from financial ruin and certain closure. His knight in shining armour (or so he thought) was Amstrad boss Alan Sugar, a man with a bruising business reputation. It wasn't long before Sugar became concerned about the goings on at Spurs – the result of a combination of rumours and Inland Revenue facts. The relationship between Venables and Sugar became increasingly uneasy. Venables was dismissed by Sugar in a blaze of publicity and, in 1993, the two men slugged it out in the High Court as Venables took legal action against his former partner. The legal proceedings were the usual claim and counter claim, including evidence suggesting that some managers accept cash bungs as part and parcel of transfer deals. Alan Sugar knew that Tottenham's troubles with the Inland Revenue were to be laid directly at Scholar's door, yet Venables felt that Sugar consistently tried to portray him as the bad guy. As manager of the team under Scholar, Venables was employed by Tottenham Hotspur FC, a subsidiary of Tottenham Hotspur PLC and each organisation had its own independent board of directors. The FA examined the evidence and cleared Venables of any wrong doing. They must have been satisfied because, two years later, they appointed him England coach.

The FA Commission of Enquiry decided Spurs had broken the regulations 'dealing with the avoidance and evasion of fees'. In all, they were found guilty of forty charges, twenty of which related to breaches of transfer regulations. The Commission announced its first findings on 14 June 1994, with Spurs escaping relegation (much to the anger of Swindon Town). They were fined £600,000, had twelve points deducted from their next season's total, were banned from the 1994/95 FA Cup and ordered to pay the costs of the enquiry.

Alan Sugar appealed and the points deficit was reduced to six along with the club's reinstatement to the FA Cup. This, and the subsequent signing of Jurgen Klinsmann, helped Sugar to win the fans over again.

One transfer under scrutiny in the ongoing enquiry was that concerning Teddy Sheringham's move from Nottingham Forest. Newspaper allegations had suggested that Brian Clough had taken a cash bung from Venables for agreeing to sell the player. The money was supposed to have been handed over at a motorway service station in a brown paper bag. Clough has threatened to sue over this on several occasions but, as yet, no legal action has ever been taken.

Particular interest was also taken in the £58,500 that was paid by Spurs to Frank McClintock's company First Wave which had issued the invoice for promotional work. McClintock's partner, Graham Smith, sent the invoice and the money was handed over. Terry Venables questioned the amount, saying that £50,000 was the true amount, not £58,500. The balance of £8,500 was returned to Tottenham where it sat in the safe for several days.

Alan Sugar was bemused by it all, as were the general public. Cash payments in football are amongst the most complicated financial transactions you can imagine. No wrong-doing was ever proved and Brian Clough, Terry Venables and Frank McClintock react with disdain to any suggestions of impropriety.

League newcomers Barnet were fined £25,000 for making irregular payments to players and were warned that any further indiscretion could cost them their League status. The inbalance of financial power in British football encourages unusual financial transactions which, if discovered, could mean significant trouble and muck-raking for a lot of clubs.

The influx of foreign players into our game, all searching for that readily available pot of gold, has opened up all sorts of cloak and dagger deal-making opportunities, with money laundering being made relatively easy by cash-hungry clubs and unscrupulous foreign 'agents'.

A three-man Premier League enquiry team, comprising Rick Parry, Steve Coppell and Robert Reid QC, was set up in 1993 to investigate transfer irregularities (in layman's terms, bungs). The FA had to be seen to be doing something as bung allegations had been filling up the back pages of newspapers for a considerable period of time. Finding the evidence was the difficult thing in the hear no evil, speak no evil, see no evil world of football.

The enquiry team were particularly interested in discrepancies arising out of deals between English and Scandinavian clubs. Nordic players were a cheaper, more value for money acquisition for a club at a time when transfer fees for even very ordinary players were rocketing to new heights. British football is greatly admired in Scandinavia and their traditional qualities of hard work and good skills were attractive to many British managers.

Although there are almost certain to be many managers who have been involved in irregularities, only one had to face the music – George Graham, Arsenal's most successful manager for years. He was sacked by the club in February 1995 following persistent rumours and some extraordinary newspaper allegations. George Graham was banned from participating in foot-ball for one year for accepting money from the Norwegian agent Rune Hauge who had been involved in brokering the sale of three players – Pal Lydersen, Anders Limpar and John Jensen – to Arsenal for inflated transfer fees.

Graham complains about being a scapegoat but there is no doubt that used bank notes were instrumental in his downfall. His version of events is described in his colourful autobiography *The Glory and the Grief* where he describes meeting Hauge at the Park Lane Hotel in December 1991: 'Hauge came into the bar carrying a hold-all. We ordered a drink and he said, "I have something here for you, George." He opened the hold-all, dipped inside and brought out several plastic envelopes. "Please put this into your briefcase," he said. "It is an appreciation of all you have done to help me open doors here in England." When I got home, I opened the envelopes to find they were filled with £50 notes. I decided to take the money straight to the bank, where it was counted. There was £140,500 in all.'

Some time later, he received a banker's draft for a further £285,000. Graham says, 'I gratefully had it credited to my Jersey bank account,' but laments in the book: 'It no doubt sounds like a Bung, and looks like a Bung, but it was a gift. And I did not ask for it.' It was a bung. He might not have asked for it but he accepted it and quickly lodged it offshore, out of reach of the taxman. He didn't even think to tell his employers.

Graham goes on: 'The ridiculous thing is that it (money) wouldn't have changed my life. I was on a good salary, but greed got the better of me. Now I wish I'd never clapped eyes on Rune Hauge. Yes, I was greedy. If it was offered to me again I would say, No, No, No!'

The FA enquiry found him guilty and banned him. Graham's defence was provided by top fraud lawyer Anthony Aldridge QC whose legal fees were estimated at £200,000. The year ban was apparently going to cost Graham £1.75 million in lost earnings and the bung money was handed back to Arsenal, with interest. Hauge cooperated with the enquiry and was also interviewed by the FA. He is currently under investigation by the Skattedirektoratet – the Norwegian tax authority – hence his silence.

Realising that nobody would believe that a hard-headed businessman like Hauge would throw money around out of pure generosity, Graham decided to shed a little more light on the matter. He claims that the money was paid to him, in part, for his role in the sale of Peter Schmeichel and Andrei Kanchel-skis to Manchester United. The Scot claims he wasn't interested in either player but told Hauge who would be.

'Arsenal had first choice on all Hauge's players and, if I did not want them, I steered them on to who did. I was offered Peter Schmeichel and Andrei Kanchelskis but turned them down and recommended Manchester United. When the deals went through Hauge said very precisely "I will not forget what you have done for me." I never thought he meant payment. I did it to maintain our good relationship. I did it so Arsenal would continue getting first choice,' he said.

Graham failed to address the most begging question of the lot: who in their right mind would turn down a brilliant winger and probably the world's top goalkeeper and sign, instead, two no-hopers like Lydersen (who hardly played) and Jensen whose speciality was passing the ball to Arsenal supporters in the North Bank upper tier? Arsenal fans must be asking questions, not least because Graham was instrumental in both players signing for Manchester United – Arsenal's biggest rivals at the time.

The FA's one year ban for Graham was extended worldwide by FIFA and Hauge was also banned worldwide for his part in the affair. George Graham feels that he is part of a sinister conspiracy to keep him out of football. In April 1996 he said, 'There are people in the corridors of power who wish I would just disappear from the scene and get on with my life. The thought of me returning to football, especially as a successful manager, frightens them to death. It's all just a little too close for comfort as far as some people are concerned. They don't want me there reminding everybody of just what goes on in football.'

If that is true, then George Graham must not be left to carry the can and face the music alone. However, Graham is visible proof that corruption is part of football. 'Don't forget that I'm still the only person who has ever been thrown to the wolves,' he said, 'but there are people within the game who go to bed every night thanking God that George Graham has taken the rap and carried the can.' Surely he should name names.

Outspoken former manager Tommy Docherty has similar forthright views, claiming, 'there are half a dozen managers I know of who have committed worse offences than Graham, yet they are going scot free.' He questions the FA's investigation saying: 'The people in power should know them and that things are being swept under the carpet. If their inquiry has been as thorough as they make out, why haven't they been exposed? All managers and ex-managers know what's going on as it's talked about in the corridors of football.'

Allegations in the press of accepting bungs are very serious and, as in the case of Graeme Souness, can be costly for the paper concerned.

In an article published in December 1994, the *Mail on Sunday* accused Souness of taking 'secret and corrupt bungs' whilst he was manager of Glasgow Rangers and Liverpool Football Club. The story said that Souness received £30,000 from Mr Pinchas Zehavi on a deal involving an overseas player whilst he was at Rangers, and £100,000 from Rune Hauge on the transfer of Torben Piechnik from FC Copenhagen to Liverpool.

The article also claimed that Souness was responsible for the transfer of numerous players to and from the football clubs of which he was then manager for the sole purpose of obtaining similar illegal payments. Souness sued the paper, saying the allegations constituted 'the very gravest libel upon him'. Anxious that the paper be exposed for telling lies and that his good name be restored, he went to court on 22 May 1995. Souness was awarded undisclosed damages (believed to be in excess of £100,000). Mr Justice French held that there was 'not a shred of truth' in the article and Associated Newspapers offered their sincere and unreserved apologies.

On 14 May 1996, Premier League chief executive Rick Parry

admitted that the bung enquiry was no nearer reaching a conclusion. He underlined the complexity of the investigation, saying: 'I had hoped our inquiries would have been finished long ago but that has not happened. It has become a bit more spasmodic because leads are few and far between. It is not as much setting a trap as following a trail – and as long as a fresh trail appears we will follow it up.'

The trail continues.

7 In Court

THE SIMILARITIES BETWEEN football and courts are striking: both have two sides, opposing teams; the judge is the equivalent of the referee; the public galleries are the terraces; barristers are the managers; the defendants and witnesses are the players; like the referee, the judge's decision is final; an appeal case is the same as a replay – the only difference is that lawyers don't exchange shirts at the end of a case.

Court appearances have a special place in the history of British football – for such a small country our 'Hall of Shame' is second to none. Football criminals have indulged in all kinds of offences but fall into two main categories, the stupid and the serious. Young professional players frequently fall into the former category whilst older and ex-players usually indulge in the more criminally insane activities. These older players never earned the telephone-number salaries that today's young superstars earn and for some, a chance to make a killing, even if it's illegal, has proved too much of a temptation.

In Britain, football and the judiciary crossed swords as early as 1314 when an Act prescribed imprisonment for anyone caught playing football in London. The popularity of the game was seen as a threat to national security as it kept bowmen from their archery practice. Modern day players fell into the trap of considering themselves untouchable in the eyes of the law, mistakenly assuming that being a soccer superstar was enough to influence judges and juries and convince them of their innocence. However, a string of legal run-ins between players and the long arm of the law in the 1994/95 season blew this arrogant view clean out of the water.

We are not alone as far as football related crime is concerned – moronic behaviour, thuggery, violence, gross stupidity and untouchable arrogance have also played their part in the legal history of football all over the world. In the 1960s, it was not uncommon for players in the Spanish League to fall foul of the law for offences committed on the pitch. Athletico Madrid's Argentinian centre back Jorge Griffa, spent an unpleasant night in a Bilbao jail in 1963; he was arrested after a game for insulting the referee – on the orders of the mayor, who had been watching the match.

Overzealous police officers played their part in one farcical incident in 1965 when the Argentine sides Independiente and Boca Juniors played each other. Independiente goalkeeper Toriani clashed with Boca's Abeledo, and on ran several police-men in riot gear who grabbed both players and dragged them into a waiting police van. The referee was powerless to inter-vene and the match continued with ten players on each side, ending in a 3-3 draw. Later, the Argentinian FA ruled that, in future, only when the referee asks for help should the police intervene.

In December 1965, Russian International Yuri Savidov was convicted of drunken driving and manslaughter after he struck and killed the eminent nuclear physicist Professor Dimitri Ryabchikov. He was jailed for ten years. Another Russian International, Eduard Strelzov, described by many as 'poten-tially the greatest Russian striker of them all', was jailed for five years and banned from football for life for attacking a young woman. On his release, he was reprieved and went on to play for his country again.

Since the Peruvian Estadio Nacional disaster of 1963 (when more than 200 people died following a pitch invasion), the police were under strict orders to get tough on any similar incidents. In March 1966, Alianza played Santos of Brazil in a friendly. Gilmar, the Santos goalkeeper, assaulted the referee for sending off his teammate Carlos Alberto following 'a splendid display of fisticuffs'. Police immediately rushed onto the pitch and dragged off the kicking and struggling Gilmar.

The next day, Santos flew home, leaving Gilmar to face the music in court. He was fined £60 and banned from playing in Peruvian football for two years.

In the same month, all eleven Velez Sarsfield players were arrested after a friendly against Emelec of Ecuador. The match had degenerated into a general brawl although no one had actually been sent off. However, a zealous official of the local sports federation left the game early to lodge a formal complaint with the police, claiming that Velez had consistently gone for their opponents rather than the ball. At the final whistle, scores of police poured onto the pitch and frog-marched the eleven bewildered Argentinians away – still wearing their strips and boots. It took a frantic protest by Velez officials, and the payment of a heavy fine, to get them out of jail in time to catch their plane home.

Top Peruvian referee Arturo Yamasaki was found guilty of dangerous driving in December 1966 after killing a policeman in an accident. He received a massive fine, forcing him to sell his house which he shared with his mother and brothers.

March 1973 saw some bizarre goings-on in Spain. Adorno, a Valencia signing from Paraguay, was forced into a battle over the legality of his passport. Only South Americans with Spanish parents were allowed to play in the Spanish League and, during the lengthy court case, Adorno decided to do a runner, escaping through a courthouse window during a recess. For some time, his whereabouts, and the legality of his passport, were a mystery – until the public address system at Valencia's stadium announced his inclusion in the team for the club's next home game ... as substitute. Adorno played, and no one mentioned his passport.

Former Murcia defender Jose Louis Ponce was arrested for carrying out an armed robbery on a bank in March 1975: a curious pastime for a former star of the Spanish game.

In March 1982, Norwegian International goalkeeper Roy Amundsen (15 caps) was sentenced to a suspended 60 day jail term for attacking a referee. Amundsen had been sent off in a Second Division game and, as a result, had already been banned from all sports for two and a half years. His trial, which made front page news in Norway, lasted three days and the severity of the referee's injuries (two broken ribs and severe bruising) were reflected in the harsh punishment.

Sometimes, football folk stick together regardless. Silvano Martina, the 29-year-old Sarajevo-born Genoa goalkeeper, was found guilty in May 1982 of common assault on Fiorentina's Italian World Cup star Giancarlo Antognoni. The pair had squared up to each other after colliding in a league game, with Antognoni suffering a fractured skull. Martina escaped being sentenced because Antognoni refused to put his name to the complaint, rendering the trial utterly worthless. In the same month, Greek player Achilles Kontandinis was jailed for 20 days and fined £45 for striking referee Andreas Petoglou. Kontandinis had raced off the bench and struck the referee after a goal had been awarded against his team. In court, he claimed he'd hit him 'by mistake'.

During 1983, Jan Berger, Czechoslovakia's 1982 World Cup midfielder, was handed a three year suspended jail sentence for his part in a bar brawl. His career was widely considered to be over but he confounded his critics by continuing to play for his club, Sparta Prague. In the same year, Bulgarian International Ivan Petrov was picked up for shoplifting two pairs of trousers on the eve of a European Championship qualifier in Cardiff. He was fined £50 by the local magistrates and sent home in disgrace.

Before the collapse of communism, players from the Eastern Bloc sometimes found it hard to resist the lure of the Aladdin's cave of the West. In 1983, ten Hadjuk Split players were arrested by Yugoslavian customs officers on their return from a pre-season trip to Italy. All ten were accused of smuggling offences after being discovered trying to bring in large numbers of portable TVs, tape and video recorders.

Sports photographer Marcelo Agost got the surprise of his life whilst taking pictures of a South American Championship match between Chile and Uruguay in late 1983. He was kicked in the face by Uruguay's Alfredo De Lus Santos and was taken to hospital suffering from concussion and an eye injury. Santos was arrested by police and bailed, the money being put up by the Uruguayan Soccer Federation. The case never went to court but, no doubt, Agost received suitable payment from the Uruguayans in return for dropping charges.

October 1984 saw three officials of the Yugoslavian First Division club Budocnost Titograd charged to appear in court for injuring a referee. The three, including manager Branco Bulatovic, were arrested following an incident at Budocnost's home match against Hadjuk Split which the visitors won 3-2. The referee, Dobrivoje Cvetkovic, was still in hospital having treatment for head and kidney injuries a month after the assault.

Cameroon's Roger Milla took the law into his own hands and turned jailer in 1993. Milla had organised a tournament at the Omnisports Stadium featuring teams comprising pygmies and, in all, 120 pygmies had travelled from villages all over the country to take part. However, Milla was soon in trouble – for keeping them imprisoned, under guard, in a room within the stadium. When asked why, a tournament spokesman said, 'you don't know the pygmies. They are extremely difficult to keep in control.' When asked why they weren't fed properly, the same person replied, 'they play better if they don't eat too much.' The tournament was a disaster; only 50 spectators turned up and all they did was hurl abuse at the pygmies.

Chelsea's Yugoslavian goalkeeper Peter Borota, a big favourite at Stamford Bridge in the 1980s, was jailed in 1994 for stealing religious icons and fine art paintings. After hanging up his gloves, Borota opened two shops in leading Belgrade hotels trading antiques and earning a reputation for himself as an artist. He enjoyed a degree of critical acclaim before it was discovered that he wasn't an artist at all; the paintings were stolen. Borota, and his partner, were last heard of languishing in Novi Sad prison, reputedly the worst of all the jails in the former Yugoslavia.

Rene Higuita is probably best known for his mesmerising 'scorpion' kick whilst playing against England at Wembley in

1996 but, in his native Colombia, he is known for other things. He was friends with cartel boss Pedro Escobar and missed the 1994 World Cup finals because of a spell in jail. Higuita was accused of acting as a go-between to secure the release of a girl who had been taken hostage by one of the drugs gangs. Colombian law forbids any assistance of this kind. Higuita explained the sudden appearance of $50,000 in his bank account by claiming, 'I helped negotiate the release of the little girl and was paid for it. Maybe it was against the law, but $50,000 appeared in my bank account without my knowing.' On 3 January 1994, he was released on £6,800 bail after serving the maximum detention time of 120 days.

In September 1995, Oussama Aytour, star of the Lebanese World Cup squad, was fined £300 after magistrates found him guilty of making an explosive device at his brother's flat in Fulham. Aytour, who was visiting London at the time, told police that he had felt bored while everybody was out and had made the device for fun. He told the court, 'I meant no harm. I just wanted to amuse myself.'

Colombian International Faustino Asprilla received a one year suspended prison sentence for possessing a firearm after he had fired a shot in a crowded bar – he then went on to fire blanks for Newcastle United. Asprilla had a reputation that went before him during his time in Italy. Whilst playing for Parma, he was long suspected of carrying firearms and often abused speed limits in his flashy sports car, but the Italian police consistently chose to turn a blind eye to his antics. Asprilla certainly wasn't as handy with firearms as the former Panithinaikos player Floros Vasilaska. He was charged with stealing over £17 million in a series of armed robberies in 1995.

One of Turkey's biggest car smuggling rackets was smashed in 1996 after former Turkish International Tanju Colak turned State's evidence. Colak had already served seven years and, if it was anything like the prison in *Midnight Express*, you can't blame him for wanting to get out.

British players seem curiously attracted to trouble, and there have been one or two players who seem to have spent as much time in court and prison as they ever did on the field of play. Players like Birmingham City's Ricky Otto got it right – he carried out a robbery and was sent to prison, but all this happened *before* he became a professional player. Leicester City's Jamie Lawrence served 26 months for armed robbery but was able to resume playing after his stretch. To some, playing football is like making a new start, it's a way of exorcising criminal demons.

Former Arsenal and England player Peter Storey deserves his own sub-chapter for a string of offences that border on the foolish and sad – Arsenal have a history of court room dramas that Perry Mason would have been proud to get his teeth into. Between the mid-80s and mid-90s, Britain has witnessed some of the most extraordinary football court cases anywhere in the world.

Names like Cantona, Ince, Mickey Thomas, Jan Molby and Duncan Ferguson illustrate the changing face of player crime and, through the outcomes of those court appearances, the changing attitudes of the courts to the stars of the national game. Long gone are the days of the high-jinks-after-a-few-pints-with-the-lads type of offences; today's offenders are a touch more sophisticated. Players find themselves under intense media scrutiny which explains the soccer show trials that have filled up so many column inches over the years.

Arsenal, a veritable giant of the English game, has had more than its fair share of court appearances: during the period 1981–86, five Arsenal players were banned from driving. In fact, the day after Charlie Nicholas was banned he sensitively took delivery of a new Porsche. Former England International Tony Woodcock was also banned for drink driving with Raphael Meade quickly following suit, having earlier been sentenced to a fortnight in prison for obstructing the police who were trying to arrest a friend of his. Graham Rix was then stripped of his captaincy as a result of his drink driving offence and Alan Sunderland was banned for a year after failing to provide a breath test although he was cleared of any blame over the deaths of two pedestrians who had stepped out in front of his car.

In June 1987, Viv Anderson and Rhys Wilmot were sternly spoken to by Portuguese police following a street fight in Albufeira. Luckily for them, there were no formal charges but Arsenal were forced to pick up the bill for the damage. Then, Paul Merson was fined and banned from driving in July 1989 after his new BMW rebounded off a lamp post and two other vehicles.

Another Arsenal player who gained notoriety off the pitch whilst under the influence of drink was Tony Adams. After going to a barbecue in 1990, the Arsenal captain was clocked doing 73 mph across a road junction. He lost control of his vehicle and ended up in a brick wall after first smashing into a telegraph pole. Adams admitted responsibility to the police and was charged to appear in Southend Crown Court where he pleaded guilty to reckless driving with an excess of alcohol. Gilbert Gray QC, defending, said: 'The offence was out of character. Adams was seen driving off with no anxiety about his condition. He recalls nothing about beginning to feel that he had had too much to drink and he cannot understand the very high level of analysis.' Judge Frank Lockheart, in his summing up, said: 'It is incredible to think that you came out of that car alive, let alone unscathed. It was merciful that nobody was killed.' Adams was sentenced to four months in Chelmsford prison, disqualified from driving for two years and ordered to pay £500 costs. In addition, Arsenal Football Club fined him £2,000.

There was more car trouble for Arsenal in the shape of Kevin Campbell who was fined £1,800 and disqualified for driving offences in 1992. A year later, youth team player Kevin Dennis was jailed for 30 months for manslaughter.

In May 1995, permed wonder Ray Parlour received a £170 fine for assaulting a Hong Kong taxi driver on the club's tour of the Far East. Last, but not least, in Arsenal's catalogue of crime is David Hillier, a member of Arsenal's FA Cup winning squad in 1993, who was arrested over the theft of luggage from a baggage carousel at Gatwick Airport.

Former Arsenal player Peter Storey started his career in crime in 1977 with a fairly innocuous misdemeanour: he was fined £65 after failing to stop at a crossing and head-butting the lollipop man who remonstrated with him. Magistrate Harry Cook accused Storey of behaving 'like a little boy'. A year later, Storey was charged with putting up £4,000 to finance a scheme to counterfeit gold half sovereigns. He went before the Old Bailey to answer the charges in September 1980 where Judge Jack Abdela QC told him: 'For a man who commanded the respect of thousands of people, to find yourself here, believe me, it is heartbreaking.' Storey was jailed for two years.

Unable to keep out of trouble, even when he was already in it, Storey was given a six month suspended jail sentence in 1979 for running a brothel and living off immoral earnings. His Counsel, John Cope, explained to the court: 'Peter is a man of good character who succumbed to temptation to make some easy money. He is just relieved it was stopped at an early stage.' Famous last words.

In 1982, whilst he was still inside, Storey got another six months, to be served concurrently, for stealing two cars back in 1978. He had sold the cars on before the hire purchase agreements had been completed. This time, Storey's defence counsel, Victor Leven, said: 'It is tragic that a man who enjoyed such an illustrious career and held such a position in the eyes of the public should have had this sort of downfall.'

After his release from prison, Storey settled down to run a market stall in London. But it wasn't long before the police were anxious to talk to him again. In 1990, he got a suspended sentence for attacking a traffic warden and in November 1990, Storey was jailed for four weeks for smuggling porn videos into Britain via the spare tyre in his car. In court, magistrate Vivienne Judd sentenced Storey with these words ringing in his ears: 'You already know what prisons are like Mr Storey.'

The roll call of dishonour for the rest of British football also makes interesting reading.

On 2 April 1915, Manchester United were in danger of relegation and faced Liverpool, who were positioned safely in mid-table. They kicked off in pouring rain and United soon took the lead through George Anderson. The match rapidly deteriorated with Liverpool showing no appetite for the game at all, much to the annoyance of their fans. Anderson scored again and the match ended 2-0 to United. However, it was such a debacle that a public outcry forced an FA enquiry which found that various players had conspired to rig the score.

'Knocker' West was the only United player to be found guilty and he was banned for life, along with four Liverpool players. Heavy betting had taken place in West's hometown of Hucknall Torknard. Disgusted with his ban, West took the FA to court (at great personal expense). He also sued three publications for libel. The court case was undoubtably going his way – until Liverpool's Jackie Sheldon appeared as a witness and admitted to a match rigging meeting in the Dog and Partridge pub in Manchester which had involved West and two other players.

The next day George Anderson, United's double scorer, gave evidence and confirmed that he had been asked to join the scam but refused. He also said that West had earned over £70 from illegal bets. In his summing up, the judge upheld West's ban and dismissed his libel claims as unsound. Undeterred, West took his grievances to the Court of Appeal in 1918 but, as there was no new evidence, it was a futile venture.

The judge took a dim view of West's economy with the truth – he'd lied in the first trial, claiming he had no relatives in Hucknall Torknard. The case was thrown out and West was ordered to pay all costs. He never played football again and died in 1965, still protesting his innocence. West's teammate, George Anderson, was imprisoned for eight months following a separate trial for his part in a large betting scam.

Former Montrose captain Gavin Hamilton was sentenced to 60 days in prison after being found guilty of making illegal payments. He offered £50 to Montrose left-back David Mooney to fix the home match against Edinburgh City on 5 December 1931. Mooney told the court that Hamilton had told him 'to lie down' and, if goals didn't come quickly enough, to give away a penalty. Mooney's brother confirmed to the court that he had also heard the conversation.

Graham French, the former Luton Town player, was given a three-year jail term in 1970 for grievous bodily harm. In 1986, he got another twelve months for obtaining property and services by deception.

A couple of bizarre football-related court cases in the 1970s included postman David Coleman who streaked naked from the waist down before a 30,000 crowd during a Wolves–Coventry game. He was fined £25 by the court and explained his actions by saying, 'I was very bored.' Violent nun Collette Duveen was arrested and charged after she kicked a lorry driver in the teeth for cheering Holland's second goal in the 1974 World Cup Final.

Fulham FC, the club that boasts supporters who chant 'We're gonna bake you a souffle' to the tune of 'Guantanamera', are often overshadowed by their near rivals Chelsea whose fans have had a reputation for outrageous behaviour for many years. One quirky event that will be forever Chelsea is the case of Tom Whattle who was fined £10 in 1976 for sticking a hot dog up the anus of a police horse called Eileen. In court, Whattle said: 'I was overcome with excitement after the match. I am a genuine animal lover.'

In the summer of 1984, George Best, the Champagne Charlie genius of English football during the late 60s and 70s, was on the straight and narrow. George's capacity to drink was legendary. His life had been booze, birds and football – three pastimes that most men would kill for. He was off the drink and looking for work. To combat his dependence on alcohol, Best took the unusual step of having the anti-drink drug Disulfiram placed in his stomach lining. This meant that if he consumed any alcohol his body would reject it and he would need urgent medical attention. By September 1984, he was drinking again – the desire for alcohol had defeated the power of science. George confessed in an interview: 'I like drink too much to give it up. It was agony on the wagon. Hopefully, the cure won't work or I might fall dead any minute.'

As sure as eggs are eggs, trouble soon followed. Best was arrested for drink-driving outside Buckingham Palace in November 1984 and was charged to appear at Bow Street Magistrates Court the following day. He failed to show up, the police issued a warrant for his arrest, and a chase of Keystone Cops' proportions ensued. Finally, Best was tracked down to his Chelsea flat where twenty police officers attempted to arrest him. Best did a runner, diving out of a rear window, shimming past policemen in the garden and running across the road to a friend's flat. The police quickly broke into the flat, arrested Best and dragged him kicking and screaming to a waiting police van. Best lashed out, punching PC Thomas Lazenby in the face. When he was eventually subdued, he yelled to onlookers: 'Tell everyone it took 25 of the bastards to get me.' He collapsed in police custody, later explaining, 'I only collapsed from all the fatigue and excitement.'

A month later, he appeared in court and was sentenced to three months in Pentonville. Magistrate William Robins sent him down with the words: 'I regard any assault on a police officer as an extremely grave offence, and it is all too prevalent in this area. I don't see any reason to distinguish you from anyone else just because you have a well-known name.'

George Best spent Christmas 1984 behind bars and got no trouble from fellow inmates – indeed, being inside for drink driving and hitting a policeman was reason enough for them to hero-worship him.

The colourful Scottish International Mo Johnston had his collar felt in 1985. It was soon after he had left Partick Thistle to join Celtic when the police arrested four men acting suspiciously in a doorway near a Glasgow sports shop. Johnston was one of the men and had been seen by the police bargaining with the other men for some tracksuits that had been illegally removed from the shop. Stipendiary magistrate Robert Hamilton found Johnston guilty of reselling three tracksuits worth a total of £85. Johnston was fined £200.

In the mid 1980s, no player was in and out of the papers more than Charlie Nicholas. In September 1986, he faced his biggest off-pitch ordeal in the case of the stolen chip. Nicholas was on holiday in Ibiza with Willie McStay when Nicholas allegedly tried to steal a chip from a holiday maker. The incident happened outside the Confusion Bar in San Antonio, the party capital of Ibiza.

Lori McElroy was on holiday with her boyfriend and claimed in the press that Nicholas and his friends had been a problem throughout their holiday. McElroy accused Nicholas of being flash, constantly guzzling champagne and always seeking attention. Nicholas allegedly stole one of her chips, provoking a verbal barrage from McElroy. The court heard that Nicholas turned violent, as McElroy told the court: 'At that point Mr Nicholas slapped my face hard and then gave me a solid punch to the jaw. As I turned away, I felt a kick and I saw Nicholas being restrained by his friends, his legs flailing towards me.'

Nicholas called upon Christopher Brown, a friend who lived in Ibiza, to act as his witness. Brown claimed it was he who had assaulted McElroy, adding that Nicholas 'was as pure as the driven snow'. Laughter engulfed the courtroom when Brown vociferously denied that he had agreed to admit to the assault in order to save his friend's skin.

Judge McDonnel said that the attack was 'an arrogant and cowardly assault'. Berating Nicholas he said, 'I am old fashioned enough to think it is particularly nasty for a man to strike a woman, especially an athletic man'.

Nicholas was ordered to pay Lori McElroy £1,300 damages but remains adamant that an injustice was done. His solicitor said at the time that Nicholas was 'bitterly disappointed because he is not a violent man'. Nicholas does not deny that an incident took place but insists that it was blown up out of all proportion. 'I still know in my heart I'm innocent,' said Charlie.

The following month, Nicholas was back in court successfully getting a previous three year drink-driving ban reduced by a year, allowing him to buy himself a new Porsche.

The passion of the Glasgow derby in 1987 got too much for some players and one of football's most famous punch-ups erupted. Four players were charged with behaviour likely to cause a breach of the peace: Chris Woods, Graham Roberts, Terry Butcher and Celtic's Frank McAvennie appeared in court in April 1988. It was the first time footballers had faced criminal proceedings as a result of actions on the field.

All four pleaded not guilty and although McAvennie and Roberts were allowed to walk away, Woods was fined £500 and Butcher £250. Sheriff Archie McKay told them: 'Your behaviour could have readily converted the crowd into two mobs and very grave consequences might have ensued. You have failed to keep your wider responsibilities.'

In 1988 Jan Molby, Danish International and vital lynch pin in Liverpool's midfield, was sent to prison for three months for serious driving offences. Molby had led the police on a car chase that made Steve McQueen's performance in *Bullet* look like a learner driver. It began when Molby was spotted by a policeman early one morning; he was driving on the wrong side of the road, with a car full of passengers, at over 100 mph. Molby's BMW was chased by three police cars, until he embarked on a game of chicken with a fourth police car coming in the opposite direction. Molby won this contest of nerves and then drove through two red lights, overtook three cars on the wrong side of the road and ignored countless keep-left bollards. His lunatic behaviour convinced the police to give up the chase in the interests of safety.

Eventually, Molby was arrested, only to claim that he had not been driving the car but had, at the time, been with a girl in Wallasey Village. He changed his story in October 1988 when he admitted in Liverpool Crown Court that he had been driving and in a 'highly dangerous way'. His lawyer described the offence as 'two minutes of madness from a man who had drunk a couple of pints of alcohol and knew he was on the borderline of the legal limit'. David Maddison, defending, went on: 'He panicked when he saw the police officers and feared that if breathalysed he might fail.'

Molby arrived in court with five other offences hanging over him, four for driving and one for an incident outside a gay club where Molby and his mates made light work of overturning a car. Sidney Moss, a Liverpool director, was called to act as a character witness saying that, if Molby was sent to jail, the future of the club would be in jeopardy. Maddison, Molby's lawyer, added that it would be 'inappropriate' to imprison his client because it could destroy a career that had brought joy to millions. Judge Crowe, however, had other ideas. He said: 'Only the mercy of providence had prevented Molby from killing another human being. Driving of this kind is to be treated harshly.' Apart from three months in prison, Molby was banned from driving for a year and ordered to pay £320 in costs. The sentence could have been more severe had it not been for the judge recording a not guilty verdict on the charge of criminal damage caused to a police car.

Whilst playing for Portsmouth, Mick Quinn spent two weeks in Winchester jail for two driving offences. He had been banned for twelve months for drink-driving but was booked again three months later for driving whilst banned, speeding and having no insurance. Another four months later he was caught by the police yet again, this time for driving whilst banned and for having no insurance. In court, Quinn's defence was interesting to say the least; on the first occasion, he'd been taking his aunt to the station after she had heard her daughter was ill; on the second, his girlfriend had been taken ill, the phone was disconnected and, as he had no money to pay for a taxi, he had driven to give her assistance.

Quinn was sent to prison and, on his release, he admitted that he'd made a big mistake and rejoined Portsmouth. In November the following year a policeman claimed he saw Quinn driving again but it transpired that the officer had been mistaken. Mick Quinn had been pretty forthright in his views after Tony Adams was sent to prison, saying to the papers: 'The one good thing that may come out of it is that the other footballers will think twice about doing anything silly with a car.' (And perhaps dogs will think twice about sniffing each other's arses.)

In 1992, Brentford striker Gary Blissett became the first professional to be prosecuted for an on-field incident after he allegedly used his elbow to break John Uzzell's cheek, effectively ending the Torquay man's career. Blissett claimed that he was going for the ball and a jury acquitted him, thanks largely to Graham Kelly's 'expert' evidence. Kelly said that in watching four matches he would expect to see around 200 similar challenges – incredible if you consider that the challenge in question almost maimed Uzzell.

There is no doubt that Duncan Ferguson is a gifted player but, unfortunately, his ability to find trouble matches his ability to find the ball and pop it in the back of the net.

In February 1992, he was convicted at Stirling Sheriff's Court for a breach of the peace and assault after head-butting a policeman. He escaped with a £125 fine. Less than a year later he was back in front of the same court, again convicted of assault, this time for punching and kicking a postman. Ferguson had attacked Paul Robertson of St Ninian (who was on crutches at the time) while he was waiting for a taxi. He escaped prison again with a £200 fine.

In August 1993, he was given twelve months probation by Cupar Sheriff's Court after being convicted of another assault, this time he had punched a stranger off a bar stool in an Anstruther pub. On the eve of the Merseyside derby, in March 1995, Ferguson was fined another £500 and banned from driving for eighteen months after failing a breath test. Ferguson scored in Everton's 2-0 win.

His luck ran out in May 1995 when he was sentenced to three months in Barlinnie jail for assaulting Raith Rovers' fullback John McStay. He was still on probation when the incident happened in a league match between Rangers and Raith in 1994. Ferguson appealed against the punishment, complaining about Sheriff Alexander Eccles' reference to his 'quite appalling record of violence', but, on 11 October 1995, Appeal Court Judge Lord Hope upheld the sentence, saying that the crucial factor was that Ferguson had been on probation at the time. Football's most famous pigeon fancier went to prison. The story goes that when Duncan Ferguson saw ITN news artist Priscilla Coleman's drawing of him in court, he was so impressed with the likeness that he asked if he could have a copy. Coleman duly obliged and Ferguson had the picture framed so it could take pride of place in his Merseyside home.

Ferguson's club manager, Joe Royle, was quick to make his feelings known: 'I'm not saying Duncan is an angel. He's been guilty of stupidity, but more often immaturity. We can't believe that in a society that seems dedicated to keeping people out of prison we're putting away a young man who is in a good job and is no danger to society. Anyone who knows Duncan will tell you he's a pleasant young man, he's not a bad lad at all.'

Perhaps a more balanced view is provided by long-time Ferguson observer Archie McGregor, editor of the Scottish fanzine *The Absolute Game*, who said: 'He was always getting into trouble. When he was up here it was bad news when he strolled into a pub. Everyone went quiet and looked away, like in Westerns when the gunslinger walks into the saloon. Latterly, he started to employ minders, so he'd have these heavies swaggering with him everywhere. The incident that got him jailed wasn't severe but the ball was a long, long way away and he just sort of turned round and went for it. The fact that the guy just got cut was more luck than judgement.'

Ferguson was released early for good behaviour and resumed his career at Everton.

In 1992, the former Manchester United, Everton, Chelsea and Leeds player Mickey Thomas was winding down his career at Wrexham. Part of his brief as senior pro was to look after the younger players and guide them through the often troublesome early years of their careers. Clearly, Thomas misinterpreted this and, in January 1992, he was charged with passing forged £10 and £20 notes to seven YTS players. He was caught after some of the players had tried to spend the forgeries in a local nightclub. Thomas had sold them to the lads at a fiver each. The court case was scheduled for the summer of 1993.

Thomas was in more trouble in August 1992 when he was attacked whilst making love to his ex-wife's sister-in-law. The woman's husband and an accomplice beat Thomas with a hammer, threatened to cut off his genitals and stabbed him in the backside with a screwdriver. The pair were convicted of GBH and jailed for two years; the female involved was ordered to do community service for conspiracy.

In July 1993, Thomas went to court for sentencing for his part in the counterfeit racket. On his way to court he joked with reporters saying, 'anyone got change for a tenner for the phone?' The smile was wiped off his face by Judge Gareth Edwards who sentenced him to eighteen months in prison stating: 'Largely because it fitted in with your self-image as a flash and daring adventurer, you betrayed the trust of your employers and you failed in your duty as a distinguished international sportsman. You should have been setting young apprentices an example in how a true professional conducts himself.'

Court action between players is frowned upon by football's powers that be, so former Chelsea player Paul Elliott's legal action against Dean Saunders ruffled more than a few feathers. Elliott's career had been prematurely ended following a tackle by Liverpool's Dean Saunders at Anfield in September 1992. Elliott took Saunders to court, claiming £1 million damages. Chelsea Chairman Ken Bates claimed in court that the Chelsea players were so incensed by the tackle that they wanted to lynch Saunders. Dennis Wise told the court that he thought Saunders had actually slowed down so that he could go over the top of the ball on Elliott.

On 10 June 1994, Justice Drake said that, in his opinion, the Chelsea evidence was unreliable and added: 'It will be no comfort to Paul Elliott that, having found against him, I offer my sympathy at the tragic way his career has ended.' Elliott was left to foot a £500,000 legal bill and commented outside court, 'I was on the verge of an England call-up when I was injured. Two years on, my knee is still very unstable. Every movement I make has to be controlled. I can't do anything spontaneously.'

Saunders was delighted with his victory, denying any malice or deliberate attempt to injure Elliott out of the game. In 1996, Paul Elliott is running a kid's soccer school and is Chelsea's youth team coach. He also does work for TV and radio. Dean Saunders is plying his trade in Turkey, playing for Galatasaray.

1995 was a vintage year for football-related courtroom action and three high-profile stars were involved in court cases that all revolved around the same theme – violence. Eric Cantona's case attracted the interest of the world. He was charged, like his teammate Paul Ince, with common assault after unbelievable scenes at Selhurst Park in January. Cantona was sent off in the game between Crystal Palace and Manchester United and reacted violently to some crowd baiting as he was walking off. He kung fu kicked Palace fan Mathew Simmons in a heart-stopping moment that would seriously threaten the rest of his career.

With all the evidence stacked against him, Cantona pleaded guilty. In his summing up, Chair of the Bench Jean Pearce told him: 'You are a high-profile public figure with undoubted gifts, and as such you are looked up to by many young people. For this reason the only sentence appropriate for this offence is two weeks imprisonment.'

Cantona successfully appealed and was ordered to serve 120 hours of Community Service coaching youngsters instead. He was also banned from all football for nine months and fined £10,000. He made his comeback in the Manchester United team in the Autumn of 1995 and his skills were there for all to see, as was his new-found restraint.

Paul Ince pleaded not guilty and he was helped by the fact that the main prosecution witness, Dennis Warren, was exposed in the trial as being a retired football hooligan. The Magistrates dismissed his evidence as unreliable and, to loud cheers in the court room, Ince was cleared.

Chelsea captain Dennis Wise was involved in a violent altercation outside former England coach Terry Venables' West London club, Scribes West. The club is a well known watering hole for players and their agents and it's rare for notorious football agent Eric 'Monster' Hall not to appear in any given 24-hour period. Hall is Wise's agent and stuck by his client in his own inimitable style throughout the whole ordeal. Wise was accused of assaulting an elderly black cab driver following a row outside the club. He was found guilty and sentenced to three months in prison. Magistrate Geoffrey Breen commented: 'You have been found guilty of assaulting a 65-year-old man in quite disgraceful circumstances. When he made it clear that he was not going to bow to your demands you resorted to violence.'

Wise eventually won an appeal against the sentence, a decision that Judge Gerald Butler arrived at with 'no enthusiasm', commenting at the time that 'Mr Wise's conduct was quite disgraceful and does him no credit.' Eric Hall celebrated outside the court and Dennis 'Lucky' Wise continued his career at Chelsea.

On 9 February 1996, James Kelly of Wolverhampton Wanderers was jailed for five years for kicking a man to death in a brawl outside a Liverpool hotel in September 1995. Kelly and his mates were barred from the hotel by porter Peter Dunphy and decided to vent their anger on him. Dunphy suffered an appalling attack that cost him his life and Kelly was reported to have shouted at the time, 'you wanted it and you got it. You should have let us in.'

The trial was held at Liverpool Crown Court where Kelly expressed deep regret for what had happened and admitted manslaughter. Ex-England and Wolves manager Graham Taylor acted as a character witness, describing Kelly as 'popular, trustworthy and with an excellent reputation'.

Spurs striker Chris Armstrong fell foul of the law in 1996 after being clocked doing 104 mph on the M54. He escaped with a £500 fine and six penalty points on his licence. The court heard that the £7,000 a week striker would have problems getting to work without his car. Tory MP David Evans claimed it was unbelievable that Armstrong didn't get banned saying, 'nonsense, he surely earns enough to buy a bus ticket on his earnings. He earns enough to buy the bus!' Good point.

Mathew Simmons, the fan who was kung fu kicked by Eric Cantona, was in court in May 1996 to answer charges of using threatening words and behaviour on that fateful night. The court heard that Cantona had launched his attack on Simmons after a torrent of obscene abuse. It was claimed that Simmons had rushed from his eleventh row seat in order to 'bait' Cantona. Prosecutor Jeffrey McCann told magistrates that

Simmons had yelled, 'You're a fucking animal' and 'You fucking French wanker. Fuck off back to France.' Simmons protested that he was simply heading for the toilet and was telling the Frenchman to take an early shower. In a statement to police, he said he had told Cantona, 'Go Cantona. Go and get an early shower', and said he was shouting 'Off', and pointing to the dressing room. 'I was doing nothing else. Suddenly Cantona kicked me square on,' he told the court.

The following day, the magistrates took five hours to find Simmons guilty of both public order offences at which point he went berserk and tried to throttle prosecutor Jeffrey McCann. He leapt over the dock and grabbed McCann round the neck, wrenching his tie askew and ripping two buttons from his shirt. Simmons was wrestled off the unfortunate Mr McCann by six policemen and two court security officials, placed in handcuffs and led away to the cells shouting, 'You're all scum.'

Later, he was brought back to the court and placed inside a perspex cage from where he sheepishly apologised. Bench chairman Mrs May Richards described the attack on Mr McCann as an 'obvious and serious contempt of court' and jailed him for seven days. He was also fined £500 and ordered to pay £200 costs for provoking Cantona with a tirade of abuse.

Less than 24 hours after his imprisonment, Simmons was free as he automatically qualified for a fifty per cent remission and prison rules forbid a weekend release. His lawyer Adam David claimed that his client's actions were all stress related – which probably also explained the time in 1993 when he was arrested with a group of shaven headed youths who burst into an anti-fascist rally shouting Nazi slogans.

Ensuring that football's court room catalogue of shame continues are a couple of cases current at the time of writing. Blackpool chairman Owen Oyston stands accused of raping two young girls, but potentially the most damaging case for football will be heard in January 1997 when John Fashanu, Hans Segers and Bruce Grobbelaar face charges of match fixing. At a hearing to fix the date of the trial on 3 May 1996, all three formally denied the charges. In the dock with them will be Malaysian businessman Heng Suan 'Richard' Lim.

Grobbelaar is accused of taking £40,000 from Fashanu to throw a Premier League game. He was quizzed by Hampshire police in November 1994 following a three month investigation by the *Sun* newspaper. Wimbledon goalkeeper Hans Segers faces a similar charge involving a payment of £19,000. All four men face a total of seven charges of conspiracy and corruption. The trial begins on 14 January, guaranteeing more in-depth scrutiny for the game that is increasingly becoming littered with criminal activity.

8 Drugs

THE VAST MAJORITY of footballers abhor drugs and view people who take them as traitors to their profession. In a game where vast sums of money swill around, it is easy for the weak-willed to succumb to temptation and empty their bulging cash-rich pockets into the seedy world of the drug dealer. The effects of drug abuse can be devastating; health damaged, lives ruined and careers ended.

FIFA works very closely with the individual football associations of the world in an ever-vigilant and rigorous programme to eradicate drugs from the game. Their doping control aims are based on three fundamental principles: preserving and defending the ethics of sport, protecting the physical and mental integrity of the player (in effect safeguarding his health) and maintaining equal opportunities for all.

In Britain, the use of hard and soft drugs is strictly controlled by the Misuse of Drugs Act 1971. It is a criminal offence to even possess these substances. All of the following are classified as hard or soft drugs: heroin, crack cocaine, cocaine, LSD, amphetamines, magic mushrooms, ecstasy and cannabis. Performance-enhancing drugs are also banned on the premise that sport is primarily founded on moral and ethical codes which preclude drug taking. Put simply, using performance-enhancing drugs is gaining an unfair advantage over opponents and is, therefore, cheating. Beta blockers, steroids, anabolic agents, narcotic analgesics, diuretics, stimulants and peptide hormones and analogues are all performance-enhancers, but the downside is that these drugs can also do massive harm to the body.

A grey area for most players up until recently has been the use of medicines. All medicines contain at least one drug, otherwise they wouldn't be medicines. Cold and flu remedies pose real problems for the players as they can contain banned substances – which is why it's essential for club doctors to be one hundred per cent au fait with the dope testing guidelines.

The war on drugs in football is absolute and the chances of evading detection are becoming less and less. Drugs testing is carried out by taking urine samples from randomly selected individuals. The sample is checked for banned substances and, if clear, is declared 'negative'. In April 1996, the English FA announced the doubling of their random dope testing for the 1996/97 season. Only 2 offenders were caught out of 300 tests in the 1995/96 season compared with 12 from 272 the previous year. The FA clearly felt that their message was getting through. Now, 500 random tests will be carried out on the 3,500 senior and youth training scheme players at England's professional clubs; it's envisaged that every club will be tested.

As drugs are a universal problem, football authorities all over the world are just as stringent; it's completely unrealistic to assume that society's problems won't transfer to football. Vast sums of money are spent discouraging young men from becoming involved. A couple of draws on a cannabis joint could easily end a career – few players realise it but cannabis can stay in the blood stream for up to eight weeks. Today, the game is quicker than ever before; legendary drink and drugs sessions should be a thing of the past because to take part in them regularly would impair performance to such a degree that a career in professional football would be impossible. However, drug-free football is, perhaps, more of an ideal than an achievable reality.

Drugs and Arsenal will be intrinsically linked in the minds of the British public following Paul Merson's shocking confession of drug abuse and gambling addiction in the 1990s. It is fair to say that Merson is by no means the only professional footballer to take hard drugs – there are other celebrated cases. To Merson's enormous credit, he admitted that he had a serious problem and needed help.

If Paul Merson had been a member of Arsenal's 1925 team, he could have got drugged up not just with the manager's approval, but actually with the manager. Leslie Knighton, a famous pre-war manager, had a book called *Behind the Scenes in Big Football* published in 1947 which lifted the lid on the goings-on in the game. Knighton was in charge at Highbury in 1925 when Arsenal met London rivals West Ham in the FA Cup. Like quite a few Arsenal managers, Knighton had very little confidence in his boys' ability to win games, until one day when he was visited by a West End doctor who just happened to be an Arsenal fan.

After hearing Knighton's football worries the doctor said that the team simply needed a courage pill. The doctor went on to explain that he occasionally administered the pills to those patients requiring abnormal stamina or resistance for a particular purpose; the pills posed no harmful effects but simply toned up reflexes to produce maximum effort. Leslie Knighton went ahead with the pills idea for his players, although admitted his concern about the story leaking out. The players were dosed up an hour before kickoff. Knighton took one as well as a demonstration of his confidence.

In his book, Knighton said that after about an hour or so he felt great, he wanted to run, jump and shout; he felt as though he could push a wall down. Everything was perfect, apart from the fact that the game was called off because of fog. On the journey home, the players were in a highly alert and excitable state but were then encompassed by a red hot thirst as the pills started to wear off. They drank gallons of water trying to satisfy their craving.

On the following Monday morning, Arsenal travelled back to West Ham, again opting to take the pills. Once again, the fog scuppered the match and the players suffered more agonies of thirst and violent restlessness. The game did eventually take place with the Arsenal lads once more consuming their 'pluck pills'. According to Knighton, 'they ran like Olympic sprinters, jumped like rockets, and crashed in shots', but the game was drawn and, again, the players suffered.

For the replay Knighton tried yet again to get the players to take the pills, but when the players saw his little red pill box the yell of protest nearly split the roof. The game was another draw. Before the second replay, the Arsenal players refused the pills. They were much the better side but conceded a last minute goal; 1-0 to West Ham. Knighton lamented in his book: 'I often wondered if we should have won if the boys had been doped for that game . . . we didn't win when we rejected them. The doctor never said what they contained but he was certain they would have taken us to the Cup Final.'

An amusing tale, but proof that there was an underlying win-at-all-costs mentality even in the 1920s.

There was a rumpus in the late 1930s when Wolves manager Stan Buckley announced that his side, who were well-known for their speed, were receiving monkey gland treatment to help them with their stamina. It was all just gamesmanship – they were only using anti-flu injections. They lost 4-1 to Portsmouth in the 1939 FA Cup Final anyway.

The permissive 60s were a watershed in modern times; post war baby boomers were in adolescence and early adulthood, there was a feeling of hope for the future and all aspects of life were changing apace. It was in the 1960s, however, that drugs first became a reality in football.

A lot of it, at first, was just unsubstantiated rumour. In 1962 Helenio Herreras quit as the manager of Italy amid rumours that Inter Milan players had been taking drugs. The Italian FA decided to try and disprove the rumours (or, at worst, confirm them) by introducing an extensive anti-drugs campaign including testing in the 1962/63 season. Following a whole series of spot checks on players, no positive indications of drug use were found. Rumour and counter rumour continued to taint European football. In 1963, Lausanne were reported to have used drugs to win the 1962 Swiss FA Cup but were officially cleared by a full enquiry.

Seven Napoli players were said to have been doped to improve their performance for a match against AC Milan in 1963. Napoli won the game 1-0 but the Italian FA's medical commission confirmed that seven players had tested positive following random checks after the game. Napoli denied the charges and the leniency of the subsequent sentences suggest that, either they had some justification, or the Italian FA had no intention of trying to stamp out the problem. Four of the seven players, Pontel, Molino, Tomeazza and Rivelino, were suspended for three weeks.

In May 1963, proud Bologna FC were cruising towards their first championship success since 1941 when disaster struck them in the shape of the Liga Nazionale's doping squad. Like the football equivalent of the SAS, the squad's members swooped silently into clubs, announcing their arrival when it was far too late for any wrongdoers to rectify their situation. Urine samples were taken from Bologna players after their win over Torino in February. Five players tested positive – Paride Tumburus, Marino Perani, Ezio Pascutti, Mirko Pavinato and Romano Fogli were all found to have taken amphetamines.

Bologna claimed that, because the samples had been handled by officials, police doctors and laboratory workers, anyone could have tampered with them in an effort to 'fix' the club. After weeks of arguments, the five players concerned were let off but the club was docked three points and their manager, Fulvio Bernardini, was suspended for two years. Rumour had it that everyone was doped in Italian football and the authorities didn't dare take strict action because of the sheer scale of the problem. One cynical journalist commented that, if the Italian FA and Cycling Federation really clamped down on drugs, the chemical industry would collapse.

All was not lost for Bologna; in May 1965 the Liga Nazionale overturned their three point penalty after deciding the five dope-tested players' samples were 'fixed'. Bologna then went on to win the title after beating Inter Milan 2-0 in a level-on-points play-off. The expert medical evidence claimed that the alleged concentration levels were, in fact, lethal – if the test results were true, the players would have been dead.

The Italian health minister, Luigi Marotti, announced legislation in November 1964 banning all stimulants from Italian sport, with immediate prison sentences for those who stepped out of line.

The 1966 World Cup finals in England were the first to include drug testing. Shortly before the tournament, Brazil received a FIFA directive telling them that coffee constituted a stimulant and would be regarded as a drug. Without their normal half-time cup of coffee Brazil faded without trace in the tournament. Curiously, England received no such warning about tea even though it contains more caffeine than coffee – we're left to wonder whether England would have won had they been denied their half-time cuppa.

The Italian FA mysteriously abandoned their drugs-testing scheme in December 1966. They had ordered a massive purge and sent doctors to 298 matches in the 1965/66 season; all tests on 1,186 players proved negative. In retrospect, this scheme was about as useful as providing a 24-hour vigil for burglars and then, because no burglaries would be committed, assuming the problem had gone away.

A minor sensation was caused in Argentina in 1972 by the resignation of San Lorenzo's club doctor, Cayetano Paglione, and his accusation that players were being given stimulating drugs before games. Despite the doctor's sensational claims an investigation by the Argentine FA proved nothing but, as a result, legislation was passed that selected two players from each league match to undergo a compulsory drugs test. It's understandable that, because of the doctor's professional stature, some credence was given to the allegations and they appeared to be reinforced by the fact that, at the time the scandal broke, San Lorenzo were eight points clear at the top of the table. About a month after the introduction of compulsory drugs tests, doubts were cast on their reliability and effectiveness when it was revealed that 'testing' matches were selected several days before the fixtures. Urine samples were taken from two or three players per side, but only after they had been into the changing rooms and had a shower. Today, players are not allowed into the changing rooms before they have given a sample.

Drugs to treat colds and flu, and painkillers, can cause problems for players. Today, the guidelines are quite clear but in 1974 Brazilian forward, Cosme de Silva Campos was suspended for 60 days after urine tests revealed a stimulant in his sample. The Brazilian Sports Federation applied the suspension pending an enquiry into claims by Campos that he had been given medicine by his club doctor to ease the pain from two broken teeth. The test showed the presence of ephedrine, which is considered a stimulant – the same drug that would cause Diego Maradona more problems a few years hence. Not all positive tested players are as innocent (in terms of intent) as Campos.

Ernst Joseph of Haiti was suspended from the 1974 World Cup finals after testing positive for the banned stimulant phenyimetrazin. His 'test game', played against Italy, marked his last appearance in the championship.

Two years later, Uruguayan football was rocked by a drugs scandal after Nacional player Juan Carraso tested positive for a banned substance. The scandal ended with a three month suspension for Carraso plus the resignation of the club's manager. A thorough police investigation of the club had been ordered following the incredible and sinister claims by Carraso that he 'had not taken drugs willingly'. Charges followed against several club officials for supplying illegal drugs to Carraso, and presumably other team members, to try to influence mental and physical performance during a game. Some referees had long held suspicions about some South American players and their use of drugs. The British referee of the infamous Battle of Santiago in the 1960s later admitted that he thought something was not quite right with some of the players. Considering some of the disgraceful incidents throughout the history of South American football it is not unreasonable to entertain the notion that these acts were not committed by professional footballers but by drug-induced madmen.

Pep pills were the downfall of Scottish International Willie Johnson who was sent home in shame from the 1978 World

Cup finals after being caught taking two tablets before the game against Peru. He was automatically banned for a year by FIFA and condemnation by the Scottish Football Association was swift: 'whatever Scotland's results on the football field might be, they will be achieved fairly'. Willie Johnson spoke about his ordeal in 1996. Giving an interview to *Goal* magazine, he said: 'those two little tablets put the lid on it. They were for hay fever and they were rife in England at the time. I wasn't fit, but people kept coming up to me and saying I would be letting my country down if I ducked out. So I took the tablets and played.'

When asked whether, on being selected for a sample, he had feared the worst, he said: 'No, I never gave it a second thought. It was me and Kenny Dalglish and the Peruvian striker, Cubillas. We all pissed in the bottle and theirs was a lot clearer than mine. I've always joked that Kenny swapped the bottles around. I told a tabloid that once. They took it seriously and were going to phone him up, but I couldn't keep a straight face. I would have loved to have heard Kenny's answer though. Seriously, all Scotland had to do was appeal and ask for another test, but I've always felt that they [SFA] were happy to see me out. It meant that they were able to blame someone for all that had gone wrong.'

Petulance is a tradition of Latin football and the general rule of thumb is, the more fiery and animated a player is, the higher the level of guilt. After a Cup Winners Cup tie in Belgium in 1979, Barcelona players refused to submit to a dope test – we can only wonder why.

January 1980 saw the rather late introduction of dope testing in Britain. Eight players from two matches (West Ham–Cardiff and Swindon–Brentford) were intercepted as they left the pitch and asked to produce urine samples – West Ham goalkeeper Phil Parkes was unable to do so. An FA spokesman explained the new testing rules, saying, 'we are pretty sure there's no drugs problem in English football, but we want to back that up with factual evidence.' An extremely optimistic viewpoint.

Dutch football was forced to examine itself in 1980 when Ajax's club doctor said that one out of every eleven players was using some form of doping – but how did he know? Was he supplying them? These questions were never answered.

In February 1981 officials of Paraguayan club Cerro Porteno suspended three of their players for two years each for taking drugs. The three players also faced judicial proceedings and the law in Paraguay punished such offences with three to five years in prison. Animosity reigned in the rest of the squad who refused to go training out of sympathy for their three colleagues. They also publicly accused Porteno's president Abraham Zapag of bribing an Ascunsion hotel waiter to put something in the drinks of visiting Peruvian team Alianza Lima in order to drug them before a Libertadores Cup match.

The Italians are notorious slow starters in major championships, so the improvement rate they demonstrated in the 1982 World Cup in Spain provoked a newspaper to run a story claiming sinister reasons for their new lease of life. Some months after the World Cup, an Italian club doctor spoke openly of the Italian national team's decision to use the muscle strengthening drug Carnitina in the 1982 World Cup. The substance was not on FIFA's blacklist but there were many complaints when the news broke.

The doctor, Professor Vecchiet, said: 'I studied the product for a year before I used it with the players. Using Carnitina is no different from administering vitamins or glucose. People are now jumping to the conclusion that we started using it after the end of the first round. They say because the team improved so much that the cause must have been some sort of dope. One of the newspapers ran a story that we organised a sort of bridge to ferry the stuff in from Italy before the second phase matches in Barcelona. All nonsense. You can buy the stuff over the counter in pharmacies in Spain. I've no doubt other teams did, as well. The only difference is that Italy happened to win the World Cup!'

Squad member Francesco Graziani had a simpler view: 'the reasons why we won the World Cup had nothing to do with mystery substances. It was simple: a simple diet . . . plus Enzo Bearzot.'

Professor Vecchiet was right, a lot of football clubs knew about Carnitina. Spanish club Real Madrid decided to experiment with the drug in May 1983. They gave it to players of their affiliate Second Division club Castilla, who were in a mid-table position and suddenly, they went shooting up the table. So was it mind over matter, coincidence or did the Italian national team know more than they were prepared to admit in 1982?

It is really sad when the greatest player of a generation turns out to be a cheat. Diego Armando Maradona, at his peak, was a football genius, a worthy champion with the world at his feet. Argentina's 1982 World Cup campaign was disappointing but hopes were high for the 1986 finals in Mexico and Argentina didn't disappoint . . . apart from once.

Their quarterfinal was against England and, in the fading shadow of the Falklands War, the Argentinians felt they had something to prove. The first goal was the controversial one; the ball flicked up off Steve Hodges' boot and looked as though it would fall to England keeper Peter Shilton. Suddenly, up jumped Maradona, extending an arm up in the air whilst desperately trying to half-hide it behind his head. Shilton went to punch the ball, only to be beaten to it by Maradona's hand; the referee awarded a goal and was immediately surrounded by England players protesting at the decision.

A few minutes later, Maradona scored a magnificent goal, the type expected from the world's greatest player. England scored a consolation goal and went out of the World Cup, not without a feeling of bitterness because of what had gone before. Maradona was summoned, along with England's Terry Butcher, for a drugs test. Terry Butcher tells an amusing anecdote about his time with Maradona in the drugs room. Once the 'hand of God' claim was out of the way, Butcher offered Maradona a tin of beer that had found its way into the room from the England dressing room. Maradona thanked Butcher but said, 'no thanks . . . I'll have a Coke.' At the time, not that funny perhaps but, in view of Maradona's subsequent drugs record, it couldn't have been more appropriate.

In December 1986, River Plate star Ramon Centurion was suspended for a year after testing positive following his side's 3-1 win over Temperley. His urine showed traces of a banned stimulant. Centurion claimed, rather foolishly, that he had taken some medicine before the match without kowing it contained the stimulant. The Argentine FA said that was impossible – there were no medicines available at the time that contained the banned stimulant.

In his ghost-written autobiography, former German goalkeeper Harald Schumacher claimed that drug taking was quite common in the Bundesliga. The weekend after his revelations, players voluntarily submitted urine samples for scrutiny as if to try to disprove his claims. Schumacher was sacked by his club Köln and was also banned from the national team at a time when he was captain and West German Footballer of the Year. The book contained some meaty stuff: Schumacher said cough mixtures containing the banned stimulant Ephedrine were the most commonly used and accused his club of double standards, saying several Köln players had taken the drug before an important match in 1984, right under the noses of club officials. Schumacher says in his book, 'the stimulated teammates ran like devils all over the pitch and, of course, we won the game'. He also recalled when, as a young professional, he went with several 'stars' to the club doctor who provided them with 'tablets and injections'.

Brazilian World Cup player Cassagrande, who had already been arrested in 1982 for cocaine possession, returned to Brazil from Italy for a holiday in 1988. He was arrested, along with fellow international Sidney and musician Ocimar De Iloveira, for stashing marijuana in his car. All three men were released after questioning following an admission by De Iloveira that the drug belonged to him.

In March 1988, Larissa were the surprise leaders of the Greek championship race, only to be docked four points after striker Georgiou Tsingov failed a dope test after a 2-1 win over Panithinaikos. The substance involved was Codeine, which was banned in Greece. A month later, in April, Greek football had to face up to the drugs problem once again when Olympiakos's new Uruguayan star Diego Aguirre failed a dope test after a match against Verria. He was banned from playing in Greece for two years for taking amphetamines. Aguirre cheekily explained his actions to the Greek press saying, 'I didn't tell anyone because I knew it was prohibited'.

Rumours and innuendo about drugs in French football had been circulating for some time when the newspaper *Libre* ran an article in February 1989 claiming an 'across the board' use of amphetamines in the French game. *Libre* said usage was widespread before big matches, but it failed to name names.

On 23 September 1990, Roma's Andrea Carnevale and Angelo Peruzzi both failed dope tests and were banned for one year. The drug the pair tested positive for was Fenermina. A lot of questions were asked about the incident and a lot of those questions remain unanswered. The two players claimed that they had taken the weight-watchers' pill Lipopill after having an expensive meal the night before the match with Bari. The meal was a celebratory one as Roma had recently beaten Benfica 1-0 in the UEFA Cup and the players were worried about putting on too much weight. They said the pills had been supplied by Peruzzi's mother. The disciplinary hearing did not believe them, mainly because they thought the drug they had tested positive for could not possibly have come from Lipopill. Carnevale added further intrigue to the saga when, in a post-hearing TV interview, he said, 'I would have told the truth from the start but the club forced me to remain silent'. Were Roma supplying players with banned substances and trying to cover their tracks by forcing the players to invent a story?

Italy's professional footballers reacted angrily to the ban saying the sentencing was too harsh as it was almost impossible to avoid taking prohibited substances because they appear everywhere. AC Milan's winger Donadoni gave an example of a near miss: he was about to take some cough mixture in the middle of the night when he decided to phone the club doctor to check it was OK and was told not to take it as it contained a banned substance.

Diego Maradona had first tried drugs in 1982 as a 22-year-old and it was only a matter of time before he would make a mistake. On 17 March 1991, it happened; he had a random dope test following a Serie 'A' game against Bari and tested positive for traces of cocaine. Maradona had slipped out of the country by the time the news broke and a disciplinary hearing dished out a fifteen month ban. Maradona was well known in the right Neopolitan circles for his love of the high life. He even managed to miss one of Napoli's European ties (against Dinamo Moscow) because he was recovering from a heavy night. Nevertheless, Napoli's fans, and the club, tolerated his erratic behaviour because of his genius on the pitch. Shortly after his drugs ban, Maradona was cited in an investigation into a Mafia-run sex and drugs ring in Naples. He went back to Buenos Aires to try and escape the glare of publicity, only to attract a lot more when he was arrested after being caught in a cocaine den. He was bailed for £10,000 after being held in custody for 30 hours and he spent the next year undergoing therapy. Napoli reluctantly realised Maradona would not be returning; it was widely thought, in Italy, that his involvement with the Mafia was responsible for his refusal to return. He was sold to Seville for £5 million. Maradona pledged he would be fit for the 1994 World Cup in America and said he would meet his destiny there – it turned out to be more trouble.

Maradona's Argentine colleague Claudio Cannigia also found himself in big trouble when, in 1993, he tested positive for traces of cocaine in his urine after playing for his club, Roma. Cannigia had already been linked with an Italian drugs ring in May 1989 when he played for Verona – the then home of the Italian cocaine industry. Cannigia was ordered by a judge to give a statement on cocaine trafficking and usage in Verona. After the positive drugs test, he was banned from all football for one year but still managed to play for Argentina in the 1994 World Cup.

In those World Cup finals it was Maradona, not Cannigia, that attracted all the attention. He got on the score sheet in a 4-0 win over Greece and celebrated by going berserk and running to a television camera to demonstrate his pumped-up feelings. After Argentina's 2-1 win over Nigeria, Maradona tested positive for a cocktail of five banned ephedrine-based substances. Medical Commission president Michel D'Hooghe said, 'tests found five prohibited substances in each urine sample. The products were ephedrine and allied substances which affect the central nervous system, increasing concentration and physical capacity. We have not found one pill which contains all five substances so we must assume the player had taken a cocktail of substances.'

Maradona's controversial dietician was a man called Daniel Cerrini who had been responsible for formulating his 'special' diet. Cerrini was a former body building champion who was known to have administered special drugs to his pupils – one of whom had been banned from a body building contest. Maradona was banned by FIFA for the remainder of the tournament, pending a full decision in the autumn. He was also fined £10,000 and spent the rest of the competition as a crazed commentator for Argentinian television.

When the chief of the Argentinian FA, Julio Grondona, was called before the government to answer questions about the team's 1994 World Cup performances he, not surprisingly, blamed Daniel Cerrini for the failure. He said Cerrini was making special concoctions and putting them into the players' food, but claimed that the mixtures did not contain any prohibited drugs. Apparently, Cerrini ran out of supplies whilst in America and bought what he thought were similar products in drug stores. Cerrini's English was not that good and this was offered up as an excuse for the purchasing of the banned substances which were eventually taken by Maradona. This might have been a good enough excuse for the Argentine MPs but it wasn't for FIFA who, on 24 August 1994, banned Maradona for fifteen months. Argentine President Carlos Menem described the ban as far too harsh. Maradona's response was a little more forthright: 'they've cut off my legs. You can tell these FIFA guys have no families.' The following day, Maradona shouted down to reporters from the balcony of his

Buenos Aires house, 'I'm not going to talk. Why should I? It's done. They screwed me, like they screw the Argentine side.'

At a press conference on 2 September 1994, Maradona compared FIFA to the Mafia: 'They've [FIFA] killed me. I'm completely dead. I don't think I will be playing any more. It's totally unfair. I said before they'd cut my legs away, I think they've now cut my whole body away. I don't know where I stand, I can't find myself . . . it used to be wonderful. I played morning and night, even when I went to bed with my wife I was training. Now, when I get up in the morning, I have no stimulant in life.'

In the summer of 1995, a novel titled *Innocente* was published in Argentina which offered the story line that Maradona's ban from the 1994 World Cup was part of a plot by the CIA who were upset with him because of his public support for Fidel Castro. What banned substance the author of the book was on isn't clear but, not surprisingly, Maradona appeared to start believing the novel, claiming the CIA and FIFA had stitched him up.

Maradonna's involvement in Argentine football is still strong in the mid-90s. One day he may even manage the national side – but for now he is committed to warning children off drugs. In April 1996, he joined an Argentine government anti-drugs programme, confessing that his addiction to cocaine was once so bad that he couldn't even get his young daughter a glass of water. 'I was, I am and I always will be a drug addict,' he told the magazine *Gente*, 'I tried drugs in football. Because in football, just like everywhere else, there are drugs. They've always been there. I wasn't the only one, a lot of players used them.'

Maradona had his supporters in the game who, apart from admiring his footballing qualities, feel that he's been a little hard done by.

At the end of 1994, José Tores, the former French International, revealed that he was given a drugs injection before the 1993 Champions Cup first round tie between his club Nantes and Rapid Vienna. Tores said, 'I'm telling this now because of

Diego Maradona. I want people to realise that the whole environment is doped. The player is caught up in a situation beyond his control but when Maradona's doctor prepares him a drugs cocktail, it is Maradona who gets the blame.'

Tores explained away his own experience with drugs by claiming that the Nantes doctor gave him an injection before the match to counteract his high temperature. Nantes won 3-1 and Tores was so wired that he had to go out running in the middle of the night to calm down.

Manchester United's Eric Cantona also spoke up for his hero Diego Maradona, commenting, 'Maradona should never have been suspended from the game that he had graced for so long.' Cantona is forceful in his opinions on drugs in football and believes that a clear distinction can be made between the player who uses drugs to improve his performance and the individual who uses a drug socially. His support for Maradona is based on the view that 'no player's private life should be of any significance; it's what they do on the pitch that matters.' In his autobiography, he states: 'When you are not playing football it is your right to live as you want to do. As if by chance, it is those who are most corrupt who are also the happiest to condemn Maradona. What hypocrisy. The important distinction is that Diego didn't take cocaine to be the best player on the field. His private life doesn't concern me.'

Cantona does not endorse the use of stimulants either, he merely makes a distinction between place-of-work drug taking and social drug taking. Football's governing bodies don't share his maverick point of view and traces of drugs showing in dope tests are considered a bannable offence regardless of when and where they were ingested. Not every player takes drugs but enough have, or still do, to warrant concern. Players in the 1990s are young men with vast amounts of cash – the perfect targets for the dealers and hangers-on.

Arsenal's Paul Merson was exactly one of those young men. For quite some time, there had been rumours of drug and alcohol abuse among Arsenal players and Paul Merson was only one of a few names that were persistently mentioned. To those in the know, it came as no surprise that a cash-rich professional footballer with lots of spare time in the afternoons should admit to a dependency on drugs and booze. Merson admitted his problems in a newspaper article that was more like a confession. One story that did the rounds was that Merson owed a lot of gambling debts and needed to raise a large sum of money quickly to satisfy his debtors who would, apparently, have rearranged his limbs, rendering his future very doubtful. Merson revealed all in December 1994 and, with the help of the FA and his club, he sought professional help to combat his alcohol, gambling and cocaine dependencies. After several months, Merson was allowed to play for his club again – a tribute to him, and his counsellors, for the speed and sincerity of his rehabilitation. Critics said Merson should have been banned, others felt his case was just one of many, only the other players hadn't been caught – yet.

In 1994, world football attention focused on Colombia. The national team were much fancied to do well in the World Cup finals but instead, they made a quick return to Colombia after a string of poor performances. When the team returned home, their problems were just about to begin. To put these events in perspective, it's important to understand the relationship between intimidation and drugs in Colombian football because the two are intricately, and worryingly, entwined.

For the last fifteen years at least, Colombian football has been completely at the beck and call of the drug cartels. It's no coincidence that Medellin is the centre of Colombian football as well as being the cartels' drugs capital. The various cartels financed different clubs and managed to set up a honeycomb of intimidation and corruption that only very recently began to be challenged by the government. Colombia's first professional league dates back to the 1920s, but it wasn't until the 1950s that the country's football attracted interest from around the world. Extravagant wages and large signing-on fees attracted international and South American stars to big clubs such as Millonarios of Bogota. Eventually, in the 1980s, Colombian club sides started making their presence felt, particularly in the

Copa Libertadores – the South American equivalent of the Champions League. In a country where drugs have permeated every level of society and which produces 30,000 murders a year, the drug cartels took no time at all to turn their attention to football.

The infiltration of the drug barons into football began in 1975 when, following an economic crash, all Colombia's big football clubs were facing bankruptcy. Raging inflation ate into gate money so the prospect of financial salvation from a sugar daddy, whatever his source of income, was irresistible. By investing in football, drug cartels had the perfect opportunity to launder money, find new customers and gain an accepted social status.

A lot of their involvement with clubs was unofficial. Pablo Escobar, the infamous leader of the Medillin cartel, supported numerous smaller regional clubs but wholly owned Athletico Nacional of Medillin although scrutinising the club's books would never confirm it. America, Millionairios, Independiente, Union Magdelena and Deportes Tolima, basically the rest of Colombia's major clubs, also fell under cartel control in the 1980s. America were the poor relations of Colombian football until their 'sponsorship' deal with Cali cartel overlords Gilberto Rodriguez Orejuela (aka the chess player) and his brother, Miguel. Their influence and dirty money turned the club into eight-times championship winners in the 1980s. Millionairios players were paid directly by 'the Mexican', Gonzalo Rodriguez Gacha, the Medillin cartel's most feared Sicario (hit-man). Union Magdelena of Santa Marta were controlled by the Davilà brothers, the heads of the marijuana cartel.

At the height of the cartels' influence, the Narco-dollar was king; clubs were easily able to attract top foreign stars, and satisfy domestic ones, by paying large sums of money for their services. Buying foreign players was a very effective way of money laundering. For the barons, transfers were registered at higher prices than were actually paid, with the balance staying in foreign bank accounts.

One club, America (i.e. the Cali cartel), was so active in the trading of foreign players that they bought far more than they needed and loaned the players out to related clubs, also owned by the cartel. The tentacles of the cartels were even rumoured to have stretched as far as the 1978 World Cup finals in Argentina where, according to legend, Miguel Orejuela sent $550,000 in cash to the Peruvian team to throw their match against the host nation. The payment was as a favour to their friends in the Argentine junta but it never arrived as it was misdirected by a Colombian airline to New York – and into the hands of the DEA (Drugs Enforcement Agency). Even Colombian drug barons can lose their luggage, it seems.

In 1989, the authorities called a halt to the Colombian season following twenty football related murders during October including three players in Medillin who were machine gunned down and the murder of referee Alvaro Ortego. No one in the game was safe. The law of the bullet had been killing Colombian football for some time. In 1982, Uriel de Jesus was shot by a rival fan as he was about to score a goal. Bureaucrats and eminent sports journalists were also murdered. Referees were bribed, drugged and kidnapped and the national side were hounded and intimidated by the barons and their henchmen. Just before the 1990 World Cup finals in Italy, Colombian coach Pacho Maturano made a plea for justice for the most talented group of players for many years. He said it was not their fault that Colombian footballers were always associated with drug barons. 'It's not my team's fault that Colombia has problems with narcotics trafficking,' said Maturano. The Colombians performed reasonably well in Italia 90 (apart from Renee Higuita gifting Cameroon's Roger Milla with a goal) but, four years later in the United States, things would take a massive turn for the worse.

Pacho Maturano resigned after the 1990 World Cup but was back in charge for USA 94. The Colombians had many talented players like Rincon, Asprilla, Higuita, Escobar and Ronald McDonald lookalike Carlos Valderarma to name but a few. Colombia failed to live up to their hype, loosing 3-1 to Romania in their first match. Maturano decided to leave defender Gabreil Gomez out of the side against the United States and replaced him with Andrés Escobar. After the Romanian game several players received death threats and Maturano received his by fax.

Andrés Escobar took his place as sweeper in the United States game and, unfortunately for him, scored at the wrong end. Upon the teams return to Colombia, Escobar was shot twelve times by a smiling assassin in the Las Palmas suburb of Medillin. He had incurred the wrath of the cartels and their organised betting syndicates who had made very heavy wagers on Colombian successes in USA 94. Within days, two petty gangsters, Munoz Castro and Santiago Gallòn Henao, were arrested and eventually convicted of murder but few people believed the government's claim that the murder of Escobar was not linked to the cartels. Mid-fielders Lozano and Alvarez were also attacked and hospitalised. According to the DEA, several members of Colombia's World Cup squad were taped (on tapped phone lines) having conversations with Cali godfather Miguel Rodriguez Orejuela only hours after arriving home – such was their concern for their own safety.

Players' consumption of the cartels' produce has long been a fact of football life in Colombia, but few top stars have ever tested positive. Dope testing in Colombia is not as stringent as other countries and the only recent defaulter was America's International defender Wilson Cabrea who tested positive for cocaine in 1995 following the introduction of regular drug testing.

In 1996, Colombia is trying to clean up its act, not least because of the determined efforts of their minister for sport, Maria Emma Meija. Pablo Escobar and Gonzalo Rodriguez Gacha are both dead, Orejuela and the Davilà brothers are locked up in a high security prison in Bogota. Clubs are now obliged to supply the government with details of every financial transaction they undertake including names of shareholders and copies of accounts.

However, the cartels' influence lives on despite the authorities' considerable success. In 1995, when police captured the

Cali cartel's number three henchman, his phone book contained the home numbers of practically every leading football administrator. The scandal that followed forced the resignation of the president of Colombia's Football Federation. The fight goes on but it's worth noting that clubs from the Cali and Medillin sphere of influence (Deportivo, Nacional and America) continue to dominate the game in Colombia – presumably still with questionable backing.

Following on from Paul Merson, British football has been tainted by drugs scandals in the mid 1990s. On 6 October 1995, Arsenal's David Hillier was charged with possesion of cannabis after a training ground check and Charlton Athletic teenagers Lee Doyner and Dean Chandler suffered the same fate.

Tottenham striker Chris Armstrong, then at Crystal Palace, was out of football for a fortnight after a test showed traces of cannabis. Tranmere Rovers' YTS trainee Jamie Hughes was handed a six month ban, suspended for two years, after becoming the first English player charged with using performance-enhancing drugs after testing positive for amphetamines. Fulham defender Tony Finnegan was found in possession of heroin and Scottish football became embroiled in its own controversy at the tail end of 1995 when St Mirren player Barry Lavety was found with traces of ecstasy in his bloodstream following a random test. Glasgow Rangers also released two young players, Roddy Kerr and Joe Robertson, for drug related incidents.

Leyton Orient defender Roger Stanislaus became the first British footballer to test positive for cocaine on 9 January 1996 after playing a match against Barnet. Leyton Orient effectively sacked Stanislaus following his one year ban by the FA. The player claimed he had not taken the drug for performance-enhancement but insisted he'd taken it at a family funeral a couple of days before he was tested.

Huddersfield Town striker Craig Whittington tested positive twice in the space of twelve months. The first time was 20 March 1995 when he tested positive for cannabis at

Huddersfield's training ground. Then, on 9 January 1996, he once more tested positive, again for cannabis, after another training session. After his first positive test, Whittington agreed to undergo a programme of clinical assessment and counselling; the programme included the player's agreement to be subjected to 'target' testing for twelve months. The second positive test was one such target test, and Whittington was instantly suspended by his club.

At the FA disciplinary hearing in March 1996, Whittington insisted that he had not knowingly taken the drug on either occasion, claiming that, on the first occasion, he may have eaten cake laced with the drug and, on the second, he had smoked a cigarette doctored by a stranger at a party on New Year's Eve. Dr David Cowan, of the King's College Drugs Control Centre, refuted his claims, saying the drug was most likely taken 24 hours before his second failure on 9 January. Initially, Huddersfield Town supported Whittington through his rehabilitation programme and expressed their 'extreme disappointment' at his subsequent relapse. On 10 April 1996, Whittington was banned for seven months for his second offence and was later sacked by Huddersfield Town.

On 16 January 1996, French International goalkeeper Fabien Barthez was banned for two months after a dope test showed traces of cannabis; he also received a further suspended two month ban from the French football authorities. Barthez's lawyer said his client had been made a scapegoat but would not challenge his punishment in order that he could complete his ban before Euro 96 in England. Four other French players tested positive for cannabis in the 1995/96 season; Stephane Paille and Franck Fontan of Bordeaux were suspended for two months in September 1995 and Paris St Germain's Oumar Dieng and Gilles Hampartzoumian of Cannes are awaiting hearings with the French doping commission.

Players don't just have to be careful about which cough and cold remedies they choose as caffeine can also get them into trouble. Bolivian International midfielder Erwin Sanchez was handed a temporary ban by the Portuguese authorities in March

1996 after a random test on the Boavista player showed an excess of caffeine in his urine. Sanchez's sample was found to have more than twice the permitted amount of caffeine when he was tested following his side's 2-1 away win over Belenese on 13 January. Boavista claimed the excess caffeine came from three bottles of Coca Cola which Sanchez drank after being substituted in the 78th minute of the match.

The question of drugs in sport is always one of interpretation. For instance, the English FA and FIFA consider cocaine to be a performance-enhancing stimulant, whilst the Institute for the Study of Drug Dependence suggests otherwise, stating that cocaine is not one of the substances commonly considered to have any particular sporting benefits. There's no doubt that it's the recreational taking of drugs that poses the most problems for players – if it happens in everyday life, it will happen in the lives of footballers. The football authorities must continue to tackle the problem forcefully but, if progress is to be made, perhaps they should listen to Eric Cantona when he says that a clear distinction must be made between social and professional conduct.

9 Sex

SHAGGING SCANDINAVIAN GIRLS on pre-season tours has always been a favourite with British footballers. Single, fit young men, and indeed some married ones, sowing their seeds with gay abandon. Faithful when they left these shores but after a few beers in a Nordic nightclub, the Club 18–30 behaviour starts.

Not surprisingly, some of these footballing Romeos continue this type of laddish behaviour after returning home. It's not just in Scandinavia either; one former England International sought 'entertainment' from geisha girls whilst on a tour of Japan – but he did phone his wife at the same time every night to tell her how much he was missing her.

There's more to sex in football than meets the eye. All forms and all fetishes make up the full picture, participated in by players, managers, officials, fans and bimbo groupies. The acceptance of homosexuality in football is hard for many to come to terms with; it's like thinking that the armed forces are gay-free just because it's frowned upon. For anyone not convinced that gay footballers exist, the next time you bump into Justin Fashanu buy him a beer and I'm sure he would be happy to tell you the truth. Fashanu claims there are far more gay players in the game than people realise; he's reluctant to name names but, more to the point, why should he?

Fans use sex as a weapon through chanting to try to unsettle opposing players. The luckless Justin Fashanu is often greeted with the chant, 'You couldn't score with your brother'; the same chant was often used to serenade Justin's brother, John.

Newcastle United's Les Ferdinand, a regular man about town, was teased for a while about his dating of the TV presenter Dani Behr when fans sang, 'He's here, he's there, he's shagging Dani Behr, Ferdinand, Ferdinand.' Whether he was or not was immaterial.

Today, Sex is used as a marketing weapon, with glamorous young footballers advertising trendy products. The marketing men aren't stupid – sex sells. World Cup winner Alan Ball wouldn't have been working very much if he had started his career a few decades later. Ball just wasn't interested in impressing girls: 'It was always football for me – when girls at school passed me love letters under the desk, I flicked them back. I never squeezed the spots on my face because I wanted to be repulsive and keep the girls away.' Newcastle's David Ginola has no such problems, complaining, 'It's very difficult to go out. All the women want to bed me.' Poor lad.

According to research first published in the magazine *Total Football*, sociologist Paul McCarthy claims that some football fans base their support or dislike of a particular team on sexual experiences. A group of lads from London have supported Sunderland ever since their 1-0 FA Cup Final victory over Leeds United in 1973 because they had an orgy with a group of female Sunderland fans. A British tourist decided to support Real Madrid after procuring the services of a Barcelona prostitute, only to discover that the lady of the night turned out to be a man in a dress. He chose Real Madrid because they are Barcelona's most hated rivals. Then there was the man who, in 1972, found Hereford United's shocking FA Cup victory over Newcastle United so exciting that he masturbated for the first time and has supported Hereford ever since.

The only time we hear sex mentioned in the same breath as players on an official level is when coaches talk about the dreaded tournament sex-ban. Usually introduced to get maximum performance from the players on the pitch, sex-bans can cause problems. The great Bill Shankly had his own views on the subject, saying in 1971: 'Of course a player can have sexual intercourse before a match and play a blinder. But if he did it for six months he'd be a decrepit old man. It takes strength away from the body.'

Sex-free World Cup training camps can be a bind for players; no sex and being away from home for long periods instils a feeling of isolation and boredom. Before the 1974 World Cup finals in West Germany, the Brazilians were locked away in a month-long, ultra strict, nookie-free camp by their coach Mario Zagalo. The enforced celibacy prompted defender Luis Pereira to complain, 'this is supposed to make us world champions. World champions of what? Masturbation?'

Controversial German goalkeeper Harald Schumacher revealed in his autobiography that, during the 1986 World Cup in Mexico, many members of the German team indulged in lurid sex sessions. Schumacher wrote: 'We are not eunuchs. Why not engage a few call girls who are medically supervised? Better to have organised love sessions than let young players scurry off to the nearest town and perhaps catch VD and foot and mouth disease in some sleazy run-down brothel.' So that's why they always do better than us in the World Cup.

Some coaches choose the more liberated approach to sex-bans. Flamengo coach Washington Rodrigues pleaded with his team in 1996 to be sensible and not to have unrestrained or wild sex before big games.

Another recent survey claimed that male sex drive is improved by watching successful football teams. Scientists at Georgia State University completed their research during the 1994 World Cup finals in America and found that testosterone levels rose by twenty-five per cent in men who watched their favoured team win; a corresponding decline was suffered by fans of losing teams.

There must have been something in the air in Malaysia during June 1995. The first scandal erupted when a player admitted faking injuries (Repetitive Groin Strain?) so that he could stay at home with his lover. This was quickly followed by the same club's Under 16 coach who was banned from football for life for serious sexual misconduct – sleeping with someone who wasn't his wife. British football would have been robbed of many eminent players and managers if Malaysian morals applied here. Jalil Dullah, of Malacca State Football Club, was caught with a woman in a men's hostel on 18 June 1995 during a national tournament. Women were not even allowed to visit the Islamic-run hostel. It is a religious offence in Malaysia for a Muslim to be in a room with a member of the opposite sex who is not related by blood or marriage.

At a Malaysian FA hearing, Jalil asked for forgiveness, saying he was not his usual self that day. 'Such an excuse does not hold', said K. Nagaratnam, the Malacca Football Association's deputy president, 'We cannot condone such behaviour . . . more so from someone who is supposed to set a good example, we want this to be a lesson to all others involved in the same.'

No such inhibitions in Turkey where belly dancer Sether Seniz was so keen to see her national side beat the West Germans in a match during the 1980s, that she offered her own very special reward to the first player to score in the match. This apparently caused much disgruntlement amongst the Turkish defensive players – whether any of the Germans came close to scoring an own goal sadly wasn't recorded.

Revelations by a British referee, who claimed he had been offered hookers and other gifts to fix matches, were made in the *News of the World* newspaper in November 1995. Retired Howard King said the bribes took place only when he was in charge of matches between top European sides. King claimed he wasn't the only referee involved and categorically denied any British involvement, saying, 'It was hard to get a cup of tea out of them. But it goes on everywhere else.'

He retired in 1994 through illness and a knee injury after officiating in 500 league games. He refereed in the Premier League for two years and had enjoyed long service with FIFA, officiating in over twenty international matches. King said the first time he was set up with a prostitute was when he was refereeing a UEFA Cup tie in Belgium. His chaperone was an ex-FIFA referee who took him across the border to a Dutch brothel. King insisted that he never fixed games in favour of clubs who attempted to bribe him but he cynically bedded the girls anyway. Clubs could hardly report him if he did nothing on the pitch as it would obviously incriminate them. If they lost there was no more hospitality and he was given the cold shoulder.

The most bizarre incident for King was the day he had sex with a stunning Czech call girl. He met the blonde at a party after a Sparta Prague game when the girl said she'd seen King refereeing the match on television. She said she wanted to have sex with King but only if he wore his referee's kit. He did, saying that it must have really turned her on as she kept tugging at it during their love-making.

Once, King tried to use his position of power to bed a girl he fancied – and it worked. He fell head-over-heels in love with a stunning girl in Moscow where he was to referee the 1986 European Championship qualifier between Russia and Norway. He danced with the girl at the pre-match banquet and, after several vodkas, plucked up the courage to ask Russian officials if they could fix him up. The girl was not a hooker and a Russian official refused to make representations to her on King's behalf. King then ignored the diplomatic niceties and made it clear that Russia needed to win and, if he didn't go home with the girl, they wouldn't. The Russians agreed that King could have one hour with the girl, who was called Tanya. Sure enough, when his hour was up he was asked to leave. The next day Russia won 4-0. King said they would have done anyway – they didn't need any assistance from him.

King puts Portugal at the top of the sweeteners league. In 1992, he was refereeing a European Cup semifinal between Benfica and Sparta Prague. The match inspector invited him to lunch where he was showered with lavish gifts. The value of any gifts is supposed to be limited to £40. He accepted them knowing full-well that he was way over this limit and was, once again, provided with a prostitute. King was offered girls wherever he travelled in Europe including Russia, Germany, Portugal, Spain, Holland and Denmark. During his 44 matches in Europe, he estimates that girls were sent to his room between twelve and fifteen times. They were usually in their twenties, very attractive and all realised exactly why they were there. King said that the practice was so common that referees enjoyed comparing notes on the various sexual favours offered by different clubs.

Another (anonymous) British referee has backed up King's story, saying, 'What Howard says about girls being available is absolutely true. It's rife. Always has been.'

Peter Storey, a stalwart of Arsenal's 1971 double winning side, was fined £700 in 1979 for running a brothel. Peter quickly moved on to other criminal activities once he realised that his future didn't lie in pimping.

Football has always had its playboys who have proved irresistible to some of the most beautiful women in the world. George Best set new standards on the pitch and in the bedroom. In fact, on one or two occasions towards the end of his career he looked exhausted, as if he'd been up all night doing what George did second best.

Charlie Nicholas was like a mini George Best – not so talented on the pitch but he would certainly have given Best a run for his money between the sheets. Suzanne Dando, ex-Olympic gymnast and former girlfriend of Nicholas, said of his exploits, 'He gets lots of women after him and when sex is offered to him on plate, he takes it. He wants to play the field.'

Managers are not averse to a bit of infidelity either. In February 1983, John Bond resigned from Manchester City and it was later revealed that the club had hired a private detective to follow Bond to the Moorside Hotel in Disley. Bond met up with a 36-year-old divorcee – and it wasn't to play dominoes. The club went to great lengths to stress that Bond's departure was totally unconnected with the liaison. John Bond commented to the press shortly after his departure, 'My wife has been magic about it.'

Ron Atkinson also enjoyed an extra marital affair and when his wife found out she said, 'As far as he's concerned, he's God. There's nobody big enough to tell him what to do.' Big Ron retorted, 'It's bloody tough being a legend.'

Tommy Docherty, one of the game's great managers, was

sacked by Manchester United in 1977 after it was revealed that he had run off with Mary Brown, the wife of the club's physiotherapist. Docherty said at the time, 'I've been punished for falling in love.' Nineteen years on, Tommy and Mary are still together.

Giuseppe Meazza, of AC Milan and Italy, was well known for his love of the high life and his womanising. Milan did not seem to mind much about his reputation and named their stadium after him – not many people know that San Siro means Randy Git.

It is only in Britain where players and personalities are exposed in the media for their sex lives or sexual misconduct. In France, Italy and Spain it is more or less accepted that men play the field and this tolerance spreads through all walks of life. A case in point is the funeral of the former French President François Mitterand which was attended by both his wife and his mistress – no one batted an eyelid.

British newspapers pride themselves on lurid exclusives and sexual revelations about the rich and famous. One story they would have definitely printed had they known about it is the one about the Scottish footballer who was given a blow job in the tunnel area at Wembley Stadium following a big game. The player met the girl involved at the ground and enjoyed her services right under the noses of some of football's most influential and powerful people.

One story the newspapers did print involved David Pleat, the then Spurs manager. On 2 July 1987, the *Sun* newspaper ran the headline, 'Peeping Pleat Paid £80 for Lesbian Acts in Car'. The story was exactly what the headline said. Pleat had paid two vice girls to perform for him in his car. Pleat arranged the sessions in a pub car park near his former club, Luton Town. He picked up prostitutes Wendy Branaghan and Sue Sealeaf in Luton's red light district. Pleat had previously picked up Branaghan for sex in a car park but this time she asked if he wanted any 'extras' and suggested a 'double-up'.

Sealeaf said: 'He was very keen on the idea even though it was expensive at £40 each. Wendy and I got in the back seat and stripped off. We simulated a lesbian act for about twenty minutes. He just sat and watched. He was a very unusual customer!'

A week later Pleat picked up Branaghan again and suggested another double-up, this time with a prostitute called Sarah. Tottenham refused to comment on the allegations and Spurs' chairman Irving Scholar stuck by his man. A few months later, on 15 October 1987, Pleat was caught kerb-crawling in Paddington. Unable to give any good reason why he was there, Pleat was arrested. The newspaper revelations meant that Spurs had no choice but to sack him, which they did on 22 October 1987.

The surprise on Nottingham Forest's Kevin Campbell's face must have been a picture when he spotted his girlfriend romping in a hard-core porn movie. Campbell confronted Lisa Thorpe and asked her about her role in the film playing a bisexual housewife. Lisa insisted she was a model not a porn star and told Campbell the girl in the film was a lookalike. It took several friends to convince Campbell that it was indeed Lisa in the film and he was not happy. Campbell and Thorpe had met at a topless beauty contest in the summer of 1995 and little did he know that she was the star of several seedy low-budget films. Campbell dumped Thorpe, who complained, 'Kevin and I fell out because of friends' comments. There is more to this than meets the eye.'

Footballer and part-time model Gary Speed finished up on the losing side the night he took two blonde beauties to his hotel bedroom. Speed was staying at the Copthorne Hotel at Salford Quays following a postponed FA Cup tie between Bolton and Leeds when he decided to go out drinking at Mulligan's wine bar and disco in Hale, Cheshire. He returned to the hotel with two blondes and proceeded to fall asleep in his room. The girls decided to rob Speed while he was asleep and stole his clothes, a £2,000 watch, his credit cards, mobile phone and £150 in cash. Under the circumstances, Speed had no option but to inform hotel staff of the theft.

Speed's recollection of the girls was pretty minimal according to Salford CID, who said that he couldn't remember their names or what they were wearing. Later, a taxi arrived at the Copthorne Hotel and the cabby handed over all of Speed's clothes – at least the girls had some heart.

Speed's next problem was explaining to his girlfriend that, not only had he been robbed, but also that it was by two five-foot five-inch blondes who were about 23-years-old and had been in his hotel room with him. The situation came to a head when the *News of the World* got wind of the story. Speed at first denied that the girls had been in his room but admitted he had been robbed. The newspaper reported that Speed's agent had phoned them in desperation offering first call on football stories in return for the story not appearing in the newspaper. On Sunday 4 February 1996, the story appeared in the *News of the World* under the headline, 'Naughty Nickers Strip Randy Gary Bare' – just about sums it up.

If there's a soccer sleaze story to be told you can bet your bottom dollar that the *News of the World* will print it. More revelations from the paper came in March 1996, when an 18-year-old girl claimed she had been invited to take part in a four-in-a-bed sex romp with Manchester United's Lee Sharpe. She had also had a liaison with Manchester City's Nicky Summerbee and alleged in the article that whilst having sex with Summerbee, several of his friends came into the bedroom to watch.

Lindsay Pender was helping a female *News of the World* reporter with an investigation into the Manchester drugs scene when they were approached by Sharpe in a bar. Lindsay had briefly dated Sharpe a few years ago and Sharpe, and a friend, were keen to renew the acquaintance. After a drink and a chat, Sharpe suggested the four of them should go to Lindsay's hotel room and, once there, the two men raided the mini-bar and started watching a porn film.

Sharpe's knowledge of drugs was second to none. The *News of the world* printed his thoughts on certain substances and how, when he retires at 32, he'll buy a yacht and sail around the Caribbean smoking a foot-long joint. Sharpe and his pal then suggested to the two girls that a four-in-a-bed sex romp might be a good idea – not knowing that the other girl was a *News of the World* reporter!

When he was approached by the paper, Sharpe said, 'You've got me by the bollocks so I'm going to have to do something. I need to speak to the gaffer and my parents. My mum will have a fit.' Summerbee denied ever knowing Lindsay Pender but, curiously, neither player threatened legal action against the newspaper.

England International Paul Gascoigne was accused by a leggy blonde of taking part in an orgy, according to the *News of the World* in September 1985. Gazza used his impish sense of humour to wriggle out of the claims. He said, 'Three-in-a-bed? . . . hang on, I think it was four!'

Players can be used for publicity reasons as well and it's without doubt that some of George Best's conquests used him as much as he did them. Whilst playing in Italy, Faustino Asprilla was rumoured to be having an affair with the Italian porn actress Petra Scharbach after he split up with his childhood sweetheart wife. Asprilla soon cottoned on to what was going on, saying, 'That was a really nice stitch up. I fell into that one like some kind of chicken. She was looking for publicity and the best way to find it was to attach herself to me.'

Another South American player who's had his fair share of female admirers and scandals is Diego Maradona. A particularly difficult time for him was in November 1986, when his fiancée announced that she was expecting a baby. The trouble was that a pregnant local girl claimed that Maradona was also the father of her child – some interesting explaining had to be done. Journalists flocked to his home to ask some pertinent questions, only to be met by a wall of silence. In 1994, when they flocked to his home to ask questions about his drugs ban from the 1994 World Cup, Maradona shot at them with his air rifle.

Sex and football have come together in surprising ways on a couple of occasions. Firstly, in 1993, when David Sullivan bought into Birmingham City. Sullivan was the owner of the infamous *Sunday Sport* – a publication containing ridiculous *X Files*-type stories with breasts on every page. His right hand woman was, and still is, Karen Brady, who chose to up her public profile in 1994 by appearing in the *News of the world* wearing only a negligée.

Spain's national team boss Ladislao Kubala nearly went one better in July 1979 but turned down the opportunity to pose nude, for lots of money, in a Spanish magazine.

Perhaps the ultimate synergy with sex was achieved by the local Venetian club who, in the 95/96 season, were sponsored by a local sex shop – they were known as Team Punto Rosso Sexy Shop.

On 19 July 1992, Chelsea fan and Heritage Minister David Mellor was exposed by the *Sunday People* for having an extra-marital affair with 'resting' actress Antonia De Sancha. Mellor was promptly labelled the Minister of Fun and had to endure days of revelations about the affair in the press. One interesting aspect of De Sancha's story was Mellor's enhanced ability to make love whilst wearing his Chelsea football shirt. Mellor resigned from his post over the affair but continues as a Member of Parliament. In 1994, Justin Fashanu made claims that he had had sexual relations with two cabinet ministers – a story that has failed to develop since.

So much rubbish has been written and said about George Best over the years. Best was a genius on the field and had a remarkable gift for attracting women. His autobiography *The Good, the Bad, and the Bubbly*, tells his story in his own words and contains the eye-opening quote, 'I've never been faithful to anyone. I find it impossible to be faithful.' That was then. Now, he's married to a former air stewardess called Alex and lives happily in West London.

Best was a product of his time, the Swinging Sixties and the Sensational Seventies. Footballers weren't corporate superstars, they were mavericks. Every team had three or four flair players and every side had its Champagne Charlies, to whom burning the candle at both ends was a way of life.

George Best's hormones got him into big trouble a month

after he quit Manchester United, when he met Marjorie Wallace, Miss World, and ended up in a police cell. It all started with a call from her agents, asking if she could be photographed with George at Slack Alice's nightclub in Manchester. Best was part-owner of the club and, naturally, agreed to the request. He got her telephone number and, the next time he was down in London, he gave her a ring. He arrived on her doorstep with his suitcase one Friday night, saying he hadn't sorted out a hotel and, of course, he never did. They went out to some of George's favourite London haunts and then went back to her flat to consummate the relationship. The following evening they did exactly the same again. Trouble started when Marjorie Wallace's boyfriend's mother phoned out of the blue. George felt it was rather insensitive of Wallace to have a phone conversation whilst they were in bed together and they had a row.

The next day they went their different ways but it wasn't the last George was to hear of the affair. The following Tuesday, a group of police officers turned up at Slack Alice's, informing Best that two Metropolitan police officers were travelling up from London to see him. Marjorie Wallace had accused Best of stealing some items from her flat during his recent stay. Best was taken to London and questioned by police during which time a few things emerged that didn't look good for Wallace. Firstly, she had got the day that Best arrived at her flat completely wrong. Secondly, George hired a detective to look into her past and found her implicated sexually not only with Tom Jones' manager, but also with a police chief inspector. The case against Best was dismissed and he was allowed to walk free 'without a stain on his character'. Marjorie Wallace flew to America – using the passport that she had accused Best of stealing.

One of George Best's greatest sexual adventures was when he achieved 'The Magnificent Seven' – bedding seven girls in 24 hours. He woke up in bed with one girl, then went to the Brown Bull pub in Manchester and spent lunchtime in bed with a girl from Granada TV. Then he met the young niece of a friend from school and went to bed with her. When she went out shopping, he had sex with her cousin. Best then went back home and called up a girl who he occasionally met for bedroom fun. In the evening he had a dinner date with another girl who he took to a casino and then back to his place. Then he went back to the casino and decided to make it lucky seven on the way home. At seven-thirty in the morning, he drove round to the house of a girl he vaguely knew; she was the girlfriend of a guy he didn't particularly like. He slept with her until lunchtime the following day and hasn't seen her since. A round of applause for George.

You know you are a real man about town when you take your girlfriend to dinner and join eight other girls at a table, only to discover that you've slept with all of them. This happened to George Best when he was dating Miss Great Britain, Carolyn Moore. On sitting down at the table George just started laughing.

Other famous Best conquests included Juliet Mills, Annette Andreé, Sinead Cusack, singer Lyndsey De Paul, Debbie Let's-have-a-look-at-the-old-scoreboard Forsyth and Georgie Lawton, the daughter of Ruth Ellis, the last woman to be hanged in Britain. He even tried to get together with Brigitte Bardot, having got her phone number from a friend, but he could only get through to her maid who didn't understand English, let alone George.

A poignant moment in George Best's wild days was when he was going out with Marie Stavin, one of his collection of Miss Worlds. They went to a casino, where George won £15,000, and then returned to a posh hotel in Bloomsbury. Best threw the money onto the bed and Stavin changed into a skimpy negligée. They ordered a bottle of Dom Perignon from room service that was duly delivered by a little man from Belfast. Best tipped the porter £50 and, as he walked out, the man turned to Best and said, 'Can I ask you something Mr Best?' He looked at the money on the bed and then at the half naked Miss World and said, 'Tell me Mr Best . . . where did it all go wrong?'

Frank Worthington was signed by Bill Shankly at Liverpool when he was twenty-three – subject to a medical test. When the club doctor took his blood pressure, he told Worthington, 'You should not be playing professional football.' Worthington had just been on a gruelling Eastern Bloc tour with England so it was decided that he should have a holiday in Majorca to relax – then he would be ready for another test. The trouble is, Worthington didn't relax at all.

First, he went to his brother's wedding in Manchester, where he hooked up with Carolyn Moore, one of Best's old flames. They spent the night together in a hotel and did what came naturally. Then, Frank headed off to Majorca. On the Spanish holiday island, he stayed at a friend's flat and one day returned to find two Swedish girls waiting for his mate, John. He ended up having sex with both of them.

Later the same day, he met a Belgian girl who came from a place called Knokke, which Worthington thought was rather funny considering her build. The inevitable happened, which wasn't good for his blood pressure. When he returned to Liverpool the doctor advised Bill Shankly to cancel the transfer on medical grounds, which he did. Frank Worthington never again got the chance to play for one of the top teams, a travesty of justice considering his superlative skills.

During his time at Birmingham City, Frank Worthington ran into a very famous woman on a train journey. On this particular journey he sat opposite Mandy Rice-Davies who'd been involved some years earlier in the Profumo scandal. Using his famous charm, he got her into bed and claims, in his autobiography *One Hump or Two*, that he now knows why Fidel Castro used to fly her over to Cuba for the night. Their fling continued and he introduced her to Jim Smith, Birmingham's manager, at the club party. 'Fuck me, it's Mandy Rice-Davies isn't it?' asked Smithy. And then, as subtle as an air raid, Smith went on, 'I can't believe it. I used to wank over you when I was a lad!'

The flamboyance of yesteryear just isn't in football anymore – the game has moved on, leaving us with a drought of real characters. How many of today's managers could top the notorious Malcolm Allison–Fiona Richmond incident at Crystal Palace?

Allison turned up with porn star Richmond, who was only wearing a fur coat, at a Palace training session hosted by one Terry Venables Esquire. Venables and the players wondered what stunt Allison was trying to pull this time and they found out when they got back to the ground for a wash and brush up after training. They had all stripped off and got into the communal bath when, out of nowhere, appeared Allison and Fiona Richmond who also stripped off and jumped into the bath. Quick as a flash, Venables jumped out, leaving the rest of the players to enjoy what they thought was a bit of innocent fun. Suddenly, a photographer appeared from nowhere and started clicking away and, sure enough, the photos were splashed all over the tabloids. Allison did not plan what happened – to him it was a bit of a giggle but, unfortunately, several Crystal Palace players' wives did not see it that simply.

More recently, there's been a spate of players implicated in various sex scandals. Surprisingly, one of Britain's most intelligent and articulate players found himself in a whole pile of trouble in the summer of 1995. Lee Chapman went on a three-day break to Ibiza with his wife, Leslie Ash. After a seven-hour binge of beer, wine and vodka, Chapman insisted the couple go on to a nightclub. His wife wanted to go back to their hotel and they had a row. Ash stormed off and Chapman hooked up with some British holidaymakers who proceeded to ply him with even more drinks.

To cut a long story short, Chapman ended up at an apartment with two girls, allegedly paralytically drunk. He said he fell asleep, fully clothed, on a sofa and woke up sometime later, dressed only in his boxer shorts, in bed with one of the girls, Cheryl Roberts. Bemused, dazed and suffering the wrath of his wife, he flew back to London, only to discover that the girls had taken photographs of him and sold the story to a national newspaper.

Chapman was in deep trouble as it was claimed he had had sex with Cheryl, a charge he furiously denied. Chapman said in an unpaid interview with the *Sun*, 'I don't know if I touched her. I think I might have done, I just can't remember. But I know I didn't have sex with her. I know the pictures look bad for me but I did not have sex with the woman.'

The two girls decided to jog Chapman's memory, with the help of the *News of the World*. Their story said that they had bundled Chapman into a taxi and spent several hours drinking with him before going back to the apartment. Cheryl claimed that she half slept with Chapman but her best friend Claire insisted Chapman was so drunk she wasn't sure that he was at all capable of performing.

Lee Chapman continued to deny any hanky panky and realised he very nearly said goodbye to his marriage over the incident. In the *News of the World* on 30 July 1995, he put the matter to bed, so to speak, saying, 'I can't believe I've been such a fool. Leslie and our two little boys are the only things in the world I really care about. I was such a selfish bastard, I can't believe I risked losing them.' Lee Chapman and Leslie Ash continue to be married – what a tolerant wife she must be.

The tangled love life of Coventry City's Zimbabwean International Peter Ndlovu became tabloid fodder after a couple of kiss and tell articles appeared in Sunday newspapers. Ndlovu has a child by an ex-girlfriend in Zimbabwe but it wasn't long after he joined Coventry that he started a relationship with seventeen-year-old Alison Jarvis. In the newspaper article, Jarvis went into detail about what a wonderful lover Ndlovu was and how he had a habit of disappearing for weeks at a time. Surely, if she wanted to check on his whereabouts all she had to do was switch on Sky Sports. Ndlovu fathered two children with Jarvis although, according to her, he failed to acknowledge his financial responsibilities. Ndlovu maintained a silence throughout the revelations and Jarvis was sent a signed football by Coventry manager, Ron Atkinson, who suggested she raffle it to raise much-needed cash.

Ndlovu's roving eye got him into more trouble in April 1996 when police woman Sharon Bent told the *News of the World* about her relationship with the Coventry star. Apparently, Ndlovu showered her with lingerie and took great delight in telling her anything she wore would be taken down.

The couple had met in the tunnel at Highfield Road and Bent recalled how Ndlovu used to eye her up whilst bending down doing stretching exercises in the pre-match warm up. Bent complained sex was less than exciting with Ndlovu (in complete contrast to Alison Jarvis) and said he seemed more interested in watching football on television. Needless to say, she had no idea about Alison Jarvis and the two kids but when she found out, the proverbial hit the fan.

After seeing mail from a former girlfriend, Bent decided to end the relationship. It didn't seem to deter Ndlovu who quickly returned to form, immediately installing another long-term girlfriend, Amina Essoff, and their one-year-old daughter Rashana into his home. If all the claims of Ndlovu being the father of all these children are true, he'd better start saving because their school fees alone are going to cost him a fortune.

Perhaps it's a sign of the times that the percentage of footballers whose personal lives are paraded all over the tabloids is a very small one. These days players are probably a lot more careful and reclusive than they used to be and are more than aware that newspapers are the media equivalent of the Inland Revenue – once they get their teeth into you they don't let go that easily. Certainly, compared to pop stars, actors and even politicians, footballers' indiscretions appear to be in a significant minority – or maybe it's just that they don't get caught.

10 Agents' Tales

UNTIL FAIRLY RECENTLY agents were not controlled, and they were able to do business pretty much on their own terms. Players undoubtedly need representation, not least for their commercial activities. They also need help in thrashing out terms with clubs which employ many former players as managers and who therefore know every self-interest trick in the book.

FIFA and the international FAs now operate a system whereby all practising agents must be registered in order to trade, and the rules are quite specific. The Agents' Charter sets out quite clearly the do's and don'ts for football agents although some wilful rule-bending does seem to go on still.

There are just over 300 practising football agents in the world, all registered with FIFA and all abiding by the same set of rules.

The regulations for the control of football agents deem that a player is entitled to receive the services of an adviser who receives remuneration for their part in any negotiations the player may have with a club. If, however, that adviser is acting solely as an agent, then he or she must be licensed with FIFA. Therefore, a person whose clearly established profession is that of a lawyer or financial adviser may advise a player on any matter without being considered an agent. This method is particularly popular with foreign players who prefer to negotiate their own contracts and then get the final agreement checked over by a lawyer. Jurgen Klinsmann's transfer to Tottenham in the summer of 1994 was carried out in this way.

However, FIFA rules state that no person may become

directly involved in negotiations with a club on behalf of a player unless he or she is a close relative of that player or is a licensed player agent. Budding agents must satisfy a number of criteria before a licence can be issued: they must have been resident for at least five years in the country they would like to trade in; proof of no criminal record should be supplied and anyone occupying a position with a national association or club is ineligible.

Individual national associations decide whether applications are admissible. Prospective agents also undergo an interview with their national association where they have to demonstrate an adequate knowledge of football regulations, a working knowledge of civil law and, furthermore, they must appear capable of advising a player who calls on the candidate's service.

If the outcome of the personal interview is positive, the national association forward the candidate's file to FIFA which has the ultimate power of veto and can block any recommendation for a licence without having to explain why.

Assuming FIFA approve the application, the agent is required to put up a bond of approximately £100,000 which is held by FIFA to compensate any party that has a justifiable claim against the agent. The interest due on the deposit is credited annually to the agent.

As soon as the bond money is received at FIFA headquarters, the agent is issued with a licence which is strictly personal and non-transferable. Under the charter, agents have the following rights:

> to contract any player who is not or no longer under contract with a club.
>
> to represent any player who requests him to negotiate and/or conclude a contract on his behalf.
>
> to manage the affairs of any player who requests him to do so.

Any agent who breaks these rules is likely to be sanctioned with a reprimand, censure or caution, face a fine or have his licence withdrawn.

Any player who uses the services of an unlicensed agent is clearly breaking the rules of the charter and can face a FIFA-generated fine of up to £25,000 or a twelve-month suspension. Any club wishing to engage the services of a player can now only negotiate with the player himself or a licensed agent. Anything else is illegal and clubs found violating transfer negotiation rules can face serious fines or even a ban.

Into the complicated world of agents, FIFA have introduced a strict code of conduct, designed to bring all transfer dealings above board. Until recently, foreign agents acted individually but also, and more often than not, as representatives of entire clubs. In Britain, agents carry out transactions on an individual basis. A Rune Hauge type transfer would be as follows: if Scandinavian club X wanted to sell player A to a British club, they would tell the player's agent how much money they want for the player. So, if club X wanted £1 million for player A, the agent would agree a purchase price with the British club of, say, £1.2 million. The balance of £200,000 would go directly to the agent for brokering the deal and all parties would be satisfied; the British club would get their player at what they perceived to be a fair price and Scandinavian club X would get the £1 million they demanded for the player. This method of one-off payments proved very fruitful for a number of foreign agents.

In Britain, dealings have never been as simplistic. The vast majority of British agents offer an all-encompassing service. They broker financial and commercial deals for players, officiate in transfer negotiations and generally nurse players throughout their careers. It is a full service in every sense of the word.

Dennis Roach is, without a doubt, the most successful of the modern day agents. His company, PRO, specialises in foreign transfers and Roach's capacity to spot deals incredibly quickly has not made him popular with his rivals. Roach got into agency work by accident after he met Johan Cruyff on a family holiday and agreed to represent the Dutchman's interests in Britain. His successful deals include Mark Hateley to AC Milan, Glenn Hoddle to Monaco, Mark Hughes to Barcelona,

Trevor Steven to Marseille, Des Walker to Sampdoria and even John Toshack moving, as a coach, to Real Madrid.

Certain clubs favour certain agents; Roach is welcome at almost every big European club and was a particular favourite of Brian Clough when he was manager at Nottingham Forest; Eric Hall and Frank McClintock were flavour of the month during Terry Venables' tenure at Spurs.

Before the introduction of the charter, the market place was unregulated and full of pitfalls. Agents and clubs were technically breaking the existing limited FIFA rules and FIFA were turning a blind eye. One agent claims that the system was so much fairer when the FA turned a blind eye to clubs paying agents directly (a practice that is still frowned upon). Players don't like paying agents and would be far happier if the clubs paid their representatives directly. The agents who were paid directly often had to submit trumped up invoices for other services such as public relations in order to gain payment. Such invoices were, in reality, for arranging a player's transfer, and just a way around the rules.

'In Britain, there are two types of agent – the legal ones and Eric Hall' as another agent put it. Technically, this statement is absolutely correct – Hall is unlicensed. Eric Hall is a flamboyant figure; the term 'low profile' is not in his vocabulary. A young-looking 59, Hall saunters around British football with his loud jackets and fat cigars talking in a dialect of English that is 'monster' difficult to understand. His background is in showbusiness where he used to be a 'plugger'. Hall's list of showbusiness successes is very long; you name them and he has worked with them. He lists amongst his triumphs his promotion of Queen's 'Bohemian Rhapsody' which became a worldwide hit – the fact that the song was patently brilliant is neither here nor there.

Hall talks a great game: 'I make the poor player rich and the rich player richer. I'm not a one-man band, I'm a one-man orchestra.' His friendship with Terry Venables goes back to the former England coach's days as a player with Chelsea and, probably, Hall's most lucrative period came from Venables' regime at Spurs. In June 1991 when Venables became chief executive at Tottenham, it was Hall who became the most favoured agent at the club and he also looked after a number of the players. When Terry Venables and Alan Sugar fell out, Hall and his players were very vociferous in their support for Venables. He claimed that all his clients would leave Spurs if Venables' dismissal was upheld in court. Only Neil Ruddock left (he was transferred to Liverpool). He got involved in a loyalty payment row with Spurs over Ruddock and eventually settled for £50,000 instead of the original figure of £150,000. Hall then became a huge Liverpool fan and claimed Graeme Souness to be the greatest manager in the world. This statement underlines Hall's claim that he 'doesn't really understand football'.

His hatred of Spurs continues unabated. Eric Hall is banned from Tottenham Hotspur as a result of his actions and outspoken views in support of Venables during his legal battle with Sugar. He views Sugar with complete contempt but claims to still represent the interests of several Tottenham players, a situation that, if true, would infuriate Sugar.

Hall's fellow agents view his activities with disdain, not least because he remains unlicensed. 'I love it, they find me a monster, monster threat,' says Hall. He thinks the necessity of a licence is a restraint of trade: 'I've been in showbusiness a long time and if Cliff Richard wants his plumber to be his agent, it's his decision,' argues Hall. All very well but, all industries have regulators, so why should football be any different?

Hall claims the FA are desperate for him to get a licence and their anxiety is easy to understand: Hall is a loud maverick and to get him to toe the line would be a good public relations exercise. Pressure from other licensed agents is coming to bear and even Hall is feeling it: 'I'm ready to get a licence and to put up a bond of £100,000,' he said in May 1996.

A potential spanner in the works would be the introduction of territory licences by the FA. Each licence would allow an agent to trade only in a single country and it's conceivable that agents would have to apply for separate licences for England,

Scotland, Ireland and Wales. A bond system would also apply, with a figure of £25,000–£50,000 most frequently mentioned. 'If that happens, I'll withdraw my bond and do that. I'll pay less,' says Hall. Either way, the FA will undoubtedly be delighted to have some regulations over Hall and his activities.

Hall remains confident that domestic licences could be free and bases his optimism on a brief conversation with Rick Parry of the Premiere League: 'Rick Parry said to me, "Why don't you get a domestic licence?" I said, "How much will that cost?" "Nothing," said Parry. I said, "Well, I'll have two of those then." '

If a new domestic licence is free then anyone could become an agent, which is why some sort of fee seems inevitable. Hall cannot escape the fact that some clubs refuse to deal with him due to his unlicensed status. However, he can and does bend the rules to suit his purposes. A favourite trick is taking a player's wife or brother into negotiations and instructing them on the type of deal he wants for his client. 'I can sit in a room but can't actively negotiate, because of FA rules, with a manager or a chairman. It's a farce,' claims Hall, 'I've never had a club not deal with me.'

As if to underline the ease with which FA rules can be broken, Hall recalls a transfer which he was involved in some years ago: 'Bobby Mimms was at Spurs and Don Mackay, at Blackburn Rovers, wanted to buy him. So I went up to do the deal but Blackburn's chairman was Bill Fox, a high ranking FA official. So when I turned up with Bobby Mimms, Don Mackay said, "Eric, what are you doing here?" I said, "I'm here because I'm Bobby's agent." Don Mackay said, "But I can't do business with you because of the rules." So I said, "OK, we'll both go back to London and forget the whole deal." Don Mackay panicked and said something like, "Please don't say you were here . . . Bill Fox is my chairman." Anyway, to cut a long story short, we eventually started negotiating and we came to a sticking point. Don Mackay had to ask Bill Fox what to do, so he telephoned him. I grabbed the phone and spoke directly to Fox and we did the deal directly over the phone. So, even in those days it was possible to do a deal.'

Hall likes to see himself as the unofficial spokesman of football. He plays up to the media to such an extent that they appear to believe him. To many, he is the unacceptable face of football although Hall sees his role as quite the reverse. One of his more serious claims is that other agents watch his business dealings very closely and have taken to implicating him in deals that he has had nothing to do with. This has resulted in a string of enquiries by Graham Noakes at the FA's licensing and registration department. Nothing untoward has ever been found.

The modus operandi of a football agent is a curious one which differs, within the rules, from agent to agent. At the time of writing, Eric Hall is not operating within the rules: 'I make managers and chairmen aware of players who are available and advise them of up-and-coming situations.' The football grapevine is an essential tool of the agent.

'I do different deals for different players,' says Hall, 'Horses for courses I call it. I take twenty per cent of all commerical earnings but I don't take a percentage of a transfer fee. We would normally sort something out; the bigger the deal, the bigger the commission.' He is extremely reluctant to talk about specific deals but champions the introduction of incentives into contracts. 'I introduced what I call "compilation" into football. It was something I did in showbusiness. When I first got into football, players maybe got loyalty payment, a signing on fee and wages. Under an incentive scheme, if a player scores X amount of goals then I want this; if a player plays for England then I want something else.'

Loan deals have been modified, says Hall: 'Normally, if a player is on loan, the club has to cover his wages bill. I try to arrange goal bonus, so if a player scores say ten goals whilst on loan, he gets a bonus payment.'

On the question of bungs, Hall is adamant that they don't take place. In all his years associated with the game, he claims he has never been involved in one or heard of one being made. By way of emphasising his point, he says his friendship with Terry Venables was tested over the sale of Steve Sedgley when he and Venables met at the Royal Garden Hotel in London to thrash out a deal and, in Hall's opinion, Venables did not offer the right terms. The two fell out until a deal was finally agreed three to four weeks later. 'It would have been the easiest thing in the world to do a deal with Terry,' says Hall, 'I won't do a deal just for the sake of it, even if he's my best mate.'

In the past, Hall has been a regular guest at Terry Venables' club Scribes West where he marshalled the Saturday night karaoke with his usual colourful personality. It was on one such occasion that Hall was having a bite to eat with Venables and his wife, Yvette. Unbeknown to Hall, Yvette, who is a master practical joker, had planted an exploding capsule in one of his giant Havana cigars. All through the meal Venables and Yvette were waiting for the explosion to happen but it never did as Hall kept picking non-doctored cigars by sheer luck.

On the Sunday morning, Hall travelled to Manchester with Paul Walsh with a view to negotiating a transfer from Portsmouth to Manchester City. The pair met City chairman Francis Lee and manager Brian Horton at an exclusive country hotel. All four men went up to a suite to negotiate the deal. Francis Lee was very nervous as the signing would be his first as the newly appointed chairman.

Lee had great difficulty understanding Hall's quick fire delivery, and spent the eight hours of negotiating twitching; at one point he got up to go to the toilet, only to open the wrong door and walk into a cupboard instead. Eventually, agreement was reached and, barring a troublesome medical the following morning, Paul Walsh was now a Manchester City player.

Francis Lee ordered some champagne to celebrate and Hall offered him one of his customary cigars. Lee took one of the Havanas for later. After a drink and a chat, Hall made his way down the M6 towards London. At 3 a.m., Hall's telephone rang – it was Francis Lee. Initially, Hall suspected there may have been a problem with the transfer but Lee quickly allayed his fears. He said he had got home, eaten the snack his wife had left him and settled down to watch the film on television with a nice relaxing brandy, trying to get Eric Hall out of his system.

He was so pleasantly relaxed that he decided to light the Havana cigar – which promptly exploded.

Lee had telephoned Hall to enquire if it was how he sealed all his transfers and was amused to learn the real story behind the exploding cigar. One thing is for sure, Francis Lee will never forget his first signing as Manchester City chairman.

If Eric Hall is the unacceptable face of football then the exact opposite must be the Smiths. Phil and Jon Smith run a company called First Artists which covers the whole gamut of sports promotions and management. The Smiths are a symphony orchestra compared to Eric Hall's one-man band. Jon Smith is the company chairman and his brother is a company director who also has his own, associated, public relations company called Double Impact.

Jon has been active in football for many years; one of his first major successes was tying up Diego Maradona's first Coke deal – the drink that is. Phil has a track record in the music industry but is a relative newcomer to football, having only been involved in promotion and agency work since 1991. It's Phil Smith who is now steering First Artists football agency work into the next millennium.

Good public relations are an essential part of any successful company and it's one aspect of business that the Smiths take very seriously. 'Incorporating Double Impact into the company gives First Artists a PR outlet for all our other activities,' said Smith and Smith, 'We don't just deal with the media when something's happening – we deal with them every day.'

Football management is the company's principal vocation although they are also involved with the England cricket team and have their own event company that imports a lot of American sport and sportsmen into Britain. They have corporate clients like Mars and Littlewoods and were even responsible for organising Mikhail Gorbachev's lecture tour. First Artists are a global organisation in every sense of the word.

The Smiths' reputation is good; both men are outwardly affable, very professional and are well-known for driving a very hard bargain. 'We feel very able to offer a complete service to clients and players, apart from managing them and handling their affairs,' said Phil.

On their books are just over 30 professional players including Les Ferdinand, Ruud Gullit (commercial transactions only), Kevin Cambell, Trevor Sinclair, Ian Rush and Liverpool Football Club. The Liverpool deal is a commercial one that operates all year round and gives First Artists a presence at the club that is unique. Plus, it gives Liverpool FC an outside company that are as close to being in-house as possible.

First Artists enjoyed a similar promotional arrangement with the England football team which was terminated after Terry Venables became England coach. According to the football grapevine, Jon Smith and Terry Venables fell out over the issue and subsequently barely exchange pleasantries.

The PR aspect of player representation forces First Artists to take the rough with the smooth. 'I think we probably keep more things out of the papers than we get in,' says Phil, 'But you can't keep everything out of the papers; if someone wants to squeal about something and cause trouble it'll go into the papers first and then you can minimise it from there – or another paper will give you the facility to redress the balance. We do that in both personal and professional circumstances.'

On an operational level, Phil Smith firmly believes that the Agents Charter was badly needed and has served to legitimise the business. He is not a fan of the bond system, referring to it as 'dead money' and an ineffective way of doing business. He believes the pressure is on agents with less cash-flow than First Artists to do rash deals to make up for the outlay of the registration fee.

On the up side, he says, 'It also broadened the parameters within which we could work, we can now work for clubs as well as the players although you can't be at two ends of the same deal.'

Arguably, there is more money to be made out of working for clubs than there is working for individual players. First Artists are player-driven more than club-driven but are gradually increasing their activities within clubs. The strict rules of the charter have made such dealings above board. Under the new rules, Phil Smith would like to see the FA and FIFA providing a full back-up service for agents by acting on their behalf in disputes with clubs over deals. 'FIFA should act as an insurance policy,' said Phil, 'We had a problem getting money from a South American deal and it was only when we got involved in a legal wrangle that the FA were forced to intervene.'

One area that is of considerable irritation to First Artists is the blind eye that is turned by the authorities to unlicensed agents like Eric Hall. 'We have no personal problem with Eric,' they said, 'In fact, I'm not sure if he's got any clients. You've got these agents that have put the money in, yet deals are still being done by people who are not genuinely part of the business. The idea of putting up the bond money signals serious intent as a football agent. We are welcome at football clubs and are no longer the tainted agent; having said that, we have to do business the right way. You can't dictate to clubs that they're going to make you wealthy if they don't like you personally.'

The question of sub-contracting under the umbrella of one licence is one that Phil Smith finds irritating. Technically, he is required to put up another bond as it's against the rules for him to operate under his brother's licence, even though he works for the same company. FIFA and the FA say the situation is under review and Phil Smith has been given jurisdiction to keep on working, for the moment at least. 'Our argument is, why should people have to do this when people are trading without licences, and people are working under the umbrella of a bond doing deals and thereby breaking FIFA regulations!' said the Smiths.

A case in point is the 1996 transfer of defender Alan Stubbs from Bolton Wanderers to Celtic. FIFA and the SFA received half a dozen official complaints over the deal which was done by two financial advisers using the shelter of a FIFA-licensed agent. If true, the rules clearly prohibit the practice. It is a test case for the brave new world of the football agent that could have serious repercussions for the parties involved. Phil Smith's anger is understandable: 'If I can't operate under my brother's licence as a director of the company, then why should they be able to do it under somebody else's licence?' Only FIFA and the SFA can answer that question.

About 70 football agents are paid-up members of the International Agents Federation. They meet every three months to try to create a working environment that is fair and they are officially linked to FIFA. Protests of rule-breaking will not go away: 'If FIFA run the activities of agents in the spirit of the agreement, that's fine. But something has to be done about rule-breakers,' said Phil, who openly hints that the Federation may be forced to break away from FIFA if something is not sorted out.

Agent unity is essential to the Smiths who believe that the marketplace is an international one. 'The money isn't in England, the big deals are the foreign deals,' they said. 'Therefore, to get a domestic licence is all well and good but the fact is that the big money passes between the big clubs overseas.' Maybe Eric Hall should rethink his strategy.

In the international marketplace, the temptation for some clubs to do underhand deals is great, especially if money is in short supply. First Artists have done deals with the Serbian FA who actively encourage home-grown talent going abroad. Transfers generate much-needed foreign currency. Sell-on clauses are more common, so if a player is resold after the first transfer, his original club gets a share of the fee.

Favours are asked of agents; items such as new kits, training equipment and even new seats for a stand are, wherever possible, supplied in the interest of good relations. 'Compassionate bungs' are essentially gifts, and quite different to the sort of bungs all of us have heard about and which, like fellow agent Eric Hall, Phil Smith insists don't happen: 'You hear about these stories. I've never come across bungs. I'm a relative novice in the game having only been in it for four years. Sometimes the price of a player suddenly goes from £500,000 to £1 million, usually because the more people who get involved, the more the parameters change. We've done deals, amicably, that have involved as many as four agents.'

Getting an agent to even entertain the notion of bungs is like getting blood out of a stone. 'As far as I will go on the subject of bungs is, if we were in the market for offering incentives for deals, they wouldn't necessarily be turned away,' said Smith. 'That's not the way we operate. We do good deals, that's why we are who we are in the marketplace. We get our players through other players recommending us, so we can't do bad deals.' Phil Smith's PR background serves him well.

The Smiths have been involved in some unusual deals, the most unusual being a transfer Jon Smith was part of some years ago. The Brazilian Roberto was playing in Argentina and his club were finding it very difficult to find the money to keep him. In an attempt to cover their costs, the club decided to advertise Roberto's body parts and limbs for sponsorship. Smith bought a share in the player's left leg for approximately £40,000. When the Argentine club sold Roberto to Italy, the sale generated a large transfer fee. Smith's return on his investment was £150,000.

When Gary Pallister moved from Middlesbrough to Manchester United, Jon Smith brokered the deal between the two clubs. The deal itself was discussed and rubber stamped in a car park at the back of a service station at Scotch Corner. Bruce Rioch, Alex Ferguson, Gary Pallister and Jon Smith met in pouring rain in the windswept car park to agree a then British record transfer fee for a central defender – £2.3 million. Smith recalls feeling a little odd at the time because in his words, 'People just wouldn't believe such a big deal was done in such a miserable location.' Alex Ferguson's only comment after the conclusion of the deal was that he could not believe that he had just paid £2.3 million for a central defender. In hindsight, he would certainly agree that he has had value for money.

Tony Cottee's transfer from West Ham to Everton is another memorable one for Jon Smith. Cottee and Smith had held talks with Arsenal as well as Everton but Colin Harvey agreed to meet the pair at the Crest Hotel at South Mimms. After exchanging the initial pleasantries, the trio enquired at reception to check the availability of a room to conclude their talks. The receptionist informed them that the hotel was full so Harvey, Smith and Cottee decided to go to the bar instead.

Football Babylon

The bar was full of football fans and it was perfectly obvious to all and sundry what was going on. People were butting into the conversation, telling Cottee to up his demands and giving him advice – the whole situation was a farce. Supporters were phoning newspapers and news agencies from the bar detailing terms and conditions in the vain hope of a tip-off payment.

Weighing up the options is a crucial part of any potential deal between a player and a club. One of Phil Smith's clients had a number of big clubs interested in him and the next move the player made would probably be the most important one of his career. It would be unfair to name the club and chairman involved for fear of ruining Smith's good relations with the club. Smith and his client arrived for talks at the club concerned and were offered a fantastic deal. Smith and the player asked the chairman if they could go for a private chat in an executive box to consider the offer. Sensing that a deal was very close, the chairman agreed. Smith and the player spent the next ten minutes just chatting about everyday things, until they were interrupted by the chairman who popped his head round the door to see if they had an answer. Somewhat flustered, the pair requested a further five minutes and spent it actually discussing the deal. To the disappointment of the chairman, they decided to keep their options open and held out for a better deal which eventually came from another premiership club. To this day, the chairman of the first club has no idea that the player and Smith spent ten minutes just chatting about nothing, instead of seriously considering his offer.

To anyone considering a future as a football agent, they would be mistaken in thinking it was a jet-set champagne lifestyle mixing with sports stars and enjoying the fruits of successful deals. The work is hard, unsociable and, on occasions, downright frustrating. A tale that amply underlines the point is the saga surrounding the transfer of Joey Beauchamp from Oxford to West Ham, a deal in which Phil Smith was the agent.

Phil and Jon Smith arranged the deal and were set to tie it up before the transfer deadline. Phil Smith maintains that the night before the deadline, he and Beauchamp were due to go to West Ham for a visit when, out of the blue, Beauchamp phoned him and said he was a bit busy and could not go. The deal had to be done by the evening of the transfer deadline, which happened to be a Thursday. Beauchamp asked Smith if the deal could be done on the Friday instead because West Ham was a bit far away from Oxford and his girlfriend wanted to see him.

Smith could not believe what Beauchamp had said but managed to keep the deal bubbling away throughout the summer. A couple of months later, Smith got a telephone call from West Ham's manager, Billy Bonds. He told Bonds that Swindon Town were very keen on Beauchamp and Bonds agreed to match their offer.

Despite his insistence that he wanted to stay close to home, Smith and Beauchamp agreed a transfer to West Ham. Beauchamp, his father, Phil and Jon Smith, Billy Bonds, Harry Redknapp and Ronnie Boyce met up in a hotel at Heathrow to finalise the deal. Everything was agreed and it was decided that Beauchamp would attend a full medical examination at Upton Park at one o'clock the following day.

Everything passed off without a hitch until around half past three in the afternoon when Smith says Beauchamp phoned him and said, 'I've signed but I'd rather be at Swindon because it's a lot nearer to home.' Smith could not believe it and said, 'Don't be silly, it's your big chance; you're now in the Premiere League.' It did not seem to cut much ice with Beauchamp who hardly entered into life at his new club with enthusiasm.

Following a fee payment of £1 million, West Ham were less than happy that Beauchamp turned up 40 minutes late to his first training session, complaining that the one and a half hour drive was too long. His willingness to go on a pre-season tour of Scotland was non-existent – it was too far away. He did not want to go but, if he had to, he wanted to go home every night.

Beauchamp was disinterested to say the least and, according to Smith, spent most of his short stay with the Hammers walking around like a zombie. News of his lack of commitment to the club slowly but surely leaked out to the fans and the last straw came at a pre-season friendly against Southend when West Ham fans tried to beat him up. The writing was on the wall; West Ham asked Phil Smith to look for a buyer and, with the help of the Professional Footballers Association, a move to Swindon was facilitated.

Even that transfer did not go smoothly. John Gorman, Swindon's manager at the time, offered Beauchamp a good deal and was stunned by the player's hesitation in signing. Gorman let Beauchamp sit outside his office for a couple of hours to ponder the move and then popped his head round the door and told Beauchamp to take it or leave it. He took it, although not for long as he then went back to Oxford United following a transfer that must have had his girlfriend hanging out the bunting.

True, a football agent's lot is not always a happy one.

11 On Tour

THE FOOTBALL TOUR. More often than not it resembles a week at Butlin's rather than a serious pre-season kick around or a semi-serious end of season wind down. Today, tours are big business and if the money's right the tour will happen. Teams are ambassadors for their country and, more importantly, for the leagues they play in.

Not so long ago, the money aspect was not the be all and end all for most clubs although the prospect of earning a few bob was always a good incentive. The financial arrangements for tours have been known to have been abused. In the 1970s, a well-known English club went on a short tour of the Far East which included Singapore. The players were only on expenses, with the younger members of the squad having to exist on about £5 a day.

The older players found themselves subsidising the younger ones with cash loans. One day the manager took three senior players to a head tennis tournament, and it wasn't just a social visit. To the amazement of the watching players, the manager was handed £5,000 by one of the tournament organisers; he was being paid an appearance fee and seemed quite happy to pocket all the money. The senior players were furious and a huge row followed. Eventually they gained an agreement from the manager that each player would receive £100 – the price for keeping quiet – and the balance was kept by the manager.

A current Liverpool player (name withheld to avoid embarrassment) has also experienced financial problems while travelling with his teammates. Whilst checking out of a hotel, he whipped out a huge wad of notes, prompting one of his teammates to ask if he had a credit card. 'No,' came the reply, 'I've never understood how they work.' 'I'll get you an application form', said his teammate. Sometime later, the player was filling out the form on the team coach and was looking puzzled. 'What's wrong?' asked the teammate. 'What do I put for "Company"?' said the player. 'Liverpool FC', came the reply. Not long afterwards, the player was looking puzzled again: 'I don't know what to put in for "Position".' 'They're playing me at the back but I prefer the wing,' came the reply.

One of the great things about being a footballer is going on tour: it's a perk-laden paradise. Usually, they provide the following twelve months with endless mickey-taking and laughs. Leicester City's tour to Barbados in the 1970s brings back particular happy memories for Frank Worthington.

Leicester were playing in a triangular tournament with Bobby Robson's Ipswich Town and the Barbadian national side. Ahead of the trip, the players were asked if they would like to be accompanied by their wives – the silence was deafening. Both British teams were staying at the Paradise Beach Club.

Worthington and his teammates quickly discovered that the top club to be seen in on the island was Alexander's and it didn't take long for Frank to work his magic. He met a Canadian air hostess and they decided to go somewhere a little more private for some fun. They jumped into a taxi and, before he could say 'Filbert Street', the girl was getting to work on his zip. Worthington was even more taken aback when her head found its way into his lap – all in full view of the taxi driver who was straining his neck to gaze at the unfolding events in the rear-view mirror. When they arrived at their hotel the taxi driver's smirk said it all and Worthington still wonders to this day how they ever managed to arrive in one piece.

On the same tour, Worthington spotted a girl who took his fancy whilst lining up for the national anthems before a game. He told a friend to tell the girl that, if she fancied a drink after the game, he would meet her at Alexander's. Sure enough, she turned up and, to Worthington's surprise, turned out to be the reigning Miss Barbados, Lindy Field. The next ten days were spent horse riding, wining and dining, attending society parties and making love along the way. Things got so hot in the days leading up to his departure that he had to tell her that he couldn't see her any more. After all, Worthington was still a married man although his Swedish wife had moved back to Sweden following a rocky patch in the marriage.

By a curious twist of fate, Ipswich were at home to Leicester in the opening game for the 1973/74 season and, after the tour to Barbados, the Ipswich boys were nervous that the news of their antics would leak out. Allan Hunter had a word with Worthington before kick-off, pleading with him to see to it that the Leicester players wouldn't say anything in front of the wives and girlfriends in the players' lounge after the match. Sure enough, one of Leicester's jokers walked straight into the lounge with a huge grin on his face and said, 'Greeeeeaaat trip' – the blood visibly drained from the Ipswich players' faces.

On a trip to Kuwait, again with Leicester, Worthington got chatting to a beautiful Eurasian girl by the hotel pool and arranged to meet her the following day for sex. One of his teammates could hardly contain himself when Worthington told him he'd pulled and asked if he could hide in the wardrobe whilst Worthington was entertaining the girl. Worthington agreed to the request and remembers that the player must have spilt some Bacardi or something because, when he climbed out of the wardrobe after the girl had gone, there was a big wet patch down the front of his trousers. The mystery player was beside himself and described his time in the wardrobe as the best hour he'd ever spent anywhere.

Boozing and high jinks are an integral part of touring, whether it be abroad or up and down the M1 for away fixtures. In 1995, the entire West Ham squad trashed a Bournemouth hotel room and urinated over seats on the team coach during an away trip. According to the hotel, food and drink were thrown, glasses smashed and bedspreads ruined. West Ham's fullback Kenny Brown confirmed the incident: 'There was a bit

of mess but we borrowed a Hoover and cleaned everything up.'
However, the cleaning up can't have been very thorough as
West Ham received a £1,000 bill from the hotel.

Coach journeys provide plenty of anecdotes worthy of going
down in football folklore. One Premiership footballer had a
very interesting introduction to life on a team coach. He was
sitting towards the back of the coach when he heard a series of
moans and groans coming out of the audio system. He thought
that somebody had put on a porn movie but then realised that
the coach did not have a video on board. His teammates were
laughing as they had experienced this type of ritual before: the
well-known manager of the team in question had put a tape
recorder under his bed whilst he was copulating with a woman
he had met in the team hotel and he was playing it back for the
rest of the team to listen to. The manager concerned, a happily
married man, is unlikely ever to admit to the story.

Even coach drivers get in on the act. One of the most famous
football coach drivers in Britain admits to being caught copulating with a woman on the team coach. His cover was blown
when the entire Spurs team lined up alongside the coach and
sang, 'We know what you're doing . . .'

Card schools are universally popular amongst players and, at
some of the top clubs, thousands of pounds have been known
to change hands on away trips. One player tells of an instance
on a coach involving one of the major European footballing
nations: one of the players was caught interfering with the pack
of cards and was immediately thrown off the coach, never to be
picked for the national side again.

A northeastern English club had their coach stopped by the
police on the A1 because they were concerned that other drivers
might be distracted by the antics of the film stars that were
clearly visible through the coach windows – the team were
watching a very graphic porn movie at the time.

Terry Venables had a very hairy time on one away trip with
Barcelona. They had been playing against their great rivals Real
Madrid and, as the players boarded the coach, a mob of Madrid
fans were howling at them from just beyond the stadium gates.

It reminded Venables of the night the Chelsea coach had been pelted with rocks after they had beaten Roma. He told the Barcelona players to pull down the window blinds and crouch on the floor. As the coach sped through the gates, all the windows were smashed by a hail of missiles.

Few clubs can hold a candle to Wimbledon for pranks and, not surprisingly, the club's coach driver hasn't escaped the crazy-gang jesters. The Dons players take perverse pleasure in deliberately guiding their driver into hotel walls as he reverses into parking spaces.

Teammates don't escape either, with one notable exception – Mick Harford. Even Vinnie Jones refused to wind up Harford because of his fearsome reputation. John Fashanu wasn't so lucky. On a club trip to Germany, the Dons were staying at an army camp in Krefeld when an announcement came over the tannoy system saying, 'In the event of the nuclear warning alarm sound, please put on the gas mask provided and leave the building immediately.' All the players were in on the joke apart from Fashanu, who was unaware that his colleagues had arranged for the warning to sound at five o'clock in the morning. Sure enough, the nuclear warning sounded bang on time and Fashanu dived out of bed, put his gas mask on and ran out of his room. All the Wimbledon players got up and looked out of the window to see Fashanu running hell for leather into the distance.

Eric Young had an annoying habit of always using the same bag to travel with; wherever Young went, so did his old Brighton and Hove Albion FA Cup Final kit bag. One day, whilst on a trip, the rest of the Wimbledon players decided to perform a ritual burning of the bag in the dressing room. Eric was not happy.

Wimbledon's MD Sam Hammam openly condones his players' behaviour and it's not uncommon for him to join in the fun. Allegedly, one of his contributions to the crazy-gang's legacy of lunacy was to scrawl obscenities on the dressing room wall at West Ham.

Wally Downes was the Don's court jester and, during a

tournament in France, decided to demonstrate his athletic prowess in a bar. He was hanging from some giant oak beams by his arms when he decided to swing his legs up and hang by his feet instead. He was smoking a big fat cigar and, after about ten seconds, lost his grip and landed flat on his face. When he stood up, the cigar was squashed all over his face in a scene reminiscent of a *Tom and Jerry* cartoon.

The great Liverpool side of the late 1970s to mid 80s had their fair share of scrapes abroad and Ray Kennedy and Jimmy Case were, more often than not, involved. During the 1978/79 season, Liverpool had a difficult away leg in the European Cup against Dynamo Tiblisi. The Reds had scraped a 2-1 win at Anfield but were completely outclassed in Tiblisi, losing 3-0. At an official post-match reception, the Liverpool team had to face the cynics of the British press but managed to find some time to enjoy the sour champagne and caviar with their Soviet hosts. Davie Johnson, who'd never tasted the Caspian Sea delicacy, said to Jimmy Case, 'stay clear of that black jam, it tastes of fish'.

Jimmy Case was less than impressed with the press contingent and marched over to their table, red with rage. He walked around the table pointing at each journalist individually saying, 'I don't like you, I don't like you, you're OK, I don't like you, I don't like you . . .' Ray Kennedy punched Case on the chin, warning him that his behaviour was getting out of order. Case apologised and bought the press pack a round of drinks. However, it wasn't long before Case started mouthing off again so, this time, Kennedy hit him solidly in the solar plexus and then carried him, over his shoulder, up to his room. Kennedy had effectively saved Case from being front as well as back page news.

Kennedy and Case were practical jokers as well: on a trip to Ipswich, they climbed through a hotel window and overturned the beds of Phil Neal and Ray Clemence who, because they had their own room keys with them, couldn't work out how it had happened.

According to Kennedy, group sex sessions were not uncommon on tours. Kennedy was involved in one such session in Amsterdam whilst on a trip following an FA Cup Final victory. Kennedy and two other players were in the middle of the romp when one of the players turned to Kennedy and said, 'If only the Queen could see you now . . .!'

The Brits-abroad spirit certainly isn't just confined to club football, as Frank Worthington can testify. On tour with England in Bulgaria, Worthington took a shine to a slim, supple New York dancer who was a guest of the Bulgarian State Ballet. The girl was staying at the same hotel as the England team but was closely chaperoned by a Bulgarian woman. The challenge for Worthington was to get rid of the chaperone, so he hatched a cunning plan with the help of some of the players. He would go up to the dancer's room and be quickly followed by his teammates who would find an excuse to spirit the chaperone away. According to the plan, this would leave Worthington and the dancer free to practise what Worthington called 'our own version of the Nutcracker'.

He went upstairs and knocked on the door; it was answered by the chaperone, who invited him in. Worthington sensed something wasn't quite right. He wasn't wrong. She explained that Ivana, the dancer, had already flown to Paris for another performance. Worthington was gutted, not least because he'd spent two days planning and plotting his conquest. All was not lost, however. As Worthington got chatting to the chaperone, she made it plain that she would succumb to his charms without much resistance. Worthington popped into the bathroom to freshen up and was just wrapping a towel around himself when he heard a commotion outside the room. It was the rest of the England players who grabbed the chaperone and dragged her down the hotel corridor. They turned to give Worthington the thumbs up, not realising that they'd just ruined his evening's entertainment.

On the pitch, the highlight of England's South American tour in 1984 was John Barnes' wonder goal against the Brazilians in the Maracana stadium. It was, without doubt, the greatest individual solo goal ever scored by an England player abroad and worthy of the post-match celebrations. The England lads were invited to a barbecue by their Brazilian hosts and some of the players were particularly taken by some of the young ladies present.

A little later, back at the team hotel, the hotel manager became upset at a commotion in one of the players' bedrooms and demanded to be let in to put a stop to it. FA official Ted Croker, was called to the bedroom where he discovered three players (names withheld to protect their embarrassment) in bed with one of the nice girls from the barbecue. The players, terrified that they would be sent home in disgrace, were summoned by manager Bobby Robson the following morning. Senior player Ray Wilkins agreed to plead their case although, in truth, he didn't have much to do – Robson was only interested in hearing a blow-by-blow account of the previous night's 'entertainment'.

Scotland's Italia 90 campaign got off to a disastrous start with a humiliating defeat by World Cup minions Costa Rica. Aberdeen's Jim Bett, held responsible by most Scottish fans for the debacle, found himself in further trouble after a night out with Mo Johnston. The *Sun* reported that Bett and Johnston turned up at a local restaurant with two Scottish girls but left in the arms of a couple of Italian girls. The inference was that both players may have had sex with the girls but had tended to concentrate more on their alcohol consumption.

Scottish manager Andy Roxburgh, who had devised a strict code of conduct concerning alcohol, ended up defending both players at a press conference. He said that no breach of discipline had taken place and that both Bett and Johnston had been given permission to have a drink. Press speculation claimed that Scottish captain Ray Aitken had been despatched to collect the two players from the restaurant in a taxi. Roxburgh assured the press that this was untrue and the players had returned to the team hotel under their own steam. Moreover, no curfew had been broken. Mo Johnston threatened legal action against the *Sun* but never followed it up.

Johnston was back in the limelight just a few weeks later

when he was sent home from Glasgow Rangers' Italian training camp in Tuscany by his manager, Graeme Souness. Johnston arrived in Glasgow sporting a gashed forehead, a grazed right eye and marks on his nose and lips and, when asked by reporters what had happened he said, 'Ask the manager, ask the manager.' Johnston had had a furious row with Souness following what witnesses described as an incident in the hotel bar. Johnston, allegedly, was injured in a fall after consuming copious amounts of alcohol. A member of the hotel staff told the *Daily Record*: 'this player who was injured had a great deal to drink'.

Gary Stevens, the former England International, enjoyed an illustrious career with Portsmouth, Tottenham and Brighton before he was injured out of the game in his late twenties. He recalls a club trip to Majorca during his time at Brighton: 'I was seventeen. I'd never been on an end of season tour so I didn't really know what to expect. We arrived at the hotel and Alan Muller said: "Right, I want you to go up to your rooms, get your swimming gear on and get back down by the pool in thirty minutes." I thought we were on to have a big meeting about what we could and couldn't do. But when I got back down to the pool, Alan had pushed a load of tables together and every one was absolutely crammed with St Miguel. He said: "Right, there's a drink to get you started. Here's your spending money, and I'll see you here, with your suitcases, at half past eight in seven days' time." I couldn't believe it. We had quite a good time, I think, but, to be honest, I don't really remember.'

The Albanians perhaps take the biscuit for the most amusing and, by the same token, most embarrassing football tour faux pas. In 1989, the Albanians zoomed in from Tirana for a World Cup qualifying game against England at Wembley which, predictably, they lost. Their flight home was from Heathrow and the Albanians were obviously impressed by London and all it had to offer. Coming from a country that was one of the last bastions of communism, their eyes must have lit up like kids' in a candy store when they saw, first hand, Western life and materialism in full swing. Before their flight, they decided to check out the duty free shop and several players were soon apprehended by police after stocking up with just about everything they could lay their hands on. None of the goods had been paid for as the Albanians had interpreted the word 'free' and taken its meaning literally. They were all let off without charge and sent on their way.

12 Drunk and Disorderly

OREIGN PLAYERS AND coaches are at a loss to comprehend how British players can call themselves professional athletes, considering how much booze they drink. To an extent, they have a point; but they will never understand the culture of this country which puts drinking and pubs as an essential ingredient of our social fabric. A trip on holiday abroad only serves to underline the point; sure, foreigners have nice drinks, but there's a distinct lack of ambient places to consume them in. Drinking is all part of the camaraderie of being a British footballer.

The Italians munch their pasta and drink wine, the Greeks glug Ouzo and stuff themselves with Feta cheese and the Germans devour sausages washed down with a stein or two of beer. For the Brits, it's a case of forget the food, eating takes up valuable drinking time.

Of course, not all players enjoy drinking to excess, but most join in to a point.

After England's World Cup semifinal defeat against Germany in Italia 90, the England players boarded the team coach armed with beer and began singing. The German team, who had booked their place in another World Cup Final, emerged from the stadium looking morose and couldn't believe what was going on in the England coach. They must have wondered what the celebrations would have been like if England had won.

That incident sums up what it's like to be a British footballer. Some have far exceeded the generally accepted standards of behaviour when consuming alcohol – some foreigners have too

– and it's these characters who provide the bulk of the following stories. From the hilarious to the sad, there's a veritable skinfull.

Charles Nicholas summed up the psyche of the British player in 1984 when he said: 'On a boys' night out after the game, the most I'll have is seven or eight pints of lager. That, to me, isn't being drunk.' Stoke City's John Ritchie was horrified at the prospect of Sunday football interfering with his social life, saying, 'Of course I'm against Sunday football. It will ruin my Saturday nights!'

Drink is ingrained in the British game.

In the 1950 FA Cup Final, Denis Compton, playing the last match of his career, inspired Arsenal to a 2-0 win over Liverpool. At half time he had a double brandy to revive him and duly set up the Londoners' second goal. Arsenal's great manager Herbert Chapman used booze to sign David Jack from Bolton for a world record fee of £11,500 when Bolton's original valuation had been £13,000. When Chapman arrived at the hotel to negotiate, he instructed the waiter to serve him gin and tonic without the gin, his assistant whisky and ginger without the whisky – and the Bolton men double measures of everything. Chapman got his man cheap – and the Bolton boys got absolutely pissed.

'Hair of the dog' rarely works, as Nottingham Forest discovered in 1909. Forest needed to beat their neighbours Leicester to avoid relegation and managed to do it by twelve goals to nil. An inquiry was set up to investigate such an unusual result and soon made a startling discovery – the day before, the Leicester players had all got very drunk at the wedding of a teammate.

The Russians have also had a reputation for an unhealthy appetite for alcohol. In 1963, three Torpedo Moscow players (Sawuschkin, Koslov and Madjakan) were suspended for life for being drunk and assaulting a young girl. Russian International Velentin Denisov was ordered to get treatment for his alcoholism in 1965 after being suspended for life. In November 1974, another Russian International, Anatoly Baidachny, was suspended for life after turning up for training with Moscow

Dynamo whilst under the influence. He was only 21 and had been one of the club's top goalscorers.

In 1973, seven Barcelona players captured all the end-of-season headlines after holding a champagne party in their hotel rooms. It all happened in the Hotel Colon in Seville, following a Spanish Cup quarterfinal which Barcelona sensationally lost 3-1.

The seven players (Marcial, Rexach, Juan Carlos, Perez, Sandurni, Reina and Marti Filosia) went to their rooms after dinner and, a little later, got together and ordered a bottle of champagne. One thing led to another and they phoned the bar asking for a second bottle of champagne to be sent up. When the waiter took the order up to the room, he was followed by Barcelona's manager, Rinus Michels, who took the tray from the waiter and knocked on the door. 'Come in waiter and serve the champagne . . . bring on the dancing girls!' shouted a voice behind the door. Michels walked in, cleared the table of empties and said to the astonished players, 'Your champagne is served gentlemen . . . I'm sorry there are no dancing girls.' Then he left.

A few days later, the eleven players who lost the quarterfinal were fined 50,000 pesetas each (about £350) for losing the match and the seven who attended the party were fined double. Two players, Reina and Marcial, were put on the transfer list.

The World Cup is not without it's boozy tales – the Holland players got drunk and swam naked in their hotel pool after beating East Germany in the 1974 World Cup.

During the 1978 World Cup in Argentina, Polish coach Jacek Gmoch said he didn't mind his players drinking and smoking 'in moderation'. The Polish delegation ordered 380 bottles of Vodka to be laid on at their headquarters in time for the start of the second phase. No wonder they were knocked out.

Tales of drink and debauchery in Scottish football are as common as sightings of the Loch Ness monster. English players are angels in comparison with their Scottish counterparts. To detail every Scottish incident would easily fill the pages of a decent sized paperback and, therefore, for the purposes of *Football Babylon*, some notable edited highlights should suffice.

In 1975, Scotland's senior squad travelled to Copenhagen for a match with Denmark. The Scots won by a solitary goal scored by Aberdeen striker Joey Harper. In their infinite wisdom, the Scottish Football Association decided to send their U23 side to Denmark as well and they also secured a victory over their hosts. The two wins were a perfect excuse for the players to let their hair down and enjoy a night on the town.

Billy Bremner led his troops on a night rarely equalled by international footballers. The drinking started in the downstairs bar of Copenhagen's Marina Hotel and then moved on to a club called Bonapartes. Bremner was accompanied by Joe Harper and three members of the U23 squad – Pat McCluskey, Willie Young and Arthur Graham. The police were called to Bonapartes following complaints of very rowdy behaviour. All five players were seriously drunk and if Bent Dorf, the barman, had instituted a swear box he could have instantly retired. Dorf attempted to reason with the players, who responded by threatening him with a good kicking. An eye witness reported that McCluskey attempted to hit a policeman but was restrained before being marched out of the club and thrown over the bonnet of a police car. McCluskey then threatened the police with one of his shoes. Eventually, the situation was brought under control and the police sent the players on their way with a warning.

Back at the Marina Hotel, more trouble followed when barmaid Anne Simonsen was on the receiving end of a double Bacardi and Coke thrown by Bremner. Simonsen claimed that Bremner had spoken to her earlier in the evening but she had ignored him and she wondered whether that had prompted the drenching. The hotel's assistant manager, Lars Borch, said he was trying to calm the rowdy players down when he heard a chant of '1-2-3' and saw Bremner throwing a drink over the barmaid. Miss Simonsen complained to the management and insisted that they call the police. Of course, official police involvement meant that any chance of keeping the incident hushed up had now gone out of the window.

At an SFA hearing on 9 September 1975, all five players were found guilty of bringing the game into serious disrepute and were told that they would never play for their country again. If the night's events are seen as an evening dinner then the dessert was the ransacking of SFA council member Jock McDonald's room in the hotel on the same night.

Bremner's playing career was abruptly brought to an end following a series of accusations of bribery in the *Sunday People* newspaper. The accusations appalled Bremner and badly affected his family life. The bribery scandal centred around comments made by two former Wolves players, Danny Hegan and Frankie Munro. Both told the *Sunday People* that Bremner had offered them money before, and during, a crucial league match between Leeds and Wolves at the end of the 1971/72 season. Hegan claimed he was offered £1,000 and swore, on oath, that he heard Bremner say, 'give us a penalty and I'll give you a grand'. Munro said he was offered £5,000.

Bremner sued the *People*'s owners, and Danny Hegan, for libel but still had to run the gauntlet of fans in his final few league games who took to screaming insults like 'fixer', 'cheat' and 'bribing bastard'. Many people started to doubt Bremner's honesty and integrity, which is why he took legal action in an attempt to clear his good name. He won his case and was awarded £100,000 damages; the evidence painted Hegan and Munro in a very sleazy light.

The case led to an early end for Bremner's playing career but, almost inevitably, he returned to Leeds United as manager a few years later. He was sacked after a series of bad results.

Jimmy Johnstone was a tiny, shaven headed winger who played in Celtic's 1967 European Cup winning side. He also played for Scotland and enjoyed a drink or ten. Probably his most famous drinking exploit happened after an all-night bender with some of his international teammates in the Ayrshire town of Largs. On the stagger back to the team hotel, Johnstone decided that he'd like to try his hand at rowing after spotting a couple of boats. In he jumped and, getting a gentle push-off from teammate Sandy Jardine, he was on his way and drifting towards Ireland. Johnstone entertained himself, and the watching players, with a rendition of Rod Stewart's 'Sailing' before losing one of the oars over the side.

It soon became apparent that Johnstone was not in control of his vessel and needed some help. A major rescue operation was launched and two local maritime experts were maydayed to help get the winger back to shore. 'I was only fishing', said Johnstone to his rescuers. Dennis Law insensitively offered Johnstone a glass of hot whisky when he came ashore – as if he hadn't had enough already.

Brian Clough was always a manager who was as revered as he was disliked for his unorthodox managerial style. On the eve of the 1979 League Cup Final against Southampton, Clough called a meeting of the Forest players at 10 p.m. The players thought it was a bit strange because meetings were not usually held before a game. When they were all gathered together, in walked four waiters carrying a dozen bottles of champagne and Clough announced, 'Come on lads, let's get tucked in.'

John O'Hare had a strange look on his face and Clough asked, 'What's the matter with you?' O'Hare said, 'I'm a pint man, Boss.' So Clough told one of the waiters to come back with fifteen pints of bitter, which he duly did. He then announced to the ensemble that no one was to leave until it was all gone. Archie Gemmill was less than happy – he liked to be in bed around nine o'clock and the drinking session raged until about two o'clock in the morning. Tony Woodcock had to be carried up to his room.

There was obviously method in Brian Clough's madness – Forest won the final 3-2 despite being a goal down at half time.

French international Patrice Loko went completely off the rails in 1995. He went wild in the early hours of a Parisian morning and was arrested for drunkenness after he was seen yelling at passing cars. When the police officers approached Loko he exposed himself to a female police inspector and, just to be on the safe side, they carted him off to a local hospital. Doctors decided there was nothing clinically wrong with him and he was discharged. Almost as soon as he left the hospital he fell ill again and the police officers took him to another hospital where Loko managed to feel well enough to assault some members of staff. Needless to say, he was charged by the police.

Wimbledon Football Club's finest hour came on 14 May 1988; it was the day the club lost its virginity according to their managing director, Sam Hammam. Bobby Gould's crazy gang won the FA Cup that day, beating Liverpool 1-0 in a final that the critics predicted would be so one-sided that Wimbledon were just there to make up the numbers.

The events of the night before go some way to helping us understand the way the club was run. On the eve of the final, the players went off for a few nerve-settling drinks at the Fox and Grapes pub on Wimbledon Common. Alan Cork claims that Bobby Gould gave him £40 to get a round of drinks in, although Gould maintains he gave Cork £200. The drinks were flowing; even the bar staff bought them a round for good luck.

Laurie Sanchez, who scored the final's only goal, claims that most of the players were in their beds by closing time although Alan Cork insists that there was a lock-in until 2 a.m. It's quite possible there was a lock-in, but only for Cork. That would explain Bobby Gould's missing £160 and support Cork's claims that he was seriously hung-over on the morning of the final. Old TV footage shows Alan Cork as the only player wearing sunglasses: well, a beer or two helps you relax, doesn't it?

Andy Thorn was a young apprentice at Wimbledon back in the 1980s and actually played in the 1988 FA Cup Final before an unsuccessful move to Newcastle United. He recalls one practical joke that was played on him by the other Wimbledon lads: 'I was an apprentice and the first team had beaten Orient 6-2 away. I went with them for the experience and it was certainly that. On the way home, the minibus stopped at an off-licence somewhere in Leyton and the players had a whipround. They got about £50 together and told me to go and get as much lager as I could carry. So I got these two cases and carried them back to the minibus. But just as I was loading it on, Wally shoves me out, slams the doors and the fuckers drive off. It took me two hours to get home, the bastards. I had to phone my mum.'

High jinks perhaps, but Wimbledon's capacity for more serious trouble shouldn't be underestimated.

The Dons were banned from a posh tennis club in September 1994 following a 'drunken spree'. A spokesman for the £900-a-year David Lloyd Tennis Club in Raynes Park, South West London, said: 'The players shouted at women walking to and from the gymnasium in leotards, saying things like, "I'd give her one", and "Come over here and we'll show you a good time." '

Present in the club were a group of 25 Wimbledon players and officials on what was supposed to be a day of relaxation. A staff member said: 'They were all in suits after a day at the races, but they were drunk before they got here. They were all swearing and cursing for three hours – there were no exceptions. They weren't actually trying to pull girls, though, they were all too busy drinking.'

Wimbledon's chief executive at the time, John Barnard, was pretty laid-back about the incident, saying,' 'We're attempting to find out which players were there. But it's not like a murder inquiry or anything.'

The previous year, Wimbledon had been banned from a Sheffield hotel after shouting obscenities, running naked through the corridors and letting off fire extinguishers after a match against Sheffield Wednesday.

On Wednesday 15 February 1995, Wimbledon's Vinnie Jones bit off part of a journalist's nose in a Dublin bar. The night had been a fateful one: England's international against Ireland at Landsdowne Road had just been abandoned following sickening scenes of mindless violence. Jones was in Jury's Hotel bar, surrounded by admirers, when he got bantering with a few journalists and BBC boys. The champagne was flowing (as an anaesthetic for what had gone before) and the bar chat was full of the question 'why?', as all and sundry searched for reasons behind the evening's shocking events.

Suddenly, Jones decided that his teeth needed some exercise and wandered over to *Daily Mirror* reporter Ted Oliver. He caressed the back of his head, and then bit off part of his nose.

Oliver stood up, confronted Jones and then concentrated on dabbing the blood away from his gaping wound. Vinnie Jones apologised within seconds and continued to do so for the rest of the night. The more Jones tried to apologise, the more Oliver stiffened.

A photographer was called out of bed to get a picture of Oliver's freshly-bitten nose and the front page of the following morning's *Daily Mirror* was complete. Jones eventually went to bed at 3 a.m. after even more apologies, but the damage was done. Jones apologised yet again the following Sunday through his *News of the World* column but still lost his job with the paper and was dropped by his manager, Joe Kinnear. Jones said afterwards: 'People ask, how can we expect the fans to behave when players are behaving like this? To be honest, I don't have the answer.'

Wimbledon's Mick Harford is one of the few new additions to the Dons who didn't undergo their traditional initiation ceremony – having his clothes sliced up and being dumped naked in a public place. Harford escaped the ritual as his reputation as something of a hard man goes before him; his glare is almost legendary. He was a member of the infamous Birmingham City side managed by Ron Saunders who played, drank and fought together. Players often used to turn up at training fresh from a night in the cells.

Tony Coton and Mick Harford were part of football's original crazy gang at Birmingham and first met in 1980. In 1987, Coton and Harford went for a drink in a pub in Hemel Hempstead. The pub had a long bar, an L-shaped room where the toilets were round a corner. Coton recalls the start of the trouble: 'I left the rest of our group to go to the toilet but, when I came out, some roadworkers started giving me the verbals.'

One of the roadworkers said to Coton, 'Are you that cunt that plays for Watford?' Coton confirmed that he did play for Watford but added that he was not a cunt. The roadworker responded, saying that his mate said that he was a cunt. Coton then turned to the second roadworker and said, 'Is that right mate? Did you call me a cunt?' The second roadworker said, quite candidly, 'Yes.'

Coton head-butted him and, before he knew it, three or four roadworkers jumped on him and it all started to get a bit nasty. Suddenly, Mick Harford flew through the air, just like he was going for a diving header. Harford head-butted one of the men and decked another three before they realised what was going on.

At the end of the fight, five or six roadworkers were laid out and two needed hospital treatment. The story made the *Sun* newspaper which printed pictures of the two injured road-workers alongside the headline, 'Soccer Stars in Fight Horror'. One roadworker was quoted in the article as saying: 'It was like walking into a war. There were fists going in everywhere.' He went on to say that it had been the drink talking, and the police dropped the charges.

The real conclusion to the story happened in the pub. Tony Coton takes up the story: 'While we were walking back to the bar, the landlord leant over and hit Mick on the back of the head with a big cosh. It sounded just like a drum being beaten. Blood started coming out of the back of his head but his knees did not buckle. He just put his hand behind his head, felt the blood trickling down, turned round and asked me to take him to hospital (where he got six stitches). He then turned back to face the bar and told the landlord that, when he came back, he'd be in a fair amount of trouble. You should have seen the look on the landlord's face.' He had just been on the receiving end of the Mick Harford glare.

George Best explains his love of alcohol quite simply: when he finished playing, he had a void that needed filling. Best compared the high he got from playing football in front of 50,000 or 60,000 fans to an orgasm and, when that feeling was gone, he had to replace it. Whilst he was playing, he drank: when he finished with the game, he deliberately tried to drink himself to oblivion. When he lived in America, he once went 26 days without food; he tried to nibble peanuts and crisps but he couldn't keep them down.

Best started drinking whilst on a youth trip with Manchester United. He had three pints in a Zurich nightclub and felt dreadful. He and his teammates had to face the problem of getting back to their hotel rooms without being seen by Sir Matt Busby and his assistant Jimmy Murphy, who used to sit in a cafe across the road counting the players back in. Best and a teammate took a taxi and spent the entire journey with his 'spinning head' stuck out of the window.

When they arrived at the hotel, the other players grabbed the sozzled pair and frog-marched them inside. Contrary to popular belief, Sir Matt Busby and Jimmy Murphy had seen the whole carry-on but refrained from saying too much the next day – Best said that he didn't need any lectures because his first experience of alcohol had put him off the idea of drinking for quite some time.

However, before too long, Best had started drinking socially and regularly, enjoying all the trappings of superstardom. He enjoyed a bevy of beautiful women and travelled the world. One regular summer haunt was Majorca, where he would often go with about 40 friends. Susan George joined him sometimes – most of those present were nothing to do with football.

On one occasion, when he was living in America, he stole money from his wife, Angie, and a total stranger – just to buy a drink.

On another occasion, whilst on a First Class flight to Australia, he fell down in an aisle and sent the drinks trolley crashing into the Economy section – he told the stewardess that he tripped.

George Best's battle with the booze is ongoing but the first time he openly tried to tackle the problem was in March 1981 when he admitted himself to an American hospital for an alcohol rehabilitation course.

No sooner had he checked in than the police came to see him. They had received a complaint from a woman who lived across the road from him in San José saying that Best had broken into their house and gone into the daughter's bedroom. There were no specific charges for assault, he was just being charged for entering the premises. On the night concerned, Best had been out with some friends and, by his own admission, he was in a state. He told the police that he would have been totally incapable of doing anything, let alone housebreaking. Nothing further was said.

Within a couple of months of being discharged from full-time rehabilitation, Best was back drinking; only this time, he was trying to hide it. Drunks are great liars and conmen but, on his final day in hospital, one of the part-time counsellors had pulled him to one side and told him, in no uncertain terms, that he might have fooled some of the staff, but not him. Best knew he was right, he knew he was going back on the booze.

Normal drinking sessions were resumed fairly quickly afterwards – to the detriment of his marriage to Angie. He tried special implants designed to help his body reject alcohol and he went to Alcoholics Anonymous, where he was constantly pestered. In the end, he decided he was going to cope with his alcoholism in his own way – if he felt like a drink he'd have one; no abstinence periods and no drinking limits.

On 19 September 1990, Best appeared as a guest on Terry Wogan's BBC Television chat show to promote his book, *The Good, The Bad and The Bubbly*. Best went on a two-hour backstage bender before his appearance, propping up the bar with actor Omar Shariff. Wogan introduced the wayward genius – the artist formerly known as sober – who sauntered onto the set to wild applause. The opening chat was about Best's time in Ford Open Prison in 1984 and the slurred nature of his speech had people reaching for empty video tapes all over the nation. Something special was happening.

Wogan wittered on, nervously listening to Best's opinions on Gazza, the England team and Italia 90, all of which were less than complimentary. Best felt that England's training methods were wrong and pointed out that England had won nothing:

TW: Not everybody has – at the risk of being sycophantic – not everybody has your talent you know . . .

GB: That's correct, yeah . . . (giggles and audience laughs) Correct! (more giggles) No, it's just a shame because I still love the game, I love it, I'll watch it, and they've got no idea what they're doing ... and they keep bringing these managers in who've got no idea what they're talking about ... (shakes head) they're talking a load of ...

TW: Please ... (laughter)

GB: Is this live?

TW: No, 'tis, very ... Well. Almost.

GB: (Touches Wogan's arm) Can I say shit? (shocked laughter)

TW: I don't think so, I don't think so, but tell me about ...

GB: (Grabs Wogan's arm and points at him) He panicked!

TW: I do, yeah. You can see it in my eyes. Tell me about ... now, you were saying it's very tough on Gazza and people like that. In your day, as a footballer, was it easier to express yourself? Was it easier to give reign to your talent?

GB: Yes, it was.

TW: Why was that?

GB: Cos we could play. (bemused laughter)

TW: You don't think players now are any good? That makes you sound very cynical and old, George.

GB: It's not cynical, it's just ... I actually believe, when I played it was nice. It was fun, it was lovely ... and I watched (grins) that show you did with Gazza ... can I say this?

TW: Well, I don't know – what are you going to say? (Audience laughter) Want to whisper it to me first? So it's not as good, it's not that you don't think it's as good? (Best laughs). Yeah, moving right along here, George. Yes, I'm spooling on. Tell me, in the book that you've written, why did you leave Old Trafford?

GB: Tommy Docherty.

TW: Tommy Docherty?

GB: Yeah.

TW: What happened?

GB: I don't like people who tell lies, and he told lies to me.

TW: What did he tell you?

GB: (Pause) I'm Irish.

TW: Get away (audience laughs). But I mean, tell me about . . .

GB: Don't (points) people bullshit . . .?

TW: Yeah.

GB: Is that live?

TW: No, no, we can edit that out in a minute.

GB: People bullshit. I don't like people who bullshit.

TW: Do you still bear a grudge?

GB: Yeah, yeah.

TW: Do you still feel that your career was cut short?

GB: No.

TW: You feel you gave your money's worth?

GB: I don't like bullshitters.

TW: Yeah . . . (Best giggles) fair enough. So tell me, in your book you were saying that, erm, you'd a reputation for knocking round with lots of girls.

GB: Screwing.

TW: Yeah.

GB: Yeah (laughs).

TW: And, erm, to put it delicately. Yes, now, in that case, you were saying that when . . .

GB: (Touches Wogan's knee) He's not sure, is he?

TW: Can you blame me? You were saying that every time any of them want to make any money they write about their years with George Best?

GB: Terry, I like screwing, all right? (Isolated laughter)

TW: All right. So what do you do with your time these days?

GB: Screw.

TW: I see (Best laughs). Ladies and gentleman, George Best! (Not so wild applause.)

Although amusing, the sadness of the situation was there for all to see; alcohol was still a terrible problem for Best. George Best continues to drink but the gaps between benders get longer. He is one of the most intelligent and eloquent speakers on football that you could ever wish to hear and there's not a bad bone in his body. He is currently working for the media and still openly admits that the three things that have dominated his life are football, sex and booze. If he had any say in the matter, booze would be a very distant third. In May 1996 he announced that he was giving up drink for a year.

If the rumours and reports are to be believed, Robin Friday was a player who could have given George Best a run for his money both on and off the pitch. Reading and Cardiff fans remember with great affection the antics of Friday. He was capable of outrageous skill and incredibly thuggish behaviour, more or less at the same time. On the pitch he was sublime but off it, he made a Faustino Asprilla look like Mother Teresa. He was the archetypal 'live fast, die young' merchant who died of uncertain causes in late 1990. You name it, he did it – boozing, brawling, smoking and pill-popping his way through his short life.

Some of his more celebrated off-pitch antics included pissing in a director's lunch box on the team coach and taking a dump in the opposition's bath after being sent off.

Whilst he was at Reading, it was common knowledge that anyone who wanted his autograph could find him on a Saturday lunchtime downing a few pints in the Spreadeagle pub just across the road from Reading's Elm Park ground.

Former Reading skipper Eamonn Dunphy remembers him as probably the best player he ever played with: 'He could have gone to the top if it weren't for his lifestyle. Off the pitch, he was a troubled spirit. He'd pop tablets, smoke joints and get pissed. He was always on the brink of self destruction but he was great fun to be with. He was a good-looking boy, a real ladies' man. He'd disappear for a week and then turn up at the training ground with a plastic bag full of clothes, toss it down on the floor and join in the game. God knows where he'd been.'

Friday left Reading to join Cardiff for a fee of £25,000 but only played 23 times for the club. More often than not he was AWOL and towards the end of his time with Cardiff his behaviour became more and more erratic. Cardiff players tell how they were woken in the middle of the night by a terrible crashing noise. When they went downstairs, they found Robin Friday standing on the snooker table in just his underpants, hurling snooker balls around the room in a very tanked-up manner.

Nothing was ever proved about his alleged dalliance with drugs but, if he did take them, it never seemed to affect his performance on the pitch. Robin Friday quit football for good on 20 December 1977, just in time for the Christmas party season.

Paul Merson was destined for the very top – until he got involved with drink and drugs. However, his rehabilitation continues apace and he just might confound the critics and fully realise his true potential.

Merson is notorious for the cocaine addiction he once suffered from. But the real reason he spent £150 a night on the drug was to complement his usual twelve pints of lager top: 'When I went out, I just had to have the drug. It made me feel so much more confident – I felt I could drink all night without feeling sick . . . I thought, this is great. I could go on drinking all night and be as right as rain the next day.'

Merson's expenditure on cocaine single-handedly rejuvenated the faltering Colombian economy. Merson has written candidly about his three addictions, booze, gambling and cocaine, in his book *Rock Bottom*.

His famous on-pitch celebration, wolfing down imaginary pints of lager, now makes him cringe. When he was drinking and at his worst, he could never just have a couple of beers – he would drink until he was paralytic.

Merson admits he's not the only footballer who likes a drink. In fact, he directly attributes England's lack of international success in recent years to alcohol. His lager binges were near legendary. He never drank ahead of games but he did drink with the fans, which explains his popularity. Merson and the Arsenal set have had more boozy nights than he cares to remember although he wasn't with Tony Adams in 1993 when he fell down the stairs in a Pizza Hut restaurant.

He did indulge in a one-night stand once, whilst completely

out of his brain, and paid the price in tabloid column inches. In the mid-90s, Paul Merson visits Alcoholics and Narcotics Anonymous on a regular basis and his wife, Lorraine, visits support groups for the families of addicts.

Paul Gascoigne is another modern-day star who has had his fair share of drink and trouble. When he was playing for Lazio, he broke his knee after being attacked in Walker's nightclub in Newcastle. Then, he was involved in an unsavoury drunken incident in the Punch and Judy pub in Covent Garden, London. Usually by Gazza's side is his spiritual adviser, Jimmy 'five bellies' Gardner, who managed to ensure Gazza maintained his old Newcastle guzzling form whilst he was in Italy. The journalist Pete Davis still maintains that, during the 1990 World Cup in Italy, Gazza bribed the waiters in the England team hotel to top up his mineral water with white wine.

Gazza's on-the-pitch performances are touched by genius and as long as he continues to deliver, the fans will be happy. However, even the most charitably minded supporter would find it hard to fathom out Gazza's actions the day his son Regan was born: Gazza spent the night of the birth downing lager with his mates, 300 miles away in Newcastle.

Mo Johnston has always been in and out of trouble and he once claimed that rumours about his activities often portrayed him as an alcoholic nymphomaniacal junkie. He was a player who enjoyed a night out and the compulsory few beers that went with it. He was found guilty at Glasgow Sheriff's court in 1987 of assault following an incident in Glasgow's Mardi Gras discotheque.

One of Johnston's Scottish teammates, Frank McAvennie, moved to West Ham United from St Mirren in 1987. When he first moved to London, he enjoyed a quiet life away from football – until his goal-scoring exploits on the pitch turned him into something of a celebrity. Then, McAvennie enjoyed wine and champagne instead of the usual footballer's tipple, beer. He succumbed to temptation and became very much a part of the Stringfellow's scene, enjoying the company of many beautiful women. McAvennie's love of women was obvious and, in the words of one Fleet Street hack, 'his tipple was nipple'.

Even when he moved back to Scotland to play for Celtic he would often incur the wrath of manager Bill McNeil for his constant clubbing trips to London. The tabloids loved him and so did the girls – although his blond hair was not natural. Liam Brady once joked that McAvennie's nickname amongst his teammates was 'ginger pubes' – yes, Frank was a bottle blond.

Perhaps one of the most senseless things ever to be said while under the influence was uttered by Manchester City's youth team coach Neil McNab in 1995 in a Stockport restaurant. McNab called all Mediterranean players 'cheats', adding, 'What do the Spanish and Italians know about football anyway . . . nothing.' Er, a lot more than Manchester City, actually.

Chris Sutton must get the modern-day award for 'most idiotic behaviour on the eve of becoming the most expensive player in Britain'. Sutton had agreed terms with Blackburn Rovers and was due to join them for the then record fee of £5 million. However, he then spent an ignominious night in police cells after an evening which began with a nightclub row, moved on to a damaging tackle on a car and ended with a policeman in a taxi chasing Sutton through the streets of Norwich, with two patrol cars in pursuit.

Sutton had been out enjoying a few drinks with some non-footballing friends and they all started to get abusive in a nightclub when they weren't being served with drinks quickly enough for their liking. Barman Ian Hankinson was serving the group lagers and double whiskies, a potent cocktail for any mortal. The group started banging their glasses and were asked to stop, much to the annoyance of Sutton who started mouthing off about who he was and how much he was worth.

Brian Gunn intervened to calm things down and Sutton apologised to the barman. The group then moved on to another of Sutton's favourite nightspots but, whilst en route, became involved in a row with a motorist who later claimed that Sutton had damaged a windscreen wiper blade and a reflector light. A uniformed policeman arrived to investigate just as Sutton and his friends left in a taxi. The officer promptly followed suit, much to the astonishment of cab driver Steven Smith who was told to 'follow that cab'.

Two patrol cars also joined in the chase, which ended about half a mile down the road with Sutton's arrest. He spent several hours being interviewed at the Bethel Street police station in Norwich. Sutton admitted damaging a car and was released with a caution the following morning. He went straight to Lancashire and signed for Blackburn Rovers.

For a while, Sutton was a magnet for trouble. On his stag night, he left half an hour before the end of the celebrations at a London nightclub. He arrived at a plush Mayfair hotel with a leggy girl who was dressed in stockings and suspenders and a fake fur coat. The couple went upstairs and when his mates got back from his stag party they spent an hour hammering on Sutton's door.

Fuelled by designer beer and champagne, the group became very rowdy, as did Sutton who screamed at them to go away. Hotel guests complained about the noise and the duty manager eventually got Sutton to open the door. The door opened and, as cool as a cucumber, the girl walked out of Sutton's room and into the lift without saying a word. Sutton and his stag night guests finally went to sleep after a warning from the duty manager.

Sutton and his teammate Graeme Le Saux were banned from an exclusive nightclub in March 1995. The police were called following a fracas that saw Le Saux wrestling with a man in the street as Sutton and fellow Blackburn player Stuart Ripley looked on. Trouble began when the three players and five friends were refused entry to Squires Rendezvous in Preston. They pleaded for over an hour to be allowed in so that they could join Le Saux's girlfriend at her birthday party. Le Saux reportedly went berserk and grabbed a man round the throat after a comment about his time at Chelsea.

The police were called but nobody was charged. The club's manageress said that the first she had heard about the trouble was when she was informed that there was £20 million outside causing trouble. 'We decided we did not want them in the club in the mood they were in,' said the manageress.

Paul McGrath is an astonishing player; his vision and

tackling are second to none and his dodgy knees seem to go on forever. It's a wonder he can see at all considering the amount of booze he's put away in his life. He was never one to shirk his drinking responsibilities. It's claimed by his estranged wife Claire that he sometimes drank a bottle of vodka *before* training. His legendary drinking has, allegedly, sometimes led him to miss matches.

McGrath went AWOL before a vital World Cup qualifying tie in Albania and pledged to give up boozing to try to help Ireland in the 1994 World Cup in the United States. Irish teammates confirmed at the time that McGrath was not drinking; in fact, he didn't even go to the bar. One team member said that in all the years he'd known McGrath, he'd never seen him drink a drop of alcohol. This was understandable as McGrath was more of a reclusive drinker. McGrath's wife Claire even attempted to take him to a private drying-out clinic after finding him blind drunk at home. In an article in the *Sunday Mirror*, she claimed that on the journey to the clinic McGrath was trying to get out of the door as the car sped along the motorway.

His drinking bouts extended into family holidays; he allegedly said to Claire on a trip to Disneyland, 'fancy paying all this money to come to a place where you can't even get a beer!' McGrath was fined £8,000 by his club, Aston Villa, for failing to turn up to an FA Cup tie against Exeter City in 1994. Rumours abounded that he went missing because of drinking and matrimonial problems. His manager, Ron Atkinson, was keen to protect the player, saying at the time that 'the matter has been dealt with and it will now stay within the club'.

McGrath offered his own explanation for his disappearance, telling the *Mail*: 'I am sick and tired of the stories. Every time I miss a game people assume the worst. I turned up for training on Friday but my knees were playing me up, really sore and the gaffer decided I should miss the game at Exeter.'

Ron Atkinson kept McGrath at Villa, signing him on a pay-as-you-play contract. The rules were simple – if he went AWOL, he wouldn't get paid.

Personal unhappiness can affect players badly, as Jimmy Greaves will testify. Greaves is a likeable man whose battle with drink involved a lot of heartache and soul searching. His performances on the football field are the stuff of legends and perhaps the only true blemishes on his life are the fact that he saved TVAM (together with Roland Rat) and his time in Milan.

When he played for Tottenham the players' pub was the Bell and Hare, just a stone's throw from White Hart Lane. Greaves and his Spurs colleagues often drank the night away in the pub following home games. It was one of his other clubs, Chelsea, that sold him to Milan.

On the day he was due to fly out to Italy for his debut against Botafogo in 1961, Greaves enjoyed some lobster and champagne at Heathrow airport with *Daily Express* sports columnist Desmond Hackett and photographer Norman Quicke. As the boys were finishing off their second bottle of champagne and considering starting a third, Quicke happened to mention that the plane had left ten minutes ago. In a panic, the three arranged to catch the next plane out and arrived six hours later than scheduled in Milan. Greaves got stuck into champagne cocktails on the flight – to give him some Dutch courage as he had a fear of flying. It was a good job the Milan welcoming committee didn't see him stepping off the plane as he was fairly light headed to say the least. He made his debut the following day and scored in a 2-2 draw.

Greaves's time in Italy was unhappy; he had been separated from his wife Irene who, for a while, stayed in Britain having given birth in July 1961. Greaves also practised a deliberate policy of non-cooperation, which eventually pushed Milan over the edge. The club turfed Greaves and his wife out of their flat to make way for the arrival of a Brazilian player who had been bought as a replacement. They were installed in a very small flat which infuriated Greaves who, at his own expense, booked into a five star hotel with his wife. Staying in the same hotel were the group of British journalists who had followed his adventures at Milan – he was now free of the regimented days of an Italian football club and the serious drinking began.

During previous nights out with the 'Brit pack', Greaves had fed them stories of his antics and bust-ups with Milan and had more or less written his own newspaper copy. They used to have two principle meeting places in the heart of Milan, La Tampa Restaurant and a club called Porta Dora. One night in particular stands out in Greaves's memory – it was the night Ian Wooldridge nearly became Miss Ina Wooldridge.

The conversation, following copious amounts of beer and wine, had got on to the subject of speed and fitness and Wooldridge claimed he was far fitter than any player. At 2 a.m., Greaves invited him to put his legs where his mouth was and, along with five other journalists, they lined up for a 100 metre race in Milan's Piazza. After 50 yards, Greaves was in the lead with Wooldridge only a couple of yards behind. Suddenly, Greaves spotted a spiked chain at about hip height stretched across the Piazza. Wooldridge didn't and sped past Greaves believing the race was his. He was struck by the chain right in the groin and somersaulted to a stop before being picked up and ushered back to the Porta Dora. After a drink he made a full recovery but he came perilously close to becoming the first female sportswriter of the year!

When Greaves moved to West Ham his drink problem was escalating and, unfortunately for him, it was not the club to go to for a drying-out period. West Ham had a drinking school that included Bobby Moore, Brian Dear, Frank Lampard, John Cushley, Jimmy Lindsay, John Charles and Harry Redknapp. Greaves was quickly accepted into the school, not only for his drinking capacity but also for his willingness to pay his own way.

West Ham went to America, to play an exhibition match in New York against Santos. The squad travelled across the Atlantic on a jumbo jet and it wasn't long before Greaves and Bobby Moore started knocking back large quantities of beer in the bar. Manager Ron Greenwood joined them and, unfortunately for him, had his Coca-Cola laced with Bacardi by Bobby Moore's business partner, Freddie Harrison. Over the course of the next hour or so, Greenwood had five or six more 'Cokes'. Finally, Greenwood cottoned on to what was happening and laughed it off. He returned to his seat where he quickly fell into a heavy, drink-induced sleep. Peter Eustace, not one of Greenwood's biggest fans, had the rest of the squad roaring with laughter as he leant over the snoring figure of Greenwood, miming as if he was telling him exactly what he thought of him.

Jimmy Greaves made up his mind to retire from football after an incident in Blackpool that was of great interest to the newspapers. On New Year's night, Greaves and Bobby Moore were having a couple of drinks in the Imperial Hotel where West Ham were staying. The following day, the Hammers were playing an FA Cup tie against the Tangerines. The two players bumped into a BBC cameraman who invited them to the 007 club which was owned by the boxer, Brian London. The cameraman said that the pitch at Bloomfield Road was iced over and the match would not be played the next day. Greaves and Moore hopped into a taxi, and off they went.

Greaves tucked into about twelve lagers and Bobby Moore had about six. They returned to the hotel with their other companions, Clyde Best and Brian Dear, at about 1.45 a.m. The following morning, they slept until ten o'clock, got up and went to Broomfield Road where the ground had been passed as playable. West Ham fans rang the club, and a newspaper, claiming that Greaves and Moore were drunk in Brian London's club on the eve of the match. West Ham fined both players and dropped them which infuriated Greaves who protested openly that they had not been drunk. The story was plastered all over the front pages of the newspapers with the players being portrayed as public enemies numbers one and two.

In his last few months at West Ham, Greaves began to shift more and more alcohol. After training at Chadwell Heath, he would go to the pub opposite Romford Greyhound stadium and drink until closing time. Football didn't matter any more; once Greaves had a few beers in him life seemed more bearable. His really bad problems came well after his retirement in 1977, when a regular pastime was rifling through his own dustbin and drinking the dregs of vodka bottles.

Greaves says that, at the height of his drinking, he was downing twelve pints of Guinness and two bottles of vodka a day. He couldn't get up in the morning until he'd drunk half a bottle of vodka. In many respects, it's a wonder he's still alive. In the mid-90s, Greaves works in the media as a pundit and personality and enjoys a good relationship with his wife Irene, who had left him at the height of his troubles. Since giving up booze some time ago, Jimmy Greaves has not touched a drop.

In May 1996, sixteen Nottingham Forest players, according to the *Sun* newspaper, trashed a holiday coach in an astonishing birds and booze rampage. Under the headline 'Soccer Aces Wreck Coach in Rampage' the players were branded worse than football hooligans after allegedly causing £2,000 worth of damage during a wild, eight hour bar crawl. The players were on an end of season trip to Majorca and paid fifteen pounds a head for the bar crawl in Magaluf. Curtains were ripped from the coach windows, seat-rests were torn from their mountings, ash trays and arm rests were hurled into the aisle and beer cans were thrown at the driver.

Tour rep Andrew Holloway, who was sacked shortly after the fracas, acted as guide to the players, some of whom 'behaved like animals'. It seems that the players grew impatient at the length of the coach journey and, fuelled by alcohol, started playing up. Holloway said: 'Some of the players were off their heads. Girls flocked round them like groupies; there was snogging all over the place. I saw a couple of players sneaking off down alleyways with girls.'

The holiday company sent Nottingham Forest a £2,000 bill for the damage. When approached by the press, manager Frank Clark said: 'This is the first I've heard of it. I was in Majorca with the players and there were no complaints as far as I was aware. We received compliments about the players' behaviour.'

The former England captain, Bryan Robson, states categorically that present-day players consume far less alcohol than when he was playing – and there is no reason to doubt him. Robson's flirtations with alcohol are well documented and some of his antics make the players of the mid-1990s look like choirboys.

Robson had a reputation for working hard and playing hard, and it is ironic that he was the man dousing the fires lit by England's Euro 96 squad on their return from a pre-tournament tour of the Far East. Banned from driving twice for drink-driving offences, Robson's most shameful alcohol-induced incident happened shortly before the England team left for what turned out to be a disastrous campaign in the 1988 European Championship in Germany.

After playing a pre-tournament friendly against Aylesbury, Robson and some England players decided to go for a few drinks in Boulevard's wine bar near the squad's High Wycombe hotel. After a night of revelry, Robson and goalkeeper Peter Shilton went for 'afters' to the nearby Orchards and Country Club. Robson got chatting at the bar to twenty-year-old Anna Csondor and enjoyed several drinks with Shilton and the club manager, Wayne Mitchell.

Robson and Shilton's capacity for drinking prompted Mitchell to comment in a newspaper article that he had never seen anybody put drink away as clinically as the two players. 'They were world class,' said Mitchell.

Allegedly, Robson staggered into the ladies toilets by mistake and confronted Csondor, who was doing her hair. Csondor described the events in a newspaper article. 'I was very shocked because he had a pee in a cubicle. I tried to ignore him but he turned round and exposed himself.

'He said, "What do you think of that then?" I laughed and replied, "Not a lot."

'He was just standing there with his trousers down, showing off. It was obvious he was getting very excited.'

According to Csondor, Peter Shilton also went into the toilet and just gave Robson the kind of look that words are not needed for. Csondor ran out of the toilet, and despite receiving no apology from Robson ended up sharing a taxi home with the two players.

Needless to say, the incident found its way to the tabloid press and when Robson was asked about the events, he said, 'I don't remember anything like that, but if anything did happen it was only a mistake. We had a pretty drunken night.'

For the 1996 European Championship, Bryan Robson was Terry Venables' right-hand man – his exemplary football track record and knowledge considered a vital part of the squad's coaching. Without doubt, he must have had 'boozy European Championship' deja vu after the events on Cathay Pacific Flight CX251. The plane was carrying the England party back to Britain from Hong Kong after a few days in the Far East. Some nine hours after the flight landed at Heathrow, allegations surfaced of £5,000 worth of damage to the Business Class section of the plane where the England players had been sitting. Reports of the incident and the damage caused varied wildly and curiously no photographic evidence was provided. It emerged that two television sets and an overhead baggage locker had been damaged. The newspapers had a field day. One paper ventured to suggest that while celebrating Paul Gascoigne's birthday, several players had attempted to put the diminutive Dennis Wise into one of the section's overhead baggage lockers. It was a claim that turned out to be total nonsense.

England coach Terry Venables, under orders from the Football Association, agreed to a thorough enquiry once the squad had gathered at their Championship HQ in Buckinghamshire. It was perceived by the media that a statement would be made and the guilty individuals would be identified and suitably punished.

FA press spokesman David Davies announced that after a thorough investigation the squad had taken 'collective responsibility' for the events on Flight CX251. In what must have been reminiscent of the classic scene in *Spartacus*, all the England players presumably professed their guilt individually to protect the real culprit or culprits.

It is always possible that Terry Venables never discovered the names of the culprits. The FA chairman, Sir Bert Millichip, hinted as much when he said, 'I understand no one has admitted responsibility.'

If the antics of the England squad amused rather than bemused other European nations taking part in Euro 96, at least the Dutch could feel a certain empathy. In 1978, when Holland's footballers were returning home from the World Cup Finals in Argentina, the whole squad got very drunk on the plane journey to Amsterdam. The paralytic players caused mayhem on the flight and several stewardesses were assaulted. The players were horrified to learn that their flight was due to be met by the Queen of Holland as a special welcome home.

In no fit state to mix with royalty, they were only saved by a fortunate turn of events when their plane had to refuel in Paris, giving them time to sober up.

Believe it or not, there is still some level of naivity amongst some players as far as alcohol is concerned. Liverpool's Jason McAteer is a perfect example. On one of his first trips with the Republic of Ireland squad, he went into a Limerick pub and asked if they sold Guinness! Bless him.

13 The Names Have Been Withheld To Protect the Guilty

THESE ARE THE stories that have either been swept under the carpet or conveniently forgotten by the perpetrators. During the course of researching *Football Babylon* a number of stories came to light that could not be reproduced on paper exactly as they were told by word of mouth. The lawyers insisted that the names be withheld to protect the guilty and, suffice it to say, it's just as well they did.

The sources of these stories are reliable (in most cases impeccable), and if you think the following is shocking you should hear the ones we had to leave out.

Given that drugs are a problem in football, it would probably come as little surprise to learn of four players with a British club who were all captured on closed circuit television partaking in a little cocaine whilst in a nightclub. The club concerned had, at one stage in its history, a problem with unsavoury characters populating the players' lounge on match days. The four players in the nightclub incident may or may not have left the club concerned but all were seriously reprimanded, leaving the club's chairman fighting a rearguard action to try to keep the story out of the tabloids. He was successful.

A player at a northern club was caught breaking a mid-week drink ban after his manager suspected the player was still going out on the razzle. The manager despatched an undercover club official to a well-known haunt of his players and caught the culprit red-handed. The player involved no longer plays for the club.

One gifted midfielder, who has a penchant for a few drinks

whenever the opportunity arises, bribed foreign waiters to add vodka to his soft drinks during team meals before a couple of important matches on foreign soil. More recently, the same player intructed a cab driver to stop at an off-licence on the fifteen minute journey home after a match. The cabby obliged and bought the player six bottles of Budweiser, which he demolished in the remaining ten minutes of the journey.

A fascination with gambling can get a footballer into trouble – just ask Paul Merson and Keith Gillespie – and no player is immune. One major European star is reported to spend an inordinate amount of money gambling on anything and every-thing. The player concerned can certainly afford it although tracking down his private bookie has proved problematic. Such is the addiction of gambling, that one British player who moved abroad to play used to fax his bets to the UK on a regular basis. Clubs' willingness to accommodate gamblers varies, although one British club intent on signing a confirmed gambler gave him his own gambling funds as part of his contract.

The stories that do the rounds regarding the shady world of bungs are numerous and it's a case of sorting the wheat from the chaff – not an easy thing to do. We've all heard them, but which ones are true?

A Fleet Street friend relayed the interesting story of a former manager who said one transfer he was involved in ended with the player involved driving away from the ground with £50,000 in used notes in a suitcase. Another cracker is the manager who signed foreign players and carved up a slice of the money between himself, an agent and a certain country's minister of sport. The amount involved is rumoured to have been around £1 million.

Players' insurance policies are useful things and have been known to have been used in dodgy deals. One manager lost his job for signing a player who had an injury that meant he wouldn't be able to perform at professional level. The manager paid the player's former club the agreed fee and the insurance cover paid off the club which had just made the purchase. The cash was shared between three people including the buying manager and the player. The purchasing club's chairman found out about the scheme and dismissed the manager concerned.

The power of the Inland Revenue is never to be under-estimated. If someone in football has large sums of money swilling around the bank accounts, the Revenue will want to know where it came from. In essence, prompt payment of any outstanding tax goes a long way towards satisfying the tax-man's curiosity. Anyone who doesn't pay their tax on time could easily find the press being tipped off and quickly facing the prospect of a trial by newspaper regardless of how innocent, or guilty, they may be.

A hard-drinking crew of a Midlands football club went out for a few drinks one evening and one of them had an argument with a pub landlord who swiftly kicked him out. The player could hardly walk so his teammates tried to get him home by taxi. Unable to let it lie, however, he jumped out of the taxi, got into another one, left it outside the pub with the meter running, ran into the pub, clocked the landlord and then got back into the taxi and went home.

On another occasion, the same bunch hailed a taxi driven by an Indian gentleman. He refused to take the players on account of them being out of their skulls on drink. Outraged at this, the players dragged the taxi driver out of his cab and dangled him over a bridge. Surprisingly, the driver relented and agreed to take them on their way.

Keeping on the same theme, a hardman midfielder was out on the town with teammates in Stavanger during an England 'B' tour. The group couldn't find anywhere to have a good time and ended up in a local bar. The bar was devoid of ladies but there was plenty of beer so they were happy. It was actually a gay bar but they hadn't realised it. The hardman had long hair and wore earrings and, while the others were at the bar, he went for a wander. Before long, he was approached by a punter who asked him to dance. 'I'll dance on your fucking head if you don't fuck off', snarled the embarrassed hardman.

Merseyside has had it's fair share of football legends and one little-known one is that Steve Nicholl was, more often than not, the butt of all the jokes during his time at Anfield. Nicholl was travelling to a game with two teammates, both of whom are very famous, when their vehicle reached Scotch Corner. It was snowing at the time and one of the mystery players asked Nicholl to get out of the car and wipe the windscreen, which he did. The two players then drove off, leaving Nicholl stranded and penniless in nothing more than a T-shirt and training shoes and in the freezing cold. The players didn't return for Nicholl who had to hitch-hike to his destination.

A certain Merseyside defender who was recovering from an injury went out partying until half past four in the morning thinking that, despite his improved condition, he wouldn't be playing the next day. At half past eight he was awoken by a phone call from his manager. 'How are you feeling?' asked the gaffer. 'Fine,' he lied. 'Were you out late last night?' asked the manager. 'Er, no not really.' 'OK, you're playing, get down here right away.' The player ended up having a pretty good game despite his hangover.

Bemused fans of a London club could not understand why their midfield general was playing on the wing for the entire first half of a match. Little did they know that it was because the player had put a lot of money on the 3.30 at a certain racecourse and had posted someone on the sidelines to shout him the result.

A few years ago, a promising young player was forced to leave his club because he was caught stealing from other players' jackets in the changing rooms. He soon found his way back into top flight football and currently enjoys a big bulging bank account – which he has amassed quite legally.

A frequently capped England International managed to crash his car on his way home. He didn't go to the police because he realised that he'd had too much to drink, so he reported the car as being stolen. The police were told by a witness that a man fitting the player's description was seen leaving the vehicle. The police decided not to take their investigations any further but said that they found a pair of lacy knickers and a bullwhip in the car's glove compartment. He hadn't been to a fancy dress party.

In the early 1980s, players from one British big city club used to have an arrangement with one of the club's evening security guards who allowed them to take girls up to the executive boxes for sex. Some famous footballing names were involved and group sex sessions were a favourite with the players.

One young player was given the nickname Bibby by colleagues after he was caught in his hotel room with sperm coming out of the sides of his mouth having just practised felatio on a teammate. Another player is reputed to masturbate before every match. He has no children.

One seasoned international was forced to leave his club after getting a girl pregnant. The girl's influential father was less than happy and one morning when the player opened his front door, he was told by a couple of heavies to leave town or he'd never walk again, let alone play football. He swiftly moved to another city.

A well-known TV presenter went to an official function at a northern club and ended up having sex with one of the club officials (a girl) in the centre circle of the hallowed turf.

International football has it's fair share of stories. One team coach, who lives on a low fat diet and consequently has the runs a lot, had a party trick of sitting on a wardrobe and defecating into a plastic cup. Sometimes he needed more than one go to get it right. One day, an official walked into the room whilst the coach was demonstrating his skill. The coach was sacked although not for the reason officially given.

An international player, admired by millions around the world, was generally loathed at one of the clubs he played for. He was seen scaling ten foot fences in order to avoid signing autographs, and his wife was once seen at a former club's reception in tears because she'd forgotten to video one of his favourite TV programmes was going to get a really hard time for it. The player was playing a European evening fixture at the time. One of his printable nicknames is shagger, given to him by his current colleagues and reflecting his appetite for women. Newspapers have been reluctant to print stories about him despite hard evidence of his illicit liaisons.

Football Babylon

A British International side, waiting in an airport departure lounge some years ago, decided to get stuck into a few beers – all except two players who spent most of their pre-flight time searching for someone with cocaine. The players were spotted by a music industry executive who also recalled how the entire squad very nearly got into a mid-flight brawl after a fellow passenger complained about their loud, insensitive behaviour at the rear of the economy cabin.

Being the manager of a football club sometimes doesn't stop the entrepreneurial spirit from taking over, however briefly. The owner of a dry cleaning shop decided to phone his local club to see if he could line up one of the players to officially open his new premises. When he telephoned, the club's receptionist informed him that none of the players were around and put him through to the commercial office. The man explained to the voice on the end of the phone what he was looking for. 'How much are you paying?' asked the voice. 'About £500', said the dry cleaning magnate. 'OK, I'll do it', said the man in the commercial department. 'Who are you?' queried the man – it was the manager of the club who just happened to pick up the phone and who was more than keen to offer his services.

Two of that manager's former players have had close shaves with authority. One was formally cautioned by police for indiscriminately firing an air-rifle in a built-up area and the other was involved in a violent dressing room punch-up after a teammate defecated in his boots. Both players were heavily fined by their club.

Two Italian players got into trouble during a World Cup tournament when they were discovered in bed together. All clubs encourage players to share rooms and, of course, room-mates have been known to innocently collapse on a bed together following a few bevvies. The Italian players were apparently involved in a different kind of bonding which, without doubt, was very much up to them. One of the players involved suffered so many jibes and personal attacks from players and fans alike that he fled Italy to live abroad. He no longer plays football.

Following a happy period as a goal scoring sensation, a Mediterranean player moved with his wife to a major European city to play for a big club. Sadly, the player did not manage to score all that prolifically for his new club but his wife had no such problems. She slept with one of the club's midfield stars and then with one of the directors. Mortified by her actions, the striker moved to another club and left his wife to go her own separate way.

Another Italian player enjoyed a very elaborate wedding reception and invited everyone at his club – apart from the club's president. Several members of a global crime ring were at the celebrations which was no surprise to the groom as they had paid for the whole bash.

The introduction of random drugs tests has made it very difficult for players to take hard or recreational drugs for fear of testing positive and facing lengthy bans. One former top club doctor privately admits that, before the introduction of random tests, he would frequently do his own medical tests on players and a significant number would show up as positive, mainly for marijuana and cocaine.

Drugs are not so prevalent in Italian football but some users are alive and well. Two players with a Rome club became very seriously addicted to cocaine, so much so that one of them was sold at a bargain basement price to another Italian club because he was so heavily debilitated by the drug. The club which bought him had no idea of his drug problem.

As time goes by, there'll be plenty more stories where these ones came from – and probably far worse. The names have been withheld to protect the guilty . . . and the innocent from guilt by association.